The Church Made Relevant

THE CHURCH MADE RELEVANT

A Commentary on
the Pastoral Constitution
of Vatican II

Peter J. Riga

FIDES PUBLISHERS, INC.
NOTRE DAME, INDIANA

FOR
Sister Jeanne d'Arc, S.C.N.

Foreword

The pastoral Constitution *Gaudium et Spes* of Vatican II is probably the largest document ever put out by the *Magisterium* of the Church (over 23,000 words). As such, it would be futile to try to give a detailed explanation of every paragraph of that document. This must, of necessity, be left to individual experts in the diverse subjects which the document touches upon and the reader must not expect a profound analysis of the conciliar document in these pages.

We have thought, however, that a general analysis covering the entire document would serve as an excellent introduction to the text itself. It is our opinion that this is all that is necessary for understanding, since the document is essentially orientated toward a practical implementation by laymen in the field. It was for this reason that the document was made so readily understandable by the Council Fathers of Vatican II. It is our hope that this short analysis will aid the reader toward this practical implementation which is the very *raison d'être* of this magnificent document.

In this commentary we have followed the plan of the document itself. It consists of a preface and two parts. The part and chapter titles of the book correspond to those of the Constitution. The commentary is set in regular type and each paragraph of the text is taken up consecutively and is set off by indentation. Comparative references to various encyclicals are similarly indented. And the two indices at the end of the book will enable the reader to locate material by subject or paragraph number.

Any author can attest to the vast amount of help and encouragement he continuously needs from friends and confreres. This is but a truism. There are, however, certain people so influential and helpful to his thought that it would border on injustice not to make mention of them. Such have been the former professors of his at the Catholic University of Louvain. After God he owes them the greatest debt of gratitude.

Peter J. Riga

University of Notre Dame
August 15, 1966

Contents

Contents

Preface

There were many discussions surrounding the title of "Pastoral Constitution" which was finally given to our text. We won't go into them again here. The prefatory note explicitly mentions the fact that many practical suggestions contained in this document would, of necessity, be subject to change and revisions as the history of men changes with the times. That is why the note explicitly says that the whole of the document must be read and "interpreted according to the general norms of theological interpretation" and that interpreters must bear in mind — especially in Part Two — the changeable circumstances which the subject matter, by its very nature, involves. The question to be answered is how and to what degree does the Church wish to engage herself in such and such a statement. For this we must carefully examine the formulas used, the historical context, the type of document employed as vehicle of the message (a conciliar document is of greater authority than an encyclical and this latter is greater than a pontifical talk to a group of specialists, etc.), whether the Pope or Council is giving an opinion or elucidating authoritatively a statement on faith and morals and so on. Our document is authoritative in that it is pastoral, since the Church using always basic doctrinal principles intends to apply them practically in the relationship between the Church and the modern world, between the Church and the men of our day.

The origin of authority in the Church is the fact that even if the people of God here below really and already participate in the divine life of God (thus forming the unique Communion of brotherhood which is the Church),[1] they still traverse this

---

1 See *Lumen Gentium,* 1, 2, 14.

1

journey here below by the theological virtue of faith. We do not as yet possess God fully for we walk in sign and sacrament which contain and give divine community but only under the sign of faith. If we were to see God as he is, he alone would rule in love, and on our part would be born the perfect submission which is born of complete love. Yet, between the Incarnation and the *parousia* the Church walks in pilgrimage where we see imperfectly through faith. Thus, in the community of the Church, authority is a basic service as a guide to Christ and guide to sanctification of its members. The authority of the Church must come from Christ himself, since otherwise we would be left as orphans, as blind men in an area where human thought cannot possibly penetrate and understand because it is the area of a radically different world, the divine dimension of God himself. The scriptures give more than abundant evidence as to the divine origin of this authority of the Church to teach, govern and offer the official cult (Matt 16:19; 18:18; Acts 20:28; 15:28; 1 Cor 5:4; 12; 7:10-12; etc.). These texts make it clear that her authority is the authority of Christ himself and he who would spurn this authority, spurns the authority of Christ. This is a radically different authority from that which exists in human society, since this authority of the Church is directly exercised *in nomine Domini* which can never be said of any other authority on earth. Thus it is that human authority comes from the fact that man must live in society, and from that fact they live by creating law and order so as to be able to carry on their human functions and aspirations. It is they who create the authority under which they wish to live and it is they who are at the origin of authority in the civic community. The Church, on the contrary, is a creation from above and as such it is the Church who creates its members at the font of baptism. It is she who gives them life in the divine sphere — the proper domain of the Church. Her authority to do so must of necessity come to her from above and not from the consent of her members. Her members, of course, cleave to her by faith, but their faith does not create this authority. Their faith is precisely in the fact that such authority is from above; for who would have faith in a purely human organization? The Church is the midwife of which St. Paul speaks when he says that he is in travail until Christ be born in each of the faithful. This image may just as well be applied to the Church for this function of service is precisely the work of the Church here below.

In the social teachings, she instructs in Christ's name, applying doctrinal principles to concrete situations of men of the present age. The difficulty begins precisely here, since it is clear in many pontifical documents that the authority on which the social teachings are based is divine and not human, coming to us from Christ the Redeemer. Yet, it is also very clear that the social teachings have been and continue to be subject to adaptation and even to change; and these characteristics cannot be fully squared with the making of each and every part of the social teachings a divine imperative. (For one example, study the evolution of the attitude of the Church toward socialism — from condemnation [Pius IX, Leo XIII] to qualifying distinctions [Pius XI, Pius XII] to overt approval [John XXIII, Paul VI].)

The usual explanation — which is not incorrect as far as it goes — is that since the order underlying political, social and economic order is moral in nature, the Church has the right as well as the obligation to clarify and to teach with divine authority the moral principles underlying these variant orders of the human community. This is clear and cannot be denied by any Catholic. Yet, the difficulty lies in applying those general principles to the concrete order of human activity and organization which is continuously in the flux of change and growth proper to all human endeavors. To what degree does the Church engage her authority, say, when she praises and recommends the UN to her faithful as a fitting instrument for peace in the modern world? Peace among men — as an extension of the inner peace between men and God and thence, from men to men — is a divine imperative for the Church. She would be remiss in her duty before God if she failed to encourage, inspire, and work for peace among men. This is clear. Yet, what of the UN when the Church recommends it (as indeed she has, many times over in the past 20 years)? We can find no such revelation in the deposit of faith (taken here in its broadest sense). The UN is obviously not of divine origin and those who direct it are not graced with any kind of divine authority. To what degree, then, can we say that such a concretization of the divine principle of peace is "authoritative," to be followed in conscience by Catholics in their struggle for peace? It is this complicated problem which we wish now to approach.

The Church's mission to the world is an essential part of her commission from Christ the Redeemer. The Church is not of the world, neither in her origins, her end, her means, nor her unifying principle who is the Holy Spirit. But she does exist in time and is influenced by the history and events of men of all ages. Without this incarnational mission of the Church to the world to activate in human history the holy ferment of the gospel — principles of brotherhood, reconciliation, and justice — the efficacy of her mission would be in grave jeopardy. For better or for worse, *the moral tone of man's life is directly affected by and through his social life*. Man does not and cannot live apart from his fellows, and what affects the social life and its operations, influences to a great extent the lives of men within that society. It is an erroneous "disincarnationalism" which would remove the Church from the agonizing and sometimes dirty affairs of men here below.

The Church is faced with a new situation, a new political, cultural, social, and economic world. She is no longer protected by the state or by an almost unique culture which she created, as in the Middle Ages. She lives in a world which she not only did not create but which was created against her and sometimes in spite of her opposition. One thinks here of the bloody religious wars of the 17th century which led to the notion of freedom of religion and tolerance, the scientific revolution of the 17th-18th century, the psychological revolution, the birth of democracy, decolonization, expanded and applied technology, the freedom of women. The culture of today is radically different — a global culture of pluralism, i.e., where there is no agreement as to the final end of man. The former cadres into which religious forms, ideas, signs and expressions were poured, as it were, are no longer adequate.

The Church must — if she is to be efficacious and faithful to her essential mission to the world — rethink these frameworks, discard anachronisms, and those institutions which no longer mean anything to modern man. She must adopt new cultural, artistic, philosophical, and even theological cadres more in conformity to the mentality of modern man. It is one thing to say — as did John XXIII — that religious dogmas of the Church do not, cannot change as to their essential signification; it is quite another to say that the forms which have encased these dogmas cannot change. To deny this is to fail to distinguish sufficiently between the human and the divine, Tradition from tradition, and, in the long run, to fall into an *ecclesiastical monophysitism* where change and real adaptation are impossible.

Seen in another way, we can view the fullness of Christ (Col 1:19; 2:9) in a twofold fashion, in order to see more clearly the essential nature of the Church's mission to the world. The one is the fullness of Christ when he shall come at the last day, the eschatological *parousia* where the Kingdom of Christ shall be fully established and he shall deliver it up to the Father (2 Cor 1:20; Eph 4:13). Here the efforts of the Spirit and of men who cooperated with him will be consumed in the total and visible establishment of the fullness of Christ's mystical body, head and members. By the same token, we may view this plenitude of sanctity and endeavor on the part of the Church as she patiently prays and labors in this valley of tears, as a dynamic growth in the Church and in humanity as well (among whom the Church is actively at work). This is so because the gospel and Christ's redemption are complete and efficacious for the salvation of men of all times to come. There can be nothing added to this aspect of God's action; yet there is the application and full development of this gospel among men by men under the eternal guidance of the Holy Spirit. In this sense, there remains much to be done "to fill up what is lacking in the passion of Christ" (Col 1:24). He has willed his Church to co-operate in the distribution of the fruits of his unique salvation and mediatorship; and in this sense, the Church fulfills continuously, cooperates really in building up the full measure of Christ until he comes. This cooperation is not a fiction but a cooperation which is totally within the one salvation and mediatorship of Christ who alone is the "one mediator between God and man, the man Jesus Christ" (1 Tim 2:5).

Thus *from man's point of view*, from the *world's point of view, there is an* ever-enlarging encompassment of Christ's *Kingdom growing in the world* from the *unique mystery of the Incarnate Word*. There is here, of course, from our part, a continuous development of Christian dogma as it is applied and learned under the guidance of the Holy Spirit who Christ promised "would guide the Church into all truth" (John 16:16). "He will teach you all things whatsoever I have spoken to you" (John 14:26). The gospel can find its fulfillment only in history among men and by the work of the Church. It would take time for these doctrines of the gospel to find their fulfillment in the social forms into which the gospel is fixed and preached. This ferment acts as a yeast in the world and like a yeast it must grow *into human fabric*.

Thus the themes of a Christian being the "light of the world," "the yeast in the dough," "the mustard seed that grows," "the salt of the earth," "the good works shining before men," and in addition that of the cosmic vision of St. Paul as he extends the salvation of Christ not only to men but to the whole of the created cosmos (Col 2:5-18), present us with the fundamental and obligatory mission of the Church to all men. This has taken time for men, even within the Church, to fully realize and accomplish. It took time, as well as the work of theologians — and even opposition, for the Church to see the implications in the social order of her own doctrines of faith. It took a long time, for instance, to see the fact that human dignity (a fundamental Christian concept) is denied by slavery, bondage of women, child labor, lack of civil rights, war, etc. It is clear, then, that efforts to promote human dignity, harmony and peace, social and international justice, alleviation of hunger and poverty are *all a fulfillment of the gospel* injunctions and insights. It is from this fundamental evangelical insight that the Church today draws her right — under the guidance of the Holy Spirit who is always with her — to speak with the authority of the gospel itself on social justice and social concerns of men here below. It is only those who fail to see this intimate connection between gospel-social order who can deny this right to the Church.

Thus Pope John XXIII stated:

Above all we affirm that the social teachings proclaimed by the Catholic Church cannot be separated from her traditional teaching regarding man's life, wherefore it is our earnest wish that more and more attention be given to this branch of learning. (*Mater et Magistra*)

And in *Pacem in Terris* the same Pope applied this:

Men should endeavor, therefore, in the light of faith and with the strength of love, to insure that the various institutions — whether economic, social, cultural, or political in purpose — will be such as not to create obstacles, but rather to facilitate the task of improving themselves both in the natural order as well as in the supernatural.

There is nothing really new in the history of the Church, but it is a new application, a fuller and more solicitous application of the evangelical principles of love and justice to a new order and a new world in its modern evolution. Thus we have here a dynamic concept of the Church which is continuously evolving toward a better understanding of her deposit, as well as its application to and for the world into which she has been sent to save. She applies an evangelical insight, but she must be attentive to the developments of men in the world through whom God also works. She must be open to *history and its lessons* — as was so clearly shown by Pope John in *Pacem in Terris;* open also to the aspect of change and evolution which the modern sciences have shown us; open as well to the questions of man, his struggles and agonies here below. It is only in the light of these facts, reflecting upon them, bringing the gospel and its dynamic principles to bear upon them, guided as she is by the Holy Spirit, that the Church makes a contribution and becomes relevant to the men of the modern age — and to every future age for that matter. If she becomes too timid here, if her children either through fear or a false disincarnationalism withdraw into a parochial and ghetto system of their own, the apostolate of the Church is in grave danger and modern man is left to drift with no direction for his works. When this happens, man becomes a giant, blind and mad, traversing the earth under the guidance of false ideologies and philosophies. This, in the final analysis, can only lead to man's ultimate destruction by the misguided works of his hands. In this context, the apostolate of the layman to the world becomes not a topic for fancy discussion under religious auspices, but a vital function of the Church in and for the world; for, after all, it is they, the laymen, who are the Church in the world. It is only with this dynamic concept of her mission to the world that the Church can become meaningful to and for the world.

Thus the building up of the Church and the fullness of human history are mutually complementary and aid each other's fulfillment. The judgment of the Church on history and its events is the judgment of Christ made in his name, *yet this judgment must be enlightened by change and events in the world* itself. The social teachings of the Church, in a sense, have been dependent on the social-human revolution of the last 150 years of man's history. This does not mean that her teachings in this regard are a simple evolutionary process of human thought adopted by the Church. We have seen that this is not so; this human situation, however, forced the Church to rethink and reapply the fundamental moral and religious evangelical principles to a new reality, a new human situation in history, with the result that we have seen the birth of a whole *corpus* of Catholic social thought in the past 70 years. From the opposite side, this thought is not a *Deus ex machina* for the Church to extricate herself from Marxist criticism of alienation and irrelevance, but rather a *fuller understanding of the gospel applied to a new historical situation*. We have here a complementary role of Church and world whereby the Church under the light of the gospel and the Spirit, purifies and elevates the progress of man and the work of the world. It forces the Church to continuously rethink and meditate the gospel mandate in the light of a new historical situation.

Hence the Church's mission to the world is both internal and external. *Internal,* insofar as she must continuously reform whatever in her structures is anachronistic and meaningless to the modern world. This is a delicate task to be done at the highest echelons of the Church's authority (Pope, Ecumenical Council), but a task which must continuously be done. *External,* also, insofar as she is in the world and *learns from God's work among men in human history*. Here her task is to purify and apply the gospel principles to new and changing situations in history. In reality, it is Christ himself who guides his Church into all truth.

The *Pastoral Constitution on the Church in the Modern World* begins by addressing itself to all men and proclaims its solidarity with all the problems and agonies of the men of our times.

1. The joys and the hopes, the griefs and the anxieties of the

men of this age, especially those who are poor or in any way afflicted, these are the joys and hopes, the griefs and anxieties of the followers of Christ. Indeed, nothing genuinely human fails to raise an echo in their hearts. For theirs is a community composed of men. United in Christ, they are led by the Holy Spirit in their journey to the Kingdom of their Father and they have welcomed the news of salvation which is meant for every man. That is why this community realizes that it is truly linked with mankind and its history by the deepest of bonds.

The Church is a solidarity with all men because she shares a common origin with them, created and redeemed by the same God in and through Christ, the Savior. The problems which afflict all men, of necessity must afflict the members of the Church as well. Christians are not separated from the men of our age in the sense that they do not share their agonies, but only in the sense that, by the pure grace of God, they have been called to a higher vocation which in no way negates — rather it reinforces out of love — their solidarity with all men of their age. That is why the Church can address herself to all men (2) concerning his agonies and problems (3) and thereby offers herself in complete oblative service to these very needs of men (4). Hence the Church is driven to this task by pure love for men, for their own good, and not by a thirst for terrestrial power (3b). The definition of the Church here given is taken from the document *Lumen Gentium,* paragraph 1:

Christ is the light of nations. It is therefore the eager desire of the Sacred Synod, gathered together in the Holy Spirit, to proclaim the gospel to every creature and thus bring to all men the light of Christ which shines brightly on the countenance of the Church. Since the Church is in Christ like a sacrament or as a sign and instrument both of very closely knit union with God and of the unity of the whole human race, it desires now to unfold more fully to the faithful of the Church and to the whole world its own nature and universal mission. This it intends to do following faithfully the teaching of previous Councils. The present day conditions of the world add greater urgency to this work of the Church, so that all men, joined more closely today by various social, technical and cultural ties, may also attain full unity in Christ.

In both Constitutions we have the Church viewed in a total and cosmic fashion much like that of St. Paul in his Epistles of the Captivity. The Church, like Christ, is in solidarity with all men — and even with all of creation insofar as it finds its fulfillment in man, who in turn finds his perfection in Christ, the Incarnate Word. Thus we have the two movements of thought in the development of Vatican II's teaching with regard to the Church: intrinsic to herself and her life in Christ (*Lumen Gentium*) and extrinsic in her relationship to the men of the modern age (*Gaudium et Spes*). This is how the latter document explains this relationship:

2. a. Hence this Second Vatican Council having probed more profoundly into the mystery of the Church, now addresses itself without hesitation, not only to the sons of the Church and to all who invoke the name of Christ, but to the whole of humanity. For the Council yearns to explain to everyone how it conceives of the presence and activity of the Church in the world of today.

b. Therefore, the Council focuses its attention on the world of men, the whole human family along with the sum of those realities in the midst of which it lives: that world which is the theater of man's history, and the heir of his energies, his tragedies and his triumphs; that world which the Christian sees as created and sustained by its Maker's love, fallen indeed into the bondage of sin, yet emancipated now by Christ, who was crucified and rose again to break the stranglehold of personified evil, so that the world might be fashioned anew according to God's design and reach its fulfillment.

We have already seen the meaning of the word "world" as used in this document (see above, pp. 4-6). Suffice it to say that in the scriptures — as is, in fact, the case here — this term often refers to the totality of creation of heaven and earth over

which man has been placed as God's lieutenant (Genesis 2).
Often, too, the term is used to express the universality of all
men whom God loves and for whom he gave his only-begotten
Son as proof of that love (John 3:16). It is in this sense that
our text employs the term "world" and not so much — as is
also found in the scriptures — the world of men who oppose
the truth of God and above all, God's Son. This is the world
of sin and reprobation from which the Christian must be separated and over which "the Prince of this World" rules. As the
Council puts it: "that world which is the theater of man's history. . . ." This is the world of all men and its history, which
our document will examine as to its meaning and direction.
Certainly, in later developments, the document will bring out
the aspects of malice, sin and rejection of God as well as its
redemption from sin and its transformation by the Resurrection
of the Incarnate Word. Thus we already have an outline of
what our document will cover in its exposition.

All this, of course, is brought out to emphasize the Church's
one objective: to be of service to man for the fulfillment of his
total vocation, both terrestrial and celestial. The Church actively
enters into these problems and agonies of modern man to understand as well as to aid in the search for solutions to them:

3. a. Though mankind is stricken with wonder at its own
discoveries and its power, it often raises anxious questions about
the current trend of the world, about the place and role of
man in the universe, about the meaning of its individual and
collective strivings, and about the ultimate destiny of reality
and of humanity. Hence, giving witness and voice to the
faith of the whole People of God gathered together by Christ,
this Council can provide no more eloquent proof of its solidarity with, as well as its respect and love for the entire human
family with which it is bound up, than by engaging with it
in conversation about these various problems. The Council
brings to mankind light kindled from the gospel, and puts at
its disposal those saving resources which the Church herself,
under the guidance of the Holy Spirit, receives from her

Founder. For the human person deserves to be preserved; human society deserves to be renewed. Hence the focal point of our total presentation will be man himself, whole and entire, body and soul, heart and conscience, mind and will.

b. Therefore, this Sacred Synod, proclaiming the noble destiny of man and championing the godlike seed which has been sown in him, offers to mankind the honest assistance of the Church in fostering that brotherhood of all men which corresponds to this destiny of theirs. Inspired by no earthly ambition, the Church seeks but a solitary goal: to carry forward the work of Christ under the lead of the befriending Spirit. And Christ entered this world to give witness to the truth, to rescue and not to sit in judgment, to serve and not to be served.

The essence here is one of dialogue since the Church admits she has no "ready-made" solutions for these problems of man; and, as such, the dialogue is twofold in direction (as must be every true dialogue) in that the Church is aided to see the problems, and in that she gives her services in an attempt to aid man in all of the ambiguities and even tragedies in modern life. She is, then, an evangelical ferment in the midst of the world.

Thus the Church "offers to mankind the honest assistance of the Church in fostering that brotherhood of all men . . . ," an offer genuine and sincere, since the Church has nothing to gain from an earthly point of view (wealth, power, etc.). This cooperation she extends to all men of good will as they agree on the common objects to be achieved among men. This community of ends on which Christians can cooperate with all men of good will was originally brought out by *Pacem in Terris* (¶ 159). Our document will insist on this cooperation throughout its text. This applies to the laymen with particular emphasis, since they are the ones directly involved in the transformation of the world. This was shown in *Lumen Gentium* as well (31b):

But the laity, by their very vocation, seek the kingdom of God by engagement in temporal affairs and by ordering them according to the plan of God. They live in the world, that is, in every secular profession and occupation. They live in the ordinary circumstances of family and social life, from which the very web of their existence is woven. They are called there by God that, exercising their proper function, and led by the Spirit of the gospel, they may work for the sanctification of the world from within as a leaven.

This invitation of work to and for the world was also brought out by *The Decree on the Apostolate of the Laity.*

The (laity) exercise a genuine apostolate by their activity on behalf of bringing the gospel and holiness to men, and on behalf of penetrating and perfecting the temporal sphere of things through the spirit of the gospel. In this way, their temporal activity can openly bear witness to Christ and promote the salvation of men. Since it is proper to the layman's state in life for him to spend his days in the midst of the world and of secular transactions, he is called by God to burn with the spirit of Christ and to exercise his apostolate in the world as a kind of leaven. (2c)

All Christians, then, are called upon in our document to give this cooperation to men of good will and to work for this common brotherhood which the Council mentions both as a fact and as an ideal in the realization of the Christian's total vocation. She actively goes out to the world of men and invites her children to do likewise while not just waiting around until the world asks her for such cooperation. The novelty here is the active manner in which the Church now goes out to the world of modern man.

The Situation of Men in the Modern World

We immediately see the newness of the Church's method and approach to the agonizing problems of man today. It is one of description, a far cry from the sure and explanatory method of all other past documents. The method has been applied by the popes during the past 70 years in the exposition of their social thought (*Rerum Novarum,* and, above all, *Mater et Magistra*). Our present document's description of the modern world is much more ample and broad than even the encyclicals of John XXIII:

4. a. To carry out such a task, the Church has always had the duty of scrutinizing the signs of the times and of interpreting them in the light of the gospel. Thus, in language intelligible to each generation, she can respond to the perennial questions which men ask about this present life and the life to come, and about the relationship of the one to the other. We must therefore recognize and understand the world in which we live, its expectations, its longings, and its often dramatic characteristics. Some of the main features of the modern world can be sketched as follows.

b. Today, the human race is involved in a new stage of history. Profound and rapid changes are spreading by degrees around the whole world. Triggered by the intelligence and creative energies of man, these changes recoil upon him, upon his decisions and desires, both individual and collective, and upon his manner of thinking and acting with respect to things and to people. Hence we can already speak of a true cultural and social transformation, one which has repercussions on man's religious life as well.

c. As happens in any crisis of growth, this transformation has brought serious difficulties in its wake. Thus while man extends his power in every direction, he does not always succeed in subjecting it to his own welfare. Striving to probe more profoundly into the deeper recesses of his own mind, he frequently appears more unsure of himself. Gradually and more precisely he lays bare the laws of society, only to be paralyzed by uncertainty about the direction to give it.

d. Never has the human race enjoyed such an abundance of wealth, resources and economic power, and yet a huge proportion of the world's citizens are still tormented by hunger and poverty, while countless numbers suffer from total illiteracy. Never before has man had so keen an understanding of freedom, yet at the same time, new forms of social and psychological slavery make their appearance. Although the world of today has a very vivid awareness of its unity and of how one man depends on another in needful solidarity, it is most grievously torn into opposing camps by conflicting forces. For political, social, economic, racial and ideological disputes still continue bitterly, and with them the peril of a war which would reduce everything to ashes. True, there is a growing exchange of ideas, but the very words by which key concepts are expressed take on quite different meanings in diverse ideological systems. Finally, man painstakingly searches for a better world, without a corresponding spiritual advancement.

e. Influenced by such a variety of complexities, many of our contemporaries are kept from accurately identifying permanent values and adjusting them properly to fresh discoveries. As a result, buffeted between hope and anxiety and pressing one another with questions about the present course of events, they are burdened down with uneasiness. This same course of events leads men to look for answers; indeed, it forces them to do so.

How does our document go about describing the situation of the modern world? We are first given the great chasm between the new social and technical abilities of man today and

the utter destitution and poverty of so much of the globe (4).
The fundamental reason for this (5) is that man has become
more and more the master of his own destiny by his technology
and his universal interdependence and "socialization." All this
has resulted in a radical transformation in man's social, cultural,
economic, and political situation in the modern world. We have
progressed from a "traditional" to a "modern" society characterized by urbanization, vast migrations of people, universal
communications systems, all making modern man more and
more interdependent. This has changed not only the so-called
"developed" nations but the underdeveloped ones as well, which
has gone so far as to affect their moral and religious traditions
(6 and 7). This has resulted in much confusion and conflict
in the modern situation of transformation and progress, particularly in collective life (8). Yet man never is so passive as to
simply accept this situation as it is; rather he continuously
attempts to overcome this imbalance present almost everywhere
in his new world. That is why all men today are asking themselves some very basic questions as to the meaning of man in
the modern situation (9). These questions, however, must be
traced to their deepest roots — which is the heart of man; man
as saved by God, but also tragically divided within himself by
sin and egoism. All this leads modern man to ask himself what,
in the final analysis is the only real question — who and what is
man and what are his goals? Once men have answered this
question we shall have had a general orientation toward a solution of all these problems facing man previously mentioned
(10). This interrogative method of the Council is in line with
its original aim of creating and engaging in a dialogue with
modern man by first specifying his problem(s) and then going
on to analyze them in its later development.

In our present paragraph we see clearly how the Church
learns of the action of God not only through the gospel but also
by reading "the signs of the times" (Luke 12:56) — its movements and direction — in which God speaks to the Church as

well (4a). The first prerequisite of this is to *understand* just what they are, before we can hope to bring aid through their solution. We must understand the world and the world must understand us as well; since, otherwise, there can be no true dialogue. Thus the document goes on to describe these problems (4b). It emphasizes the modern world's glories as well as its absurdities and contradictions. Man is at once the greatest of all of creation and its crown; but he is also overwhelmed by contradictions and death (4c). The result of this universal change in man's cultural, political, social, economic, and even moral structures is that we must find a new way of thinking of man in the modern world, and that the old cadres will simply not do. Modern men experience a profound malaise from this transformation, as they marvel before the world which they themselves have produced (4d). This anxiety is not altogether an evil; as a matter of fact, it may be looked upon as a good in the sense that it has caused men to ask themselves some very fundamental questions on where all of this is leading them and what the effects will be (4e).

All of this progress has resulted from the application of man's intelligence to the mastering and ordering of creation to serve his purposes. It is the technological spirit of modern man which has transformed the earth in a literal sense:

5. a. Today's spiritual agitation and the changing conditions of life are part of a broader and deeper revolution. As a result of the latter, intellectual formation is ever increasingly based on the mathematical and natural sciences and on those dealing with man himself, while in the practical order the technology which stems from these sciences takes on mounting importance.

b. This scientific spirit has a new kind of impact on the cultural sphere and on modes of thought. Technology is now transforming the face of the earth, and is already trying to master outer space. To a certain extent, the human intellect is also broadening its dominion over time: over the past by means of historical knowledge; over the future, by the art of projecting and by planning.

c. Advances in biology, psychology, and the social sciences not only bring men hope of improved self-knowledge; in conjunction with technical methods, they are helping men exert direct influence on the life of social groups.

d. At the same time, the human race is giving steadily increasing thought to forecasting and regulating its own population growth. History itself speeds along on so rapid a course that an individual person can scarcely keep abreast of it. The destiny of the human community has become all of a piece, where once the various groups of men had a kind of private history of their own.

e. Thus, the human race has passed from a rather static concept of reality to a more dynamic, evolutionary one. In consequence there has arisen a new series of problems, a series as numerous as can be, calling for new efforts of analysis and synthesis.

The terms "science" and "technology" are not the same — but are used here to describe a certain spirit of man which has come to dominate nature by rationalizing it for human purposes. "Science" is habitually used in a much broader sense to include all of the pure and applied sciences, while "technology" is used almost exclusively to mean the practical application of science. In our present context, the two are used almost indiscriminately — as the "common man" of the streets understands the terms. This problem, more than any other, is peculiar to modern man. Development in the sciences during the past 200 years has far outstripped the combined advances in all previous history. It has affected man not only in a quantitative measure but to an even greater degree in a qualitative measure. As the Constitution observes (5b), through the advance of the social sciences, it has become more and more possible to regulate as well as dominate the course of social events. This is called "socialization" as both *Mater et Magistra* and our present document describe it, and which includes such aspects as organization of insurances on a much broader basis, unemployment benefits, just distribution of wealth by taxes which hit the rich more heavily than the poor, and so forth. This aspect of the social sciences is indispensable in making the benefits of technology accessible to the great majority of people in a particular or even in our universal civilization (5c). As a result, for the first time in history, all men can collaborate in mastering nature and in advancing truly human goals. The future generations as well as the present have now become more and more interdependent. Technology has brought us an era of humanity which is effectively universal. This common life has made us more cosmopolitan and even a cosmic civilization. Such a process, however, has brought men further problems to contend with (5e).

The first problem is that of the industrial society which all nations have actually reached (so-called developed nations) or to which others feverishly aspire (underdeveloped nations):

6. a. By this very circumstance, the traditional local communities such as families, clans, tribes, villages, various groups and associations stemming from social contacts, experience more thorough changes every day.

b. The industrial type of society is gradually being spread, leading some nations to economic affluence, and radically transforming ideas and social conditions established for centuries.

c. Likewise, the cult and pursuit of city living has grown, either because of a multiplication of cities and their inhabitants, or by a transplantation of city life to rural settings.

d. New and more efficient media of social communication are contributing to the knowledge of events; by setting off chain reactions they are giving the swiftest and widest possible circulation to styles of thought and feeling.

e. It is also noteworthy how many men are being induced to migrate on various counts, and are thereby changing their manner of life. Thus a man's ties with his fellows are constantly being multiplied, and at the same time "socialization" brings further ties, without, however, always promoting appropriate personal development and truly personal relationships.

f. This kind of evolution can be seen more clearly in those

nations which already enjoy the conveniences of economic and technological progress, though it is also astir among peoples still striving for such progress and eager to secure for themselves the advantages of an industrialized and urbanized society. These peoples, especially those among them who are attached to older traditions, are simultaneously undergoing a movement toward more mature and personal exercise of liberty.

Here the Council speaks of the passing from what many political theorists call "traditional society" to "modernization." It gives some very general characteristics of this profound change: unity of economic production which is now distinct from the family — or the extended family or tribe. Families can no longer produce "all they need" but now rely upon the whole complicated strata of society which itself depends on a social distribution and division of labor. For this it is necessary to have concentration of large capital expenditures around which must concentrate a whole metropolis for easy access to work and production. Thus the phenomenon of ever-increasing urbanization (6c), a development which is everywhere in evidence no matter what the particular political organization (e.g., in governmental structures as diverse as the Soviet Union and the United States). It is evident in countries professing capitalism as well as the various shades of socialism. In other words, all societies are progressing from a civilization built upon custom, tradition, to one of rationalized and organized mutations of the relations between men on both a national and an international level. Both industrial (modern) as well as traditional society today exist side by side, but rapidly the swing of the pendulum of modern history is toward the former in almost every country — with the many problems this brings with it (see 69b and 86). This is a fact and there is little anyone can do about it; the Council recognizes that it is precisely in this type of civilization that the modern Christian must work. This solidarity of mankind, for better or for worse, is upon us, and it is toward the solution of the problems of this moment of history and in this new type of civilization that Christians must work. It is not only futile but positively harmful for Christians to think that they can attempt to build or rebuild a civilization of a past age.

This brings the Constitution to a discussion of the concept of socialization (6e) which Pope John had already developed in his encyclical *Mater et Magistra*. The only difference is that our document actively uses the term while Pope John did not. Here, as in the Pope's encyclical, we must not confuse it with "socialism." The old debate about the use of "socialization" has now been solved in favor of the term, whereas John XXIII never really used it in an explicit manner. In any case, in both documents, the word is employed in the sense that modern sociologists use the term, namely, as a type of global and universal interaction of persons and of things. The concept involves a complicated intertwining of many and varied relationships in the economic, social and technological fields. Since these relationships affect all peoples throughout the world, men have become increasingly interdependent socially in a great number of institutions and associations. This dependency manifests itself in many ways in each of these fields, especially in the economic and social sectors. These relationships are what might be called elements of fact which have united mankind in a unity never before thought possible (*Mater*, 47-49). This is the process of what our document calls "socialization." The essential problem here, as it was in Pope John's encyclicals, was that of rendering this new global situation free and *personalizing;* that is, helping man to become more of what he is in his human dignity. These changes have had a profound effect on the social life of modern man and can have some stultifying effects on the free initiative and liberty of man (6e). Pope John gave recommendations on how to maximize the good effects and minimize the harmful (*Mater*, 50-51), namely, by the establishment and growth of various intermediary groups which will assume the freedom of initiative and which, as a result, will be conducive to the freedom of individuals. This alone, however, is not sufficient. The wealth of power needed to cope with this problem of regulation in such manifold relationships must ultimately be lodged with the public authority. The upshot of all this is that socialization can and must be employed to promote personalization of modern man. Every temporal expression of man's personality in space and in time must be continuously evaluated and reexamined in the light of humanizing and christianizing principles to prevent deviation from its proper end: the promotion of the dignity of the men involved in the institution or enterprise along with its effects on the human community in which it exists. For this major principle of social philosophy is the sole legitimate one for any Christian examining the social order in a moral context. John XXIII never tired of repeating this throughout his two encyclicals (*Mater,* 18, 21, 55, 62, 74, 91, 106-107, 125, 142, 149, 157, 209, etc.; *Pacem,* 9-18, 20, 24, 26, 28, 34, 41, 44, 47, 65, 73, 79, 139, etc.). It is this which our document has in mind when it speaks of "personalization" (6e).

This process then has changed and continues to change the thinking — social, economic, moral — of peoples experiencing such a process of modernization. The document describes it thus:

7. a. A change in attitudes and in human structures frequently calls accepted values into question, especially among young people, who have grown impatient on more than one occasion, and indeed become rebels in their distress. Aware of their own influence in the life of society, they want a part in it sooner. This frequently causes parents and educators to experience greater difficulties day by day in discharging their tasks. The institutions, laws and modes of thinking and feeling as handed down from previous generations do not always seem to be well adapted to the contemporary state of affairs; hence arises an upheaval in the manner and even the norms of behavior.

b. Finally, these new conditions have their impact on religion. On the one hand, a more critical ability to distinguish religion from a magical view of the world and from the superstitions which still circulate purifies it and exacts day by day a more personal and explicit adherence to faith. As a result many persons are achieving a more vivid sense of God. On the other hand, growing numbers of people are abandoning religion in practice. Unlike former days, the denial of God or of religion, or the abandonment of them, are no longer unusual and individual occurrences. For today it is not rare for such things to be presented as requirements of scientific progress or of a certain new humanism. In numerous places these views are voiced not only in the teachings of philosophers, but on every side they influence literature, the arts, the interpretation of the humanities and of history and civil laws themselves. As a consequence, many people are shaken.

We may summarize this change in attitudes in the following way:

1. The universal desire for emancipation from Western imperialism has been and continues to be a shock from which the first bursts of revolutionary fever came forth. The structures of economic, social, and cultural bases left by the colonizers have been more or less of benefit for the process of modernization, depending on the colonial power, viz., Belgium has indirectly created chaos in the Congo by not having properly prepared an elite managerial and technical middle class for the transition of that power. There are very few skilled politicians with a national outlook. Tribalism is still rampant. This was less true of England with regard to India where the metropolis has left and formed a fairly stable middle-class substructure and a managerial and technical elite.

Emancipation also has resulted from an intense nationalism which in the underdeveloped countries is presently seen as the ideology around which unity within the country can be accomplished. This has forced leaders to play the great powers one against the other not only for self-defense but also for indirect aid to desperately needed economic development. Thus the cold war between the great powers can be called an indirect cause of modernization, at least in the underdeveloped countries. This type of nationalism has led to a psychological will of the people to throw off traditional values and adopt "Western values," which are enumerated in detail below.

We may summarize by saying that Western values (self-government, dignity of the human person, industrialization) have created a substructure of ferment in these underdeveloped countries. Independence has intensified their desire to break out of old traditions opposed to the universal spread of these values within the country, in order to develop the bureaucracy and industrialization for achieving these goals.

2. Economic development and its diverse bases for its development is the hub around which the whole concept of modernization is taking place. This is the source of the "revolution of rising expectation" to which all national elites aspire.

3. To accomplish #2 there are two requirements:

(a) Modernization of agriculture, since industrialization requires the release of great numbers of workers who must in turn be fed in cities. Presently, 85% of the population live on farms out of sheer necessity for production of food with the consequent result that the industrial base must be minute. To enlarge it, modernization of agriculture is imperative.

(b) The destruction (and/or) the evolution of certain traditional and religious values which are opposed to or at least obstruct industrialization. Thus laws regarding Sacred Cows are changed by the Indian Government; polygamy is practically forbidden in Pakistan; and the "transcendental" vision of Buddhism must be redirected to interests in the "here below."

4. Because of the complexification of industrialized life, one of the signs of modernization is a more intense socialization of the economic and social life of the countries. People are thus

free from intense fear of poverty, exploitation by the very rich and controlling elites, and receive the benefit of social security, pensions in old age, and so forth. Without such socialization, whole masses of the population are thrown on their own (*laissez-faire* principles) and the political stability of the country becomes problematic.

5. Communication (transportation) of a more intense nature as well as social mobility within the population. Without broader communication, (a) the output-input functions with regard to central authority become factional tribalism, (b) the concept of nationalism on a broader scale is impossible to inject, (c) the industrial-social base is impossible or retarded. Without social mobility and training of a managerial and technical class, it is impossible to have any modernization understood in Western terms.

6. Formation of diverse subgroups, voluntary infra-organizations which voice their particular interest in the political arena. This has reference to #4 but with this specification: that the whole base of substructured groups of a modern society be represented as power functions. It is true, however, that subgroups already exist (tribes, castes of ethnic and religious origin) and are often at the root of social dislocation as a result of the introduction of these new values which we have mentioned above.

As to the specifically religious changes brought about by socialization in all of its forms — this has not all been a bad thing. Much of traditional religion has been mixed with superstition in the cultures of many people; and with the introduction of science, we can now — more than ever before — distinguish religion from magic and cultural patterns. It took Christianity a long agony to come to this purification (Galileo affair, evolution, birth control) but other religions in the underdeveloped world are going through and must go through this evolutionary process. This is a good effect of socialization and modernization (7b). The Council speaks of a "new humanism" and it will come back to this subject at length later on in its exposition (19-23). The modern world, says our document, has had an ambiguous effect on men of our age: it has both purified the notion of religion as a value, thus drawing man to a more personal and personalizing faith, and it has had the effect of taking men away from God by a new humanism. This ambiguity of the modern world was already stressed by Pope John XXIII in his opening speech to the Council Fathers of Vatican II:

> It is easy to discern this reality [a new order of human relations] if we consider attentively the world of today, which is so busy with politics and controversies in the economic order that it does not find time to attend to the care of spiritual reality, with which the Church's *magisterium* is concerned. Such a way of acting is certainly not right, and must justly be disapproved. It cannot be denied, however, that these new conditions of modern life have at least the advantage of having eliminated these innumerable obstacles by which, at one time, the sons of this world impeded the free action of the Church. . . . The princes of this world, indeed, sometimes in all sincerity, intended thus to protect the Church. But more frequently this occurred not without spiritual damage and danger, since their interest therein was guided by the views of a selfish and perilous policy.

Thus, there has followed a certain purification of the faith as it has had to confront the problems of modernity.

All of this is compounded by the terrible social and economic imbalances in the modern world:

> 8. a. This development coming so rapidly and often in a disorderly fashion, combined with keener awareness itself of the inequalities in the world beget or intensify contradictions and imbalances.
> b. Within the individual person there develops rather frequently an imbalance between an intellect which is modern in practical matters and a theoretical system of thought which can neither master the sum total of its ideas, nor arrange them

adequately into a synthesis. Likewise, an imbalance arises between a concern for practicality and efficiency, and the demands of moral conscience; also very often between the conditions of collective existence and the requisites of personal thought, and even of contemplation. At length there develops an imbalance between specialized human activity and a comprehensive view of reality.

c. As for the family, discord results from population, economic and social pressures, or from difficulties which arise between succeeding generations, or from new social relationships between men and women.

d. Differences crop up too between races and between various kinds of social orders; between wealthy nations and those which are less influential or are needy; finally, between international institutions born of the popular desire for peace, and the ambition to propagate one's own ideology, as well as collective greed existing in nations or other groups.

e. What results is mutual distrust, enmities, conflicts and hardships. Of such is man at once the cause and the victim.

We have here a cursory glance at the manifold disturbances of the modern world: poverty, racial and ethnic discrimination, the problem of the unity of man's knowledge today, moral concerns over ends and means, overpopulation, the emergence of woman in today's world, and so forth. All of these problems have brought many forms of discord and strife (8e). Our document will deal with each of these problems in a particular way later in its exposition.

These problems display, however, a certain universal consciousness of the rights and dignity of all men. This is all to the good — but with various ambiguities:

9. a. Meanwhile the conviction grows not only that humanity can and should increasingly consolidate its control over creation, but even more, that it devolves on humanity to establish a political, social and economic order which will increasingly serve man and help individuals as well as groups to affirm and develop the dignity proper to them.

b. As a result many persons are quite aggressively demanding those benefits of which with vivid awareness they judge themselves to be deprived either through injustice or unequal distribution. Nations on the road to progress, like those recently made independent, desire to participate in the goods of modern civilization, not only in the political field but also economically, and to play their part freely on the world scene. Still they continually fall behind while very often their economic and other forms of dependence on wealthier nations increases more rapidly.

c. People hounded by hunger call upon those better off. Where they have not yet won it, women claim for themselves an equity with men before the law and in fact. Laborers and farmers seek not only to provide for the necessities of life, but to develop the gifts of their personality by their labors and indeed to take part in regulating economic, social, political and cultural life. Now for the first time in human history all people are convinced that the benefits of culture ought to be and actually can be extended to everyone.

d. Still, beneath all these demands lies a deeper and more widespread longing: persons and societies thirst for a full and free life worthy of man; one in which they can subject to their own welfare all that the modern world can offer them so abundantly. In addition nations try harder every day to bring about a kind of universal community.

e. Since all these things are so, the modern world shows itself at once powerful and weak, capable of the noblest deeds or the foulest; before it lies the path to freedom or to slavery, to progress or retreat, to brotherhood or hatred. Moreover, man is becoming aware that it is his responsibility to guide aright the forces which he has unleashed and which can enslave him or minister to him. That is why he is putting questions to himself.

No matter what the particular system — social, economic, political — may be, it must be used to promote the dignity of man. Later in our document, the Church will make it quite clear that she is tied to no one culture, no one political or social system, but that respecting each of their particular riches, she seeks this unique object: the promotion of the human person (3b, 42b, 75-76). As a matter of fact, Vatican II went so far as to express fear that the Church would become identified with any particular social or economic system (42d, 76b).

In any case, the Church recognizes the universal aspirations of practically all of mankind today. *Pacem* had given the same aspirations of the modern world which the Pope called the basic "characteristics of the Present Day" (39-45). He mentions the emergence of the working class from being considered mere cogs in productive machinery to the dignity of human persons; secondly, the emergence and position of woman today; and lastly, the fact that many nations have become independent in our day (up from colonialism). The Pope considered these the more perfect manifestation of the basic rights of man as it reveals itself throughout the globe in the lives of modern man. These characteristics are held together by the recognition of the human person's sacred rights. Man thus is both an interiority and an intentionality. He alone is endowed with intelligence and free will. From this flow his rights which the Pope enumerates in the first part of the same encyclical (8-27): the right to life and a worthy manner of living, the right to work and security, the right of association and freedom of conscience, the right to participate in the political and civil order as befits human responsibility, the right of emigration and immigration, and so forth. Man is becoming ever more conscious of these rights as well as the fact that traditional structures in the relationship between men and nations must change (9b), if these rights are to be effectively implemented. Nations will no longer permit other nations to dominate them economically or politically; nor will one class dominate another because of an accidental trait of wealth, class, social position, or racial or ethnic difference. The basic criterion must always be the human dignity of the human person (9e). Man will no longer permit himself to be treated as an object or thing. We are thus confronted with a truly revolutionary situation in the modern world. It is evident that our text, in this respect, was influenced by the bishops from the "third world" who claimed the original text was too occidental, and not enough was made of the emerging nations of this area (which, in fact, includes almost two-thirds of the world's population). This is evident in 9b, where it mentions "other forms of dependence on wealthier nations." This is not the only place where the problem was brought up. We may see this in 8d where our document speaks of the basic inequalities between the rich and the poor which is a scandal for the Christian. In a world which has the resources and potential to overcome this situation, it is scandalous to see a few with so much and the many with so little (4; see also 29, 63, 83). Here, as elsewhere, our document recognizes the legitimate aspirations of these millions of people and gives it her stamp of approval much in line with that of John XXIII who saw in them "the signs of the times" (see above, pp. 6-8). In many ways, however, these peoples — while free politically — are dominated socially, culturally and even economically by the richer countries. This is brought out in our document in 85a. These people, however, feel the great need to act independently, in their own right (6). These manifold contradictions afflict the modern world in almost every respect (9e) since, as we shall see later in the text, man's progress and technology are inherently ambiguous. This, in its turn brings us to the next paragraph:

10.   a.   The truth is that the imbalances under which the modern world labors are linked with that more basic imbalance which is rooted in the heart of man. For in man himself many elements wrestle with one another. Thus, on the one hand, as a creature he experiences his limitations in a multitude of ways; on the other he feels himself to be boundless in his desires and summoned to a higher life.

b.   Pulled by manifold attractions he is constantly forced to choose among them and to renounce some. Indeed, as a weak and sinful being, he often does what he would not, and fails to do what he would. Hence he suffers from internal divisions, and from these flow so many and such great discords in society.

c.   No doubt many whose lives are infected with a practical materialism are blinded against any sharp insight into this kind of dramatic situation; or else, weighed down by unhappiness they are prevented from giving the matter any thought.

d. Thinking they have found serenity in an interpretation of reality everywhere proposed these days, many look forward to a genuine and total emancipation of humanity wrought solely by human effort; they are convinced that the future rule of man over the earth will satisfy every desire of his heart.

e. Nor are there lacking men who despair of any meeting to life and praise the boldness of those who think that human existence is devoid of any inherent significance and strive to confer a total meaning on it by their own ingenuity alone.

f. Nevertheless, in the face of the modern development of the world the number constantly swells of the people who raise the most basic questions or recognize them with a new sharpness: what is man? What is this sense of sorrow, of evil, of death, which continues to exist despite so much progress? What purpose have these victories secured at so high a cost? What can man offer to society? What can he expect from it? What follows this earthly life?

g. The Church firmly believes that Christ, who died and was raised up for all, can through his Spirit offer man the light and the strength to measure up to his supreme destiny. Nor has any other name under heaven been given to man by which it is fitting for him to be saved. She likewise holds that in her most benign Lord and Master can be found the key, the focal point and the goal of man, as well as of all human history. The Church also maintains that beneath all changes there are many realities which do not change and which have their ultimate foundation in Christ, who is the same yesterday and today, yes, and forever. Hence under the light of Christ, the image of the unseen God, the firstborn of every creature, the Council wishes to speak to all men in order to shed light on the mystery of man and to cooperate in finding the solution to the outstanding problems of our time.

The problem of the ambiguities of modern man is not to be found in the world or in man's progress but in man himself and the ways in which he uses these improvements. The other view would be a practical Manicheism where the world is viewed as a quasi-principle of evil. Nothing could be further from the theology of our document, and so we must look for the imbalances in man and in his divided being (10a). Man, in fact, has been divided by sin, by his disobedience to God which in its own turn — by a type of talion law — has produced disorder in him and even in creation itself. This paragraph is proof enough against those who said that our document was too optimistic, not having taken sufficiently into consideration sinfulness and its consequent disorder in man. The Council does speak of this, and we have here the very concept of original sin; since man "often does what he would not, and fails to do what he would."

Some have answered this problem by either giving it little thought in a type of practical materialism or in a humanism which, in the thought of these men, will overcome the anxiety and division in man as man frees himself from "alienation" (10a). Our document will speak of this latter aspect more at length later in its exposition (19-22). This atheistic humanism has been popularized to a great degree by Camus and Sartre.

No matter how we phrase or rephrase the problem, we continuously return to the basic question of who and what man is (10b). For on this question will depend the ultimate signification of the progress and constructs of man. This question of basic anthropology must be answered if man is to find a correct orientation to the modern world.

The Catholic faith has never wavered in its own view on how man and his progress should be viewed (10c). The universe is basically Christocentric, for whom and in whom all things have been created in heaven and on earth. Christ is not simply some personality who appeared at a specific point *within* human history; he is the central point of both sacred and human history, and without him, history has no meaning and man no direction for himself or his works here on earth. The Council then speaks from this vantage point which gives Christianity at least a general direction in its search for terrestrial meaning. This certainly does not mean that Christianity will have, by that fact, ready answers to the vast problems of modern man; it must "cooperate in finding the solution to the outstanding problems of our time."

Yet, the Christian has at least this advantage; he knows that
the terrestrial task and the engagement of man within the world
does find meaning and signification in Christ, the Incarnate
Word. That gives the Christian a distinct optimism in facing
the problems of the modern world.

PART I

The Church and Man's Calling

This section may well be named a Christian anthropology or teaching about man. This vocation is seen, however, in its total context of Christian engagement and as such cannot be separated from man's heavenly calling (11a). The fundamental condition today as it exists is not one of "natural" man — but of men called concretely to salvation in Christ. That is why in this section there must be a rather detailed answer to atheistic humanism which is so prevalent in our day; and this can be done only by delineating a total view of man — that is, his unique vocation manifested in its terrestrial and celestial aspects. The Church looks out upon the world in this spirit of receptivity and openness to its values and aspirations:

11. a. The People of God believe that it is led by the Lord's Spirit, who fills the earth. Motivated by this faith, it labors to decipher authentic signs of God's presence and purpose in the happenings, needs and desires in which this People has a part along with other men of our age. For faith throws a new light on everything, manifests God's design for man's total vocation, and thus directs the mind to solutions which are fully human.

b. This Council, first of all, wishes to assess in this light those values which are most highly prized today and to relate them to their divine source. Insofar as they stem from endowments conferred by God on man, these values are exceedingly good. Yet they are often wrenched from their rightful function by the taint in man's heart, and hence stand in need of purification.

c. What does the Church think of man? What needs to

be recommended for the upbuilding of contemporary society? What is the ultimate significance of human activity throughout the world? People are waiting for an answer to these questions. From the answers it will be increasingly clear that the People of God and the human race in whose midst it lives render service to each other. Thus the mission of the Church will show its religious, and by that very fact, its supremely human character.

The life of faith does not exist extrinsic to the concrete life of man here below. As a matter of fact, as we saw above, human and secular history have no meaning beyond the focal center who is Christ. Faith is certainly a new light (11a) which is distinct from the terrestrial task; yet it does give us a direction and orientation as to the correct use of terrestrial realities. Thus the receptivity and openness to the values of man here below in the light of this faith does not replace the tasks themselves but rather orientates them towards their final and true end (11b). And yet, without this new light of faith, precisely because of the ambiguity inherent in these constructs of man or rather in man himself, there is grave danger of man misusing the product of his hands, as has happened many times in the past (11b). We are brought back to the fundamental question, which our text once again asks in 11c: "What does the Church think of man?" and consequently of his creation. Secular history is not strange to the Christian but is the very field of action where he must engage his principles in concrete action for the men of his day. This can be escaped only at the price of a disincarnational Christianity. For the Church, such is the meaning of terrestrial realities.

CHAPTER 1

The Dignity
of the Human Person

This section of our document is of crucial importance, since it is upon this response that we can construct what the terrestrial city should be and the work of man within it; upon it will also depend how and even "if" we can have a true dialogue with all men of good will. The dignity of man must be such a premise for further serious discussion on marriage, culture, the state, war and peace. This dignity must reach all aspects of man: body and soul, conscience and intelligence, free will and free responsibility.

12. a. According to the almost unanimous opinion of believers and unbelievers alike, all things on earth should be related to man as their center and crown.

b. But what is man? About himself he has expressed, and continues to express, many divergent and even contradictory opinions. In these he often exalts himself as the absolute measure of all things or debases himself to the point of despair. The result is doubt and anxiety. The Church certainly understands these problems. Endowed with light from God, she can offer solutions to them, so that man's true situation can be portrayed and his defects explained, while at the same time his dignity and destiny are justly acknowledged.

c. For Sacred Scripture teaches that man was created "to the image of God," is capable of knowing and loving his Creator, and was appointed by him as master of all earthly creatures that he might subdue them and use them to God's glory. "What is man that you should care for him? You have made him little less than the angels, and crowned him with glory and honor. You have given him rule over the works of your hands, putting all things under his feet" (Ps 8:5-7).

d. But God did not create man to be alone, for from the beginning "male and female he created them" (Gen 1:27). Their companionship produces the primary form of inter-personal communion. For by his innermost nature man is a social being, and unless he relates himself to others he can neither live nor develop his potential.

e. Therefore, as we read elsewhere in Holy Scripture, God saw "all that he had made, and it was very good" (Gen 1:31).

The similarity between this document and that of John XXIII's *Pacem in Terris* is striking. Both documents construct the whole basis of their doctrine on exactly this premise: the rights and dignity of the human person. It is man himself who is the very center of preoccupation of the modern world. Man is ever increasingly more aware of his dignity in the modern world, as we saw above in the characteristics of the modern world. It is he who is overcoming the disorders of nature, and by his control and technology orientating it toward human and cultural ends for man. It is no longer money or wealth, neither nationalism, race or social class which is becoming more the measure of the worth of man. It is man who is the measure of all things and for whom all things were created. In *Pacem,* John XXIII stated clearly that there is a basic core of humanity which must be respected if peace is to be achieved. He defined this core as the inviolate, inalienable, and universal rights of the human person (8-25). These are essential for any sane conception of order in the modern world. They belong to every human being — man or woman, black or white, rich or poor, strong or weak — by the very fact that each person possesses a human nature. These rights are not to be violated by government or by other individuals. In a true sense, this encyclical was a forceful justification of all the rights of the human person.

The Church in our present document understands and encourages this modern trend of the men of our day. She has certain insights to give to the men of our age which come from God (12b); and this ought to be understood well so that no misinterpretation can deter some men of good will. As we have already said, Christian faith gives the Christian the assurance that all things are good and are orientated, finally, to the Incarnate Word of God. From this follows an optimism and general orientation of which the Christian is certain. Thus this Christian revelation tells him that man is called, in a sense, to collaborate with God in the work of creation. Man is God's lieutenant who is to dominate "the fish of the sea, the birds of the air, the animals and all the earth" precisely because man is created "in the image and likeness of God." Man's image and likeness to God is precisely that, like God, man has a share in the domination of the earth. And in a very true sense, man will continue creation by his further activity over what has been initially given him by God. Thus, creation is good in a double sense; good in its divine origin and good also in all the potentialities which are derived from this initial creation by the further ordering of man. Man's vocation as the image of his Maker (12c) is intimately bound up with his task in the world.

Yet this faith of the Christian, even if it gives him certitude as to the fundamental and final meaning of things cannot and does not give him a "blueprint" of ready-made solutions to the many problems of the modern world. He is not and cannot be excused from engaging himself in the tasks of the world in cooperation with all men who sincerely seek concrete solutions to these very real problems. Thus Christian faith is no excuse for escaping the world and its problems — but is rather the greatest incentive: out of love for men to be engaged in the world, for men. It is God's will which is revealed to the Christian as he engages himself in the world at the service of man where he is both subject and object, where he questions and receives a response in the works of the world as well as having and possessing a fundamental meaning for the world. Thus, for the Christian, his faith is a type of three-way dialectic between himself, God, and the world. In this context, the Council could view man and the world in a certain optimism where "his defects are explained, while at the same time his dignity and destiny are justly acknowledged" (12b).

Finally (12d) our text relates man first of all to the fundamental orientations of his nature: the cosmos in which man has been set as lord of creation, to dominate it and use it for human ends; secondly to others, the first manifestation of which is the family (the document will speak of this later at length); and finally to God, insofar as God is the end toward which all are orientated and in whom all will be consummated by and through his incarnate Word. Thus, man is essentially social; he is by nature "orientated to" other men, the cosmos, and God. Man is a relationship with all three and none can be eliminated without a destruction of man himself. This theme of man as the "microcosmos" was brought out many times by the earliest Fathers of the Church.

Yet all is not perfect with man for he suffers from an interior division of his being. This is shown very clearly in the next paragraph:

13. a. Although he was made by God in a state of holiness, from the very beginning of his history man abused his liberty, at the urging of the Evil One. Man set himself against God and sought to attain his goal apart from God. Although they knew God, they did not glorify him as God, but their senseless minds were darkened and they served the creature rather than the Creator. What divine revelation makes known to us conforms with experience. Examining his heart, man finds that he has inclinations toward evil, too, and is engulfed by manifold ills which cannot come from his good Creator. Often refusing to acknowledge God as his beginning, man has disrupted also his proper relationship to his own ultimate goal as well as his whole relationship toward himself and others and all created things.

b. Therefore man is split within himself. As a result,

all of human life, whether individual or collective, shows itself to be a dramatic struggle between good and evil, between light and darkness. Indeed, man finds that by himself he is incapable of battling the assaults of evil successfully, so that everyone feels as though he is bound by chains. But the Lord himself came to free and strengthen man, renewing him inwardly and casting out that "prince of this world" (John 12:31) who held him in the bondage of sin. For sin has diminished man, blocking his path to fulfillment.

c. The call to grandeur and the depths of misery, both of which are a part of human experience, find their ultimate and simultaneous explanation in the light of this revelation.

We must set this statement next to that of John XXIII in *Pacem in Terris* where the saintly pontiff noted the reason for the turmoil in our world:

Peace on earth, which men of every era have so eagerly yearned for, can be firmly established only if the order laid down by God be dutifully observed.

The progress of learning and the inventions of technology clearly show that, both in living things and in the forces of nature, an astonishing order reigns and they also bear witness to the greatness of man, who can understand that order and create suitable instruments to harness these forces of nature and use them to his benefit.

But the progress of science and the inventions of technology show above all the infinite goodness of God, who created the universe and man himself. He created all things out of nothing, pouring into them the abundance of his wisdom and goodness so that the holy psalmist praises God in these words: O Lord, our Lord, how glorious is your name over all the earth. . . .

How strongly does the turmoil of individual men and peoples contrast with the perfect order of the universe! It is as if the relationships which bind them together could be controlled by force (1-4).

The theology of both documents is practically the same. The causes of human conflicts are traced to their fundamental roots, that is to the sinfulness and selfishness of man as a historical being. No real peace can come to man — at least in the long run — unless men attempt to root out these egotistical passions from the human heart. This must be emphasized by any document of the Church to the modern world, else she, too, fall into the dangerous error of seeing man's progress as a type of building up of a terrestrial messianism for alienated man. This is one of the fundamental errors of marxism and modern atheism; and the Church could not but emphasize that man's ultimate end is God, and he alone; and that, wounded by pride and sin, man is in continuous danger of overlooking his end which is God. Such a tragic fate falls to modern man who does not recognize that the source of his evils comes not from alienation but from selfishness and pride which cause him to disregard the "brotherhood." This basic theology must be a part of any relationship between the Church and the modern world. She must, of necessity, avoid all false optimism which would tend to overlook the terrible ambiguities of man and of his works. The fact is that the mystery of evil is still at work in the world of man, wounded as he is by the original fall and constituted in a state of *hubris* (pride) which can transform all his works into means of destruction and desolation. This cannot and must not be forgotten by the Church or her members. The Church must never cease teaching man this fact, continually educating him toward the good and toward the redemption from sin which Christ came to earth to give all men. The text uses the Augustinian notion of alienation (13a) in a progression of cause and effect: man who disobeys God is alienated from the very source of his being; consequently, the cosmos and the constructs of man rebel against him in a disorder which is then complete. Man, by integrating himself into Christ and away from sin, can fittingly and worthily use the cosmos and the works of his hands. By separating himself from God, man disassociates himself from the fullness of his being, which can only have disastrous results even during his life in the earthly city (13b). Yet the Church as mother and teacher of men, recalls to man the grandeur of what he is, what he is called to, and, through the grace of God, what he can attain even here below (13c).

This vocation of man, however, is not a platonic one. He was created and called to respond to God in the totality of his being, both body and soul:

14. a. Though made of body and soul, man is one. Through his bodily composition he gathers to himself the elements of the material world thus they reach their crown through him, and through him raise their voice in free praise of the Creator. For this reason man is not allowed to despise his bodily life, rather he is obliged to regard his body as good and honorable since God has created it and will raise it up on the last day. Nevertheless, wounded by sin, man experiences rebellious stirrings in his body. But the very dignity of man postulates that man glorify God in his body and forbids it to serve the evil inclinations of his heart.

b. Now, man is not wrong when he regards himself as superior to bodily concerns, and as more than a speck of nature or a nameless constituent of the city of man. For by his interior qualities he outstrips the whole sum of mere things. He plunges into the depths of reality whenever he enters into his own heart; God, who probes the heart, awaits him there; there he discerns his proper destiny beneath the eyes of God. Thus, when he recognizes in himself a spiritual and immortal soul, he is not being mocked by a fantasy born only of physical or social influences, but is rather laying hold of the proper truth of the matter.

So often in the past, Christian writers have tended to disincarnate man into "spiritual" pursuits away from the "temporal" and "bodily activities" of man. For St. Paul, for instance, the word *pneuma* (spirit) means primarily God himself as communicated to men. The word is also used in scripture referring to man insofar as he uses his faculties according to God's designs (*pneumatikos*). It signifies, more particularly, the intelligence of man illuminated by the gift of God, by his divine grace.

"Pneumatic" (spiritual), then, means that all man's faculties (inclusive of his mind, body, desires, tendencies) are used according to God's plan and wish. It does not mean the "intellectual" as opposed to the "physical," the immaterial as opposed to the material. On the contrary, a proud man may be very "intellectual" philosophically; but he is by no means "spiritual," since his intelligence is not directed by the Holy Spirit, but by his egoism and pride. Even the body and its desires are "spiritual," when, for instance, the Christian abstains from fornication since his body is the temple of the Holy Spirit (1 Cor 2:10-16). By "flesh," St. Paul (and other New Testament writers) designates those who are led not by the Spirit but by their own light of reason, by their own desires and wishes as opposed to those of God. "Flesh" is all that resists the kingdom of the spirit. In the epistle to the Galatians (5:19-21), St. Paul makes a summary list of the works of the flesh. Among these are found some things that are in no way "flesh" in the physical sense, e.g., envy, hate, disputes, dissensions, and so on. Above all, this distinction of St. Paul must not be confused with the Greek concepts of "body-soul" and the dichotomy between the realities signified by these concepts. Semitic thought knew little of such a dichotomy. Paul's analysis is not that of the Greek philosophers of matter (body) and of the spiritual principle (soul), nor could it be. *A fortiori*, neither St. Paul nor any of the writers of the New Testament even conceived of a gnostic dualism where the soul is imprisoned in a quasi-evil principle, the body. For these writers, the body was simply an integral part of man, who was created as one whole by God, destined entirely either for death or life. This point is central, for it radically distinguishes the thought of the bible from Greek philosophy.

The conciliar text faithfully follows the train of biblical thought (14a). The body is not simply a pure instrumentality but part and parcel of the very personality of man. All dualism is radically eliminated even if man is split apart *as a totality* by sin and its effects on man (14b). In a certain manner of speaking, following modern philosophy, man relates by his body to the world whereby he communicates and learns with that world. He is, by his body, consubstantial with the cosmos and forms thereby a fraternity with all his brothers in the world. He is, in the words of St. Hilary, the microcosmos of the whole universe. It was St. Paul who saw Adam as the type of Christ in a strange inversion of historical perspective: "But death reigned from Adam unto Moses, even over them who have not sinned after the similitude of the transgression of Adam, who is the figure of him who was to come" (Rom 5:14). Man even in his carnal existence is an image of Christ, and in this way, man's flesh, through Christ, comes to the salvation and redemption of God. Thus man, by his body, is established in his relationship with God, with the cosmos, and with his brothers. The resurrection of the flesh is not an afterthought of Christian thought and reality, but an integral part of the redemptive order. Yet the body is also a limitation on man since he is thus specified in time and space, subject to the physical, psychological, and even sociological laws which regulate his bio-sociological life on earth. His very dependency on others betrays his essentially social nature. Even his rebellion by sin has had its effects on this aspect of his life (14b) alienating man from himself, from God, and from his brothers. Thus man, taught in this respect by the gospel and the Church, must come, by the grace of God, to master himself and his tendencies. It is in this way that the text avoids all forms of dualism as well as materialism in its understanding of the unique reality who is man in historical existence. Man — by his spiritual principle — is therefore not a slave of matter or of determinism but remains a rational and free agent. This was a constant temptation of some of the Council Fathers, namely, a dualism between matter and spirit, natural and supernatural, body and soul. Although the proper distinctions are made in our document (particularly in the area of man's true division: sin), there are no traces of dualism of any kind. Man in his entirety is within the world, perfecting himself as he constructs the world in which he finds himself both as an integral part and its summing glory. The Christian thus contributes to this process of "humanization" not by external moralism or "religious activity" in addition to this human activity in the world, but rather by an active engagement in this fundamental work of man. This is one of the fundamental pivotal points of our conciliar document.

Following the teaching of St. Thomas, the Council attributes this mastery of man over the cosmos to the light of man's reason, by the rationalizing and ordering process of his mind:

15. a. Man judges rightly that by his intellect he surpasses the material universe, for he shares in the light of the divine mind. By relentlessly employing his talents through the ages he has indeed made progress in the practical sciences and in technology and the liberal arts. In our times he has won superlative victories, especially in his probing of the material world and in subjecting it to himself. Still he has always searched for more penetrating truths, and finds them. For his intelligence is not confined to observable data alone, but can with genuine certitude attain to reality itself as knowable, though in consequence of sin that certitude is partly obscured and weakened.

b. The intellectual nature of the human person is perfected by wisdom and needs to be, for wisdom gently attracts the mind of man to a quest and a love for what is true and good. Steeped in wisdom, man passes through visible realities to those which are unseen.

c. Our era needs such wisdom more than bygone ages if the discoveries made by man are to be further humanized. For the future of the world stands in peril unless wiser men are forthcoming. It should also be pointed out that many nations, poorer in economic goods, are quite rich in wisdom and can offer noteworthy advantages to others.

d. It is finally, through the gift of the Holy Spirit that man comes by faith to the contemplation and appreciation of the divine plan.

Man's constructs need to be informed by wisdom (15c),

that is, by the guiding principle of who man is and where he is going. Without this direction, man is mad and not identified. This is the great fault of the modern world — not having a direction and ordering principle for the works of its hands. This being so, these very works are in danger of destroying man himself as he proceeds from the rational universe (in which man is in control) to the technocratic world (where man's instruments are now in control of him). Indeed, man by his reason and technology has mastered and continues to master the world and the cosmos; but lacking wisdom, man is now becoming the slave of the works of his hands. The Council here gives at once the proper dignity and respect to human reason but also notes with Vatican I how it has been wounded by sin (15b), lacks wisdom (15c), and is, therefore, in need of God's grace for this direction and orientation (15d). By his reason, man escapes the determinism of the physical laws of nature (see *Pacem*, 3-4). St. Thomas would say that by his reason, man participates in the very providence of God and thus is radically distinguished from the actions of the rest of creation. Reasoning here means the same as having his destiny in his own hands. Man determines his own destiny under God; he is not a slave to instinct as are the animals, nor to determinism as is inanimate creation, nor to the subconscious forces of his own being, nor to the irrational forces of society. To discover God's ways and laws, man has been given the gift of reason, and only in the use of reason can he control his own destiny under God. In the words of St. Thomas, reason in man is an imprint of the divine light guiding him to this end! Therefore, this use of reason is not a static quality but a continuous searching aspect of man ever more penetrating what the will of God is for him. It is, as the moderns would say, a historical quality; and man is a historical creature. It is only man who has a history since only he can unite the past with the present and so prepare himself all the more perfectly for the future.

The modern period has brought out this aspect well, insofar as it applies itself to the governing and ordering of the universe by the application of reason called technology. This has been put at the service of man particularly in that process which the Council will later describe at length: socialization. Yet, as we have seen, without wisdom from above, it can be used to destroy man. In this sense, the natural world has changed for man and is no longer what it was in times past for him.

The law of nature (*lex naturae*) has, in traditional Catholic moral theology, been used to justify moral acts as being the "proximate norm of morality" while the will of God alone is the "ultimate norm" for all action. It is stipulated that by discovering the "laws of nature" we, at least indirectly, attain the will of the Creator of nature; and hence, we can thereby determine the "goodness" or "badness" of any particular moral action. This has been at the base of traditional "objective" moral theology, since, in such a case, the only alternative was seen as "subjective," that is, situation ethics. This last option has been unacceptable to the vast majority of Catholic moral theologians as well as by, it would seem, the ordinary teaching authority of the popes (especially by Pius XII).

Yet, this view of the "law of nature" as the proximate norm of morality is not without its serious difficulties. Two objections can be formulated against it. The first is that of precision of meaning. In what sense are we speaking of "nature" and "law of nature"? These are very ambiguous terms, to say the least, since the concept of nature which we have today is one over which man exercises more and more domination. Even Catholic theology today speaks of man as God's lieutenant in creation, prolonging and continuing the original act of creation of God given in Genesis. This trend in theology emphasizes the fact that God became man, and that somehow all nature has become sanctified by that fact. In creation, God commanded man to continue his own work by "dominating" the earth and all therein, by being God's lieutenant. In a very true sense, then, man continues the work of creation by working, controlling, and dominating nature given to him by God. In what sense, then, does the Catholic moralist today speak of "nature," since modern Christian and non-Christian men speak of it as the prolongation of man's domination over the brute forces bringing it rationality and culture? (see Chapter II, Part II, of our document).

A more fundamental question here, however, is how to read the will of God in and by such a procedure. The moral manuals insist on the discovery of a finality or teleology within nature which can lead us to such a conclusion. Such a systematization is used for a whole complexus of moral problems in society from the nationalization of industries to the regulation of births by the anovulant periods. The whole discussion on the legitimacy of rhythm is based on this argumentation as contra-distinguished from the "frustration" of nature by the use of mechanical means of contraception. Here we encounter the greatest difficulties, since what is meant by "natural" more or less corresponds to the deepest instincts of man among which the sexual drive is one of the most prominent in individual lives. We are thus led, in a sense, to confuse "natural" with "instinctive." This simply will not do, since man's sexual drives are governed by moral values which are much more subject to the spirit than to man's instinctive life, at least if we are speaking of man as a moral and responsible being. It is evident that procreation is of the very essence of the sexual drive, yet can we call it "natural"? If we do, then why is not Christian virginity and celibacy against nature? The reason in both cases is that we cannot reduce man's moral life to a mere instinct, even if such instincts appear to be among the most embedded in man's being as an incarnate spirit. In such a case, why is it "against nature" to employ mechanical contraceptives and, on the other hand, "according to nature" to use the rhythm system or pills?

We are faced here with a double misunderstanding of the term "nature." In reality, we must not forget the fact that it is not exactly the order of nature "itself" which reveals God's will, but rather that God's will is expressed indirectly and imperfectly through this "order of nature" (in the traditional exposition of this position). Thus, according to St. Thomas Aquinas, the moral perfection of man consists in submitting his will to the will of God, in the concrete case, to enter into the grand design of God for man in the universe which God has intended for man. In other words, the world and all that is in it has been created and continues to exist in its essential orientation for man, for his perfection, goodness and love — and for no other reason: "the sabbath has been created for man, not man for the sabbath." God loves man and has created all for his good, and his development, body and soul, for the Creator. "Let us make mankind in our image and likeness; and let him have domination over the fish of the sea, the birds of the air, the cattle, over all wild animals and every creature that crawls on the earth" (Gen 1:26).

This, of course, brings us to the whole problem of modern man's relationship to nature and the forces of nature. We have already pointed out how this has changed, since man no longer lives in an agricultural-passive society and culture, but rather in a technico-industrial-active one which has totally changed his relationship to "nature" and to its laws. This is one of the principal reasons why modern man — even Christian modern man — understands nothing or very little when traditional theologians speak to him of the "laws" or teleology of the natural processes. This, in its turn, has thrown the whole birth control debate (and particularly the question of the anovulants) into such a terminological and theological confusion. Let us dwell for a few moments on the basic (some would say fundamental) difficulty in this crucial debate of modern man's relationship to nature.

The relationship of man today toward nature is termed by various authors (Chenu, Schillebeeckx, Bonhoeffer) as a nature "desacralized," that is, completely disassociated from reference to God and following its own laws which man must master and direct. There is an ambiguity implied in this manner of viewing nature, for it can lend itself both to an atheistic as well as a theistic interpretation. The atheist would claim that such a view of nature releases man from the bane of superstitions of nature, the worship of unexplained causality on which Christianity is essentially predicated. The Christian, however, explains that such a view of nature frees religion from superstition, from specific cultural (agricultural, rural, passive) forms to a more spiritualized notion of religion which is beyond the natural workings of nature and its "laws." We are thus freed from naturalistic religions whose existence is predicated on fear, the unknown, the humanly inexplicable (at least for the present), and nature's contingency and violence. In this sense, the human conscience is elevated from a naturalistic mode of language and consideration to a spiritual consideration that "God is Love" and the true worshipers of God are those who do so "in spirit and in truth." After all, the first philosophers were those who elevated themselves from such a naturalistic milieu to one of rational causes, and thus incurred the hostility of their milieus as being "atheistic" (Socrates). Christianity would be seen as a purifying stage in this process of separation of man's conscience from the slavery of "nature" and its laws by elevating man from such considerations (Compte). Naturalistic religions are therefore doomed to disappear (as is even Christianity) to the degree that man sees his active relationship with nature as a force which he uses for his liberation and not for his alienation.

Thus we have reached a crucial point in our examination of man's relationship to nature which has led us to this "desacralization" of nature and man's relationship to it. Not only does modern man *not* understand the searching for God's will "in nature's teleology," as is the habit with traditional moral theologians, but he has, moreover, a positive, dominative approach to this violent and external force called nature. Technology and industrialization of modern society (achieved to a great degree in western countries and being feverishly pursued in the economically underdeveloped countries of the "third world," both communist and noncommunist) have eliminated the naturalistic concept of localization of the divine as well as of the sacred. In ancient societies, religion was predicated precisely on this relationship to nature with its seasons and harvests, its disturbances and violence, its appeasements and worshiping of these forces in nature. The divinity was seen as implicated and manifested in these natural forces, and, as such, it is doomed to extinction when the modern view of man's relationship to nature becomes fully conscious to him. By such a process, man becomes freed from those forces over which he had no control and to which he gave himself in variant forms of worship. Now man assumes total responsibility for himself, and by his work and rationality, he is fully master of his universe. It may well be that it will crush him, and by its violence, ultimately destroy him; but it will be totally himself who will die in the struggle, fully free and unalienated by the "divine forces" of nature before which, in former times, he bowed and scraped as a virtual slave. Nature is no longer a source of the sacred and it is man who now determines his own destiny by manipulating nature.

It should be evident how deeply divergent is such a view from the method pursued by the moral theologian in his quest to find God's will (indirectly) revealed to man in the direction of nature and of nature's forces. Such a search makes no sense as the "proximate norm of morality." And this is true not only for modern atheistic man but for modern Christian man as well. Christian man cannot be separated from the *zeitgeist* of his own times.

Thus this attitude toward nature can be seen as an ambiguous movement either away from those aspects of Christianity which have been involved with pagan naturalistic religions or a mounting tide toward atheism. Man simply no longer progresses from a contemplation of the "order" and "design" of the universe to the cause (supreme) of the universe, much like the great clockmaker of Voltaire or other Deists. This attitude is as dead as the proverbial "door nail," for man today sees his relationship not to the "beyond" and the transcendental, but to man himself, to the "here below" and he has learned the pragmatics of applying it to further man's freedom and well-being. It remains true that man's world is threatened today — no longer by the "mysterious forces of nature" but by man himself. The cosmos, the Sun, Moon and rain (floods) which were once feared, are no longer looked upon with mysterious awe to be worshiped — but rather they are recognized as violent forces to be conquered and used for man's own good and well-being. The age of deistic and naturalistic aspects of religion or sacred sentiment is gone. Atheism represents a breaking away of this concept of man's relationship to nature; and to the degree that Christianity itself continues such referential points, the dialogue with the unbelieving world becomes all the more difficult. We simply live in a world where everything has lost its sacred sense and has become a technical, manipulated world, where the God of nature, or of heaven and earth is simply no longer credible to modern man. This was the God where the terrors of nature made man tremble, where its violence in the form of tornadoes, floods, cataclysms brought men to their knees in fervent supplication ("From hunger, pestilence and war, deliver us, O Lord"). This God was the master of the seasons (harvest feasts, resurrection ceremonials in the spring) as well as fertility itself (Astartes of Canaan). Today all this has been radically replaced by hormones and strip farming, dams and irrigation, flood control and erosion conservation. The hope of man is in man; the face of the earth is not changed by the Spirit but, literally, by the technology and industry of man.

Some Christians would object when this view is applied to the spiritual concept of Christianity which has been, to a great degree, responsible for desacralizing nature from superstitions acquired through paganism and the religion of nature. This, of course, is true — but only to a certain degree (one of the exceptions, the critics would say, is contraception; according to the traditional moralists, the proximate norm of morality is the "law of nature" where God's will is indirectly revealed to us). It remains true, nonetheless, that Christianity has desacralized the concepts of the economy, the state, even nature itself by full and complete acceptance of technology, and modernization as a goal which can promote man's freedom and well-being.

Our document then moves on to consider this law written in man's heart and then to explain it.

16. In the depths of his conscience, man detects a law which he does not impose upon himself, but which holds him to obedience. Always summoning him to love good and avoid evil, the voice of conscience when necessary speaks to his heart: do this, shun that. For man has in his heart a law written by God; to obey it is the very dignity of man; according to it he will be judged. Conscience is the most secret core and sanctuary of a man. There he is alone with God, whose voice echoes in his depths. In a wonderful manner conscience reveals that law which is fulfilled by love of God and neighbor. In fidelity to conscience, Christians are joined with the rest of men in the search for truth, and for the genuine solution to the numerous problems which arise in the life of individuals and from social relationships. Hence the more correct conscience holds sway, the more persons and groups turn aside from blind choice and strive to be guided by the objective norms of morality. Conscience frequently errs from invincible ignorance without losing its dignity. The same cannot be said for a man who cares but little for truth and goodness, or for a conscience which by degrees grows practically sightless as a result of habitual sin.

This "law of conscience" was fully discussed by *Pacem in Terris,* paragraph 5:

But the Creator of the world has imprinted in man's heart an order which his conscience reveals to him and enjoins him to obey: they show the work of the law written in their hearts. Their conscience bears witness to them. And how could it be otherwise? For whatever God has made shows forth his

infinite wisdom, and it is manifested more clearly in the things
which have greater perfection.

Both documents are at pains to avoid all forms of relativism in
determining the law of God written in the history of man and
understood by him ever more perfectly in the course of history.
Many times, those who speak of "conscience" speak of a certain
type of subjectivism of the objective moral order. Conscience
— the proximate norm for all man's moral actions — must be
guided as closely as possible by the remote norm for moral action,
namely, the will of God. This, admittedly, is sometimes very
difficult to do, since, as we have seen, we are continuously understanding nature and man's own self ever more perfectly —
a dynamic concept. And yet, this does not negate the objective
will of God for all men, discernible by the light of reason; and,
therefore, in consortium with all men of good will, such norms
must be patiently and sometimes painfully searched for. Our
present document then, wishes at once to discard all forms of
subjectivism as well as to join with all men of good will in the
continuous discovery of these norms. The Church cannot be
accused here of a type of physical immobilism which, somehow,
had only to search this law "written in the hearts of men" and
thus come up with solutions once and for all. In this, the Church
admits that she, along with all men of good will, must search
more deeply into the continuing flux which is man's historical
existence. Once again, the Church implicitly confesses that she
has no ready-made solutions for all the problems which continuously face the world. What we know is that man must do
good, that he has reason reflecting on his historical experience.
Thus, the Council recognizes this historical aspect of human
conscience in its continuing search for solutions to man's moral
problems. The search for truth and goodness is never a ready-
made nor a "once and for all" discovery but rather a growing
and dynamic search in historical evolution.

This search of its very nature can be conducted only in freedom which, in a sense, defines man himself:

17. a. Only in freedom can man direct himself toward goodness. Our contemporaries make much of this freedom and pursue it eagerly; and rightly to be sure. Often, however, they foster it perversely as a license for doing whatever pleases them, even if it is evil. For its part, authentic freedom is an exceptional sign of the divine image within man. For God has willed that man remain "under the control of his own decisions," so that he can seek his Creator spontaneously, and come freely to utter and blissful perfection through loyalty to him. Hence man's dignity demands that he act according to a knowing and free choice that is personally motivated and prompted from within, not under blind internal impulse nor by mere external pressure.

b. Man achieves such dignity when, emancipating himself from all captivity to passion, he pursue his goal in a spontaneous choice of what is good and procures for himself, through effective and skillful action, aids to that end. Since man's freedom has been damaged by sin, only by the aid of God's grace can he bring such a relationship with God into full flower. Before the judgment seat of God each man must render an account of his own life, whether he has done good or evil.

We have here the maturity of both human decision and divine faith. Man's life — both natural and supernatural — does not have a truly human character without a personalized engagement of self, known and realized in a free human decision. Faith which comes simply from being born within it or from a cultural milieu which protects it, is simply not enough. The maturity of all human action is that it be a personal engagement, intellectually justified to the self who makes such an engagement. In this sense, freedom is a *sine qua non* of this engagement — the means — as well as *the end* for which man exists. "You shall know the truth and the truth shall make you free." Negatively speaking, freedom means a lack of force or restraint from outside forces, but from a positive point of view, an engagement for human fulfillment. Freedom, then, is not to be seen as simply one property of man alongside many others. Man, like God, is defined by freedom and, as we have said, man exists by and for freedom. In this sense above all, man is the image and likeness of God who is infinite freedom and love in personalized form — tri-personalized as a matter of fact. Thus man, made in this image, is fully free when he conforms himself to the exemplar after whom he was created, even physically: Christ. In this way, the Christian escapes every definition of a freedom which is nothing more than mere license ("I can do what I want"); it is neither arbitrariness nor caprice but a liberation of man by love as he conforms himself to the divine image. In a paradox which is Christianity, he saves his life by losing it, and he becomes free by engaging himself in the will of God as given to him in the thousand manifestations of this will in life. Thus, an engagement from love equals full freedom of the Son of God on earth. By identifying himself with Christ and his work, the essence of the Christian's freedom is attained. This self-engagement through love, freedom, has become a major motif of modern philosophy. It has aided Christians to come to a greater comprehension of what they already receive in the scriptures.

This finally leads us to the eternal question of where man is headed; his ultimate fate, and his death:

18. a. It is in the face of death that the riddle of human existence grows most acute. Not only is man tormented by pain and by the advancing deterioration of his body, but even more so by a dread of perpetual extinction. He rightly follows the intuition of his heart when he abhors and repudiates the utter ruin and total disappearance of his own person. He rebels against death because he bears in himself an external seed which cannot be reduced to sheer matter. All the endeavors of technology, though useful in the extreme, cannot calm his anxiety; for a prolongation of biological life is unable to satisfy that desire for a higher life which is inescapably lodged in his breast.

b. Although the mystery of death utterly beggars the

imagination, the Church has been taught by divine revelation and firmly teaches that man has been created by God for a blissful purpose beyond the reach of earthly misery. In addition, that bodily death from which man would have been immune had he not sinned will be vanquished, according to the Christian faith, when man who was ruined by his own doing is restored to wholeness by an almighty and merciful Savior.

c. For God has called man and still calls him so that with his entire being he might be joined to him in an endless sharing of a divine life beyond all corruption. Christ won this victory when he rose to life, for by his death he freed man from death. Hence to every thoughtful man a solidly established faith provides the answer to his anxiety about what the future holds for him. At the same time faith gives him the power to be united in Christ with his loved ones who have already been snatched away by death; faith arouses the hope that they have found true life with God.

The document fully describes the *angst* of modern man (18a) and the consequent failure of everything else — inclusive of affluence and technology — to fill up these deep voids. Our text, following other documents of the Church, avoids taking sides on whether there would have been any death (and its consequent *angst*) if there had been no sin. It simply describes the universal and most common of all human phenomena: human death and its inevitability. The Christ answer to this *angst* is clear: the resurrection (18b). In and through Christ, the Christian has passed from death to life by his baptism and the divine life by the work of the Holy Spirit who dwells in our hearts. This, of course, refers above all to the spiritual death of sin and the spiritual (i.e., according to the Holy Spirit) life in Christ. Yet, as Christian teaching firmly holds, this continues its effects even to the resurrection of the body, as the Creed holds very clearly. We do not know in exactly what manner this resurrection of the body is to take place, but Christian faith is most certain of its ultimate reality. All this has been accomplished for us once and for all by the mystery of the Incarnate Word into whose mystery Christians have been baptized. Death (physical) is not an end-all for the Christian but a beginning of the fullness of the life we have already begun here below. Thus the paradox of life and death, which is the Christian answer to modern *angst* over death. The Church cannot but confess her faith here before the whole world. Modern philosophy sees that man is made for death ("a being for death") and from this has come despair or a neo-stoicism of acceptance of this inevitable human condition. The Christian response is that life is not *after* death but the divine life which has already entered the man of faith which thus constitutes a victory (even now) *over* death. Just as Christ freely accepted this mortal condition of death, he has, by that very fact, changed its signification for all those who believe in him. St. John, for instance, never speaks of the "crucifixion" of Christ, but only of his "glorification," for Christ has radically changed the meaning of these human events for men who would come to believe in him and in his work. The physical aspect of death for the Christian remains but the end of the beginning, the entrance into the fullness of what he has lived only by sign and by faith. He has thus been freed from its terrors and its finality. His death is but a complete freedom given to God throughout his mortal life.

Yet we also ought to note — something our text does not do — the greatness of spirit of some atheists who generously accept the inevitability of death and prepare for it by a life of self-giving to their fellow men. This is a fact that cannot be denied and, as we shall see in our discussion on atheism, this itself may well be God's way of working in them.

We now begin the detailed discussion of atheism by the conciliar document. We may refer the reader back to incipient discussions of this paramount question in 7c and 10a. This section seeks to answer — as did the encyclical *Ecclesiam Suam* of Paul VI — the profound reasons for the widespread atheism of our day and what idea its professors have of God. Its nature and cause is of supreme importance for Christians today. Without knowledge of these, we are left in the dark and further *anathemas* will serve no good purpose but will only further embitter the already charged atmosphere between believer and unbeliever.

19. a. The basic source of human dignity lies in man's call to communion with God. From the very circumstance of his origin man is already invited to converse with God. For man would not exist were he not created by God's love and constantly preserved by it; and he cannot live fully according to truth unless he freely acknowledges that love and devotes himself to his Creator.

b. Still, many of our contemporaries have never recognized this intimate and vital link with God, or have explicitly rejected it. Thus atheism must be accounted among the most serious problems of this age, and is deserving of closer examination.

c. The word atheism is applied to phenomena which are quite distinct from one another. For while God is expressly denied by some, others believe that man can assert absolutely nothing about him. Still others use such a method to scrutinize the question of God as to make it seem devoid of meaning. Man, unduly transgressing the limits of the positive sciences, contend that everything can be explained by this kind of scientific reasoning alone or, by contrast, they altogether disallow the fact that there is any absolute truth.

d. Some laud man so extravagantly that their faith in God lapses into a kind of anemia, though they seem more inclined to affirm man than to deny God. Again some form for themselves such a fallacious idea of God that when they repudiate this figment they are by no means rejecting the God of the gospel. Some never get to the point of raising questions about God, since they seem to experience no religious stirrings nor do they see why they should trouble themselves about religion.

e. Moreover, atheism results not rarely from a violent protest against the evil in this world, or from the absolute character with which certain human values are unduly invested, and which thereby already accords them the stature of God. Modern civilization itself often complicates the approach to

God not for any essential reason but because it is so heavily engrossed in earthly affairs.

f. Undeniably, those who willfully shut out God from their hearts and try to dodge religious question are not following the dictates of their consciences, and hence are not free of blame; yet believers themselves frequently bear some responsibility for this situation.

g. For, taken as a whole, atheism is not a spontaneous development but stems from a variety of causes, including a critical reaction against religious beliefs, and in some places against the Christian religion in particular. Hence believers can have more than a little to do with the birth of atheism. To the extent that they neglect their own training in the faith or teach erroneous doctrine, or are deficient in their religious, moral or social life, they must be said to conceal rather than reveal the authentic face of God and religion.

The text refuses to condemn; rather, it encourages knowledge of diverse forms of atheism and an understanding of their origin. Negative atheism, for example, holds the impossibility of proving the existence of God, or at least to know anything for certain about it. George Duhamel and Martin de Gard would be in this category. Among them, a certain number would rather explain everything by the exact sciences. Others wish much more to affirm man than to deny God, as the philosopher Maurice Merleau-Ponty seems to think. Some, like Albert Camus, are atheists with a vigorous protest as much against the moral evil as the physical evil which fills the world; others still, impressed by a deep sense of the power of man over the world, are less easily led to grasp the reality of the pilgrimage toward God; and finally, there are others, like the characters of Françoise Sagan, who "never think of God."

It is unnecessary to recall that the names just mentioned are not in the text of the Constitution; they are mentioned here as examples of these different forms of atheism.

Systematic atheism is then analyzed; this is what one might call "positive atheism." Sartre has asserted that "atheism is a humanism" in the sense that the inexistence of God is a condition of the reality of man and of his commitment in the earthly city. It is the same famous commentary of Malraux on a sentence of Nietzsche: "God is dead; therefore, man is born." The characteristic mark of this widespread form of atheism is an instinctive distrust of any religious faith; for religion would imply an attempted evasion, a flight, rather than a confrontation with the realities of this world in which men are hungry and thirsty, cold and sick. Man should be "the sole artisan of his destiny" and of humanity so that his energies be truly applied to the concrete realities of society and of history. Our document specifies that this form of atheism is more often propagated and imposed by political regimes; for this end, they use means of pressure known and described by sociology.

It is important to repeat: the Council refused to launch any anathemas. The very enumeration of the diverse forms of unbelief, as we have summarized them, suffices to show that the purpose is to understand and to discover the causes of atheism, both those which come from the state of secular or religious society and those resulting from the fundamental experiences of such and such a man. The Council even refused to quote explicitly marxism and communism since terms with multiple meanings in which philosophical, economic, political, and sociological elements are mixed with religious elements, might be misunderstood.

In any case, our present paragraph gives us this general description of the modern phenomenon of atheism. The fact is, that no matter how noble individual atheists may be, of itself, atheism is an injustice to both God and man (19a), since man is, in fact, destined to live with God forever. Thus faith in God is not something a man can accept or reject, as he pleases. It is a constitutive part of the human vocation itself. To deny this is to reject the essence of the vocation of man on earth. It is a part of objective reality, which, by definition, the atheist does not have. Christian faith then is not some sort of "consolation" or "opium" but a constitutive part of man and of the very objective reality in which man — all men — are implicated.

The document (19b) makes it very clear that under its nomination of "atheism," it understands the term in a global sense and not just of marxism. There are other types of atheism as well, such as agnosticism, positivism, scientism, and practical materialism which must each be distinguished as to their cause and effect on the modern world.

Finally, Christians themselves must recognize their own responsibility in this modern phenomenon (19c). The Christian must admit that he might have given others false images of who and what God is, by means of superstition, neglect of the poor and destitute, or a wrong view of nature and man's relation to it. The document does not go into detail on this point, but it is easy to make one's own conclusions here: false images created by the Crusades, bigotry, and nontolerance; religious wars fought in God's name; the inquisition; distrust of science (Galileo); the neglect of the working man in the 19th century; the scandalous conduct of Christians in racial discrimination; and many others as well. Each Christian is here called upon to examine his own conscience in light of these deeds.

The document then goes on to describe systematic atheism:

20. a. Modern atheism often takes on a systematic expression which, in addition to other causes, stretches the desire for human independence to such a point that it poses difficulties against any kind of dependence on God. Those who profess atheism of this sort maintain that it gives man freedom to be an end unto himself, the sole artisan and creator of his own history. They claim that this freedom cannot be reconciled with the affirmation of a Lord who is author and purpose of all things, or at least that this freedom makes such an affirmation altogether superfluous. The sense of power which modern technical progress generates in man can nourish this belief.

b. Not to be overlooked among the forms of modern atheism is that which anticipates the liberation of man especially through his economic and social emancipation. This form argues that by its nature religion thwarts this liberation by arousing man's hope for a deceptive future life, thereby diverting him from the constructing of the earthly city. Consequently when the proponents of this doctrine gain governmental power they vigorously fight against religion, and promote atheism by using, especially in the education of youth, those means of pressure which public power has at its disposal.

The text makes a clear distinction between atheistic humanism (20a) and marxism (20b). The first is a refusal to affirm God because of a fear of denial of liberty and of human dignity. The second is a type of redemption and a freeing of man by means of material and economic progress. No new condemnations were made in spite of the fact that a sizeable minority wanted a condemnation of marxism. This was rejected as incompatible with the document itself as well as with the wishes of John XXIII and Paul VI; in short, it would have been inimical to the hoped-for dialogue which was to ensue from this document. The note to this paragraph, however, contains references to former condemnations of marxism and insofar as modern marxism is faithful to the same philosophical premises, they remain in full effect. Yet they were not introduced into the text itself which indicates the seriousness with which our document wishes to engage all men — irrespective of political or ideological backgrounds. This concept of dialogue will dominate the long section which follows:

21. a. In her loyal devotion to God and men, the Church has already repudiated and cannot cease repudiating, sorrowfully but as firmly as possible, those poisonous doctrines and actions which contradict reason and the common experience of humanity, and dethrone man from his native excellence.

b. Still, she strives to detect in the atheistic mind the hidden causes for the denial of God; conscious of how weighty are the questions which atheism raises, and motivated by love for all men, she believes these questions ought to be examined seriously and more profoundly.

c. The Church holds that the recognition of God is in no way hostile to man's dignity, since this dignity is rooted and perfected in God. For man was made an intelligent and free member of society by the God who created him; but even more important, he is called as a son to commune with God and share in his happiness. She further teaches that a hope related to the end of time does not diminish the importance of intervening duties but rather undergirds the acquittal of them with fresh incentives. By contrast, when a divine substructure and the hope of life eternal are wanting, man's dignity is most grievously lacerated, as current events often attest; the riddles of life and death, of guilt and of grief go unsolved, with the frequent result that men succumb to despair.

d. Meanwhile every man remains to himself an unsolved puzzle, however obscurely he may perceive it. For on certain occasions no one can entirely escape the kind of self-questioning mentioned earlier, especially when life's major events take place. To this questioning only God fully and most certainly provides an answer as he summons man to higher knowledge and humbler probing.

e. The remedy which must be applied to atheism, however, is to be sought in a proper presentation of the Church's teaching as well as in the integral life of the Church and her members. For it is the function of the Church, led by the Holy Spirit who renews and purifies her ceaselessly, to make God the Father and his Incarnate Son present and in a sense visible.

f. This result is achieved chiefly by the witness of a living and mature faith, namely, one trained to see difficulties clearly and to master them. Many martyrs have given luminous witness to this faith and continue to do so. This faith needs to prove its fruitfulness by penetrating the believer's entire life, including its worldly dimensions and by activating him toward justice and love, especially regarding the needy. What does the most to reveal God's presence, however, is the brotherly charity of the faithful who are united in spirit as they work together for the faith of the gospel and who prove themselves a sign of unity.

g. While rejecting atheism, root and branch, the Church sincerely professes that all men, believers and unbelievers alike, ought to work for the rightful betterment of this world in which all alike live; such an ideal cannot be realized, however, apart from sincere and prudent dialogue. Hence the Church

protests against the distinction which some state authorities
make between believers and unbelievers, with prejudice to the
fundamental rights of the human person. The Church calls
for the active freedom of believers to build up in this world
God's temple too. She courteously invites atheists to examine
the gospel of Christ with an open mind.

h. Above all the Church knows that her message is in
harmony with the most secret desires of the human heart when
she champions the dignity of the human vocation, restoring
hope to those who have already despaired of anything higher
than their present lot. Far from diminishing man, her message
brings to his development light, life and freedom. Apart from
the message nothing will avail to fill up the heart of man:
"Thou has made us for thyself," O Lord, "and our hearts are
restless till they rest in thee."

It must clearly be stated at the outset that, because the
Church wishes to initiate such a dialogue and even begins such
an initiative herself without waiting for the other side, this does
not imply any form of indifference on her part. We have seen
quite the contrary in earlier developments of this section. She
simply demands a modicum of good will; that is, a respect of
liberty on both sides which is simply not so in many countries
behind the Iron Curtain (21a). Yet, this refutation of atheism
must not degenerate into a polemic which it has done too often
in the past (21e). It is, above all, in the Christian testimony
of its own life that the indirect refutation of atheism will reside.

After all, to be a Christian means not purely to serve God;
it also means to espouse a dynamic social ethic, a service to mankind. It is not a matter merely of theology but also of anthropology. And although Christianity is directed to the "beyond,"
it is also directed toward action in the realm of the "here below"
— to the fostering of science and to the promotion of civilization. Solidarity with the agonies and problems of modern man
becomes the sacrament of God's saving presence in the midst
of the world: "I was naked and you clothed me; I was in prison
and you came to me" (Matt 25:36-40).

The widespread representation of Christianity as the antagonist of communist society, or of any social organization, is very dangerous. It creates the impression that the Christian faith is primarily a negative and conservative force in social matters — the strongest bulwark of the capitalist concept of society and the distributor of wealth. Christianity thereby loses almost all the creative value of the social revolution embedded in its own doctrines.

This is unfortunate, even tragic, since real fidelity to the Christian gospel, *by Christians,* can revolutionize the world, can make the Church meaningful to modern man and his problems. The Christian Churches can contribute vitally to the reorganization of today's world. Yet this force can be effectively applied only when Christians pay heed to the true causes of the social malaise and fight the evil at its roots. We have seen clear evidence of this in the recently-held international conference — the *Pacem in Terris* Convocation in New York — to discuss prospects for peace. It was attended by Christians of every denomination, communists, atheists, Buddhists, Hindus and Moslems. It was a historic event in a world where mutual respect is beginning to penetrate the universal clouds of total destruction hanging over all our heads. The marxists must recognize this evolution if they are to enter into dialogue with what, up to date, they have persecuted in the name of "alienation." Is a Christianity of this sort necessarily an "alienation" of man from his city and task here below? It does not seem probable, and if man is logical, he will have to admit that he is beating to death a 19th-century carcass. There is a possibility of dialogue here which goes beyond slogans to reality, and it ought not to be missed by marxists.

But Christians should realize there is the other side of the dialogue: the understanding of the goals of atheistic marxism and the studying of its true characteristics.

It is clear that in the midst of the struggle for a new and better community — for a more deeply developed man — no

Christian can stand aloof. Wherever a man's life, work or dignity is threatened, Christian values are at stake. When a man is treated inhumanly, Christ suffers with him.

Christians should therefore recognize that the values challenged today are truly their own, and they are rooted in the Christian heritage. As Christians, we should not be misled by the fact that these values are not expressed in traditional terminology. The struggle for *true* values in the social order has often divorced itself from those personal ones which have become discredited by making religion a private affair. The self-centered values of some Christians are embarrassing. From the point of view of the Christian who has created a religion in his own image and likeness, the entire struggle for peace, freedom and universal brotherhood, as it is being lived and suffered by mankind today, must seem utterly foreign. Other Christians are right to point out that those who strive most courageously and effectively toward the ideal of peace, freedom, unity, and human dignity do not always stand on the ground of Christianity.

The situation has become incomprehensible in character; words and slogans give only a poor or incomplete picture. Christians must not be misled by the atheistic character of some currents in the world's struggles; they must analyze the situation more deeply so as to understand the jeopardy in each case. A superficial understanding is unworthy of a Christian. Every individual must open his eyes and evaluate, through faith and without prejudice, the reality in which he lives.

For the theoreticians of communist doctrine and for those who constitute the moving force of present-day communism, the perfect society of the future will be essentially atheistic. The transition to a communistic society will be the result not only of a certain program, conventionally established by the organization of work and the distribution of goods, but will also flow from the ontological necessity of things themselves. In order to understand such a theory, one must not think of an opposition between materialism and spiritualism but rather of a materialistic monism; he must consider the unity and autonomy of the empirical world, by which and in which man arises as the supreme conscious manifestation. Man thus perfects himself by working on the world in the ambience of its socio-economic relations following the laws of dialectic evolution according to which the future will absorb anterior states. The perfection of this future is compared by the marxists to the light of a true intuition, the means by which the human person inserts himself into total reality. Such an integration is, in reality, a communion, not an opposition or division. Submission constitutes liberation. The objective order brings about the maturity of the subject. Society signifies the free expansion of each individual within the expansion of all others. Ideally, this perfection will be the humanistic reduction to reality of every potential and possibility of man, attainable only by a society which refers to all those values, i.e., the spiritual values.

The result will be that man shall be neither fully conscious of his power nor able to reduce all his possibilities to practice. Either by ignorance or by the deficiency of technical and social evolution and organization (by virtue of which some will usurp that which fully belongs to all), man cannot be fully realized as yet; he will remain alienated. He must realize himself more fully in the plenitude of social life by freedom from the pressures and dominion of these alienations. The state of alienation is expressed in ideologies (philosophical, moral, or sociological) which elevate to an absolute what is only relative, transferring that which is really in the hands of men to some supernatural category. Every ideology is an abstract system, superimposed on man, an intentional holding-back of the liberating revolution which certainly attempts to retard it (by class division, by private and public divisions, by divisions between time and eternity). Against a truly human evolution, ideologies subordinate man to nature or to other men or to God.

Religion is concerned with the dependence of man on a

feigned relationship to a divine order; it formulates a patient submission to a superior will which offers man consolation by evasion. Religion makes man search outside of himself for himself — which is, of course, pure illusion; it represents a secondary division or defective socio-economic harmony, an expression of alienated man. Thus in religion there is no special value. There is, rather, a nefarious influence on man.

The negation of religion and the consequent reduction of man to the socio-temporal life is not considered by the marxists as an act of renunciation; either man does not know what he must hope for or do (as among the agnostics), or he denies that aspirations have any content (pessimistic existentialism). Contrarily, the aspirations which are projected on God in an illusory manner are not in themselves unreal; they can be reduced to reality in the future ideal society which will absorb in itself the "divine values."

This new form of society has dedicated itself in a united effort toward a new humanism. Christianity is not bound to a particular social system. The socialist system offers one of several possible solutions to the economic problems of a state. But for Christians there is a catch in socialism. In contrast to the preceding social orders, socialism does not rely on religion for the building up of society. On the contrary, it labels religion useless, and even dangerous and harmful. The Church seems to be losing her place. A new situation is being created for the Church and Christians. For the first time in her history, the Church is encountering an integral, programmed atheism.

Atheism is an organic part of the marxist world view, which is the main ideological basis of the socialist state. Marxist atheism is derived from a detailed analysis of the manifestations of religion in the 19th century, and its negation of religions has a predominantly social character.

Therefore we must take into account two things: 1) Atheism has within itself its own eschatology and we must judge it in this light. The "terrestrial paradise of messianism" is not a stimulating utopia; 2) In its own way, marxism recognizes, whether we like it or not, the reality of the aspirations which religion itself recognizes. Subjectivity is something — a mode of reality. Logically, if in the future society as perfectly realized — some aspirations are transcended, we must consider transcendence as a human constituent and must, therefore, necessarily admit that objective reality corresponds to subjective reality.

We must not approach this whole gamut of explanation as polemic or apologetic. It must be used as a way to dialogue. Pope Paul VI noted that we must hope to accomplish something by fidelity to logic. The anti-agnostic bent and the realistic spirit of marxism can lead to a positive dialogue which, until now, because of lack of a sincere and open love of truth, has been impossible. Precisely because the marxists tend to recognize the fullness of human reality, we must invite them to consider this tendency to God not as an alienation but rather as a dynamic perfection of man.

Christians sometimes see in the concept of atheism the negation of all moral and religious values; an atheist is seen as a conglomerate of everything negative. It is true — and an honest and sensitive atheist is able to admit it — that people have often resorted to atheism to get rid of all moral values and norms. Even today we see such cases. But such an atheism is not the subject of our present analysis. We must distinguish even among the various forms of atheism. It is a gross simplification to identify atheism as a whole with its negative form. The sweeping declaration that atheists are "beyond good and evil" is an effort by Christians to relieve themselves of the obligation in truth to penetrate more deeply to the precise nature of atheism and to ask if it was not their poor example that prompted it. Our daily contact with various kinds of atheists forces us to recognize that marxist atheism is not merely a biased denial of religion from a trifling encounter with some shallow-souled believer (which kind of encounter, incidentally, gives little witness to faith), not that such an atheism represents instead a struggle from a new starting point for a solution of moral problems and, in fact, of the basic questions of life. Marxist atheism appears as a humanistic view of the life claiming the whole man and seeking to solve all his problems, thus giving him a certitude and moral norm for living such as that found through faith.

Marxist atheism is more than simply an anti-church or anti-religious campaign. If we were to judge marxist atheism in our country solely on the basis of its propaganda, the picture would be just as poor as would be a judgment of religious consciousness based on attendance figures for Sunday Mass. Marxist atheism is striving for a revolutionary world view. It is trying, in the spirit of our times, to restore to people a purpose in life and to give the whole struggle of mankind a higher meaning. We cannot ignore this effort to the extent that it is directed at human and moral progress.

Even more to the point, marxist atheism makes a crushing indictment of Christians. If we examine its criticism, we can recognize that its most important argument is the fact that Christianity, during its almost two thousand years of existence, has failed to do away with poverty, servitude, wars, and social disorder. Christians have betrayed their mission in the world. They have allowed their faith to be used to support the powerful against the weak, to contribute to their bondage. They cannot erase these facts from the history of Christianity. They can only learn, and in a spirit of deep humility before the Father and his Son, Jesus Christ, acknowledge the guilt of past generations.

From all this, two consequences: 1) The marxists' interpretations of the human vocation and of religion are, in the empirical order, inadequate. Marxists' accusations are painful because of their incompleteness. But is it possible, they must ask themselves, that at least in part, their system was constructed with a view of religion which, in reality, is not religion at all, but a false religion? We must study the hidden causes which have led them to a denial of God. Religion is not an alienation; even if some — or many Christians have made it appear in the eyes of many as an evasion of human problems and an evasion from involvement with man's concrete aspirations and agonies. We must continuously purify religion of that particular class of alienating factors (individualism, clericalism, spiritual non-involvement) which have become united to the eschatology of Christianity. We must call particular attention to the forgetfulness of the social demands of charity and of religious morality which gives possibility to construct a better world for man. Marxist doctrine, formulated in the past century, has not changed at all, even if reality has changed; we must hope that slowly it will change and end by opting for a dialogue with the Church.

There can be no question that atheism and religion are irreconcilable antagonists. But each must seek as deep an understanding as possible of the other's ends and causes. We cannot ignore permanently the atheist's struggle for his goals. Christians must take atheism into account not only as a criticism of their own practices, but even as a possible answer to the question of life. This is not suggesting that for Christians the atheistic answer is on the same plane as the Christian; but the time has come to take into account the Christian response to the question of life in the world which is formulated through the grace of belief. Can the Christian be certain, in fact, that it is not his own unfaithfulness to the heritage of Christ that has prompted some to say "No" to God's calling?

The Christian must strive for a deeper evaluation of atheism and its consequences. He must recognize in particular the fact that many atheists take questions of life as seriously and earnestly as he does, that they often struggle equally as much to subdue all that is brutal in them and to realize the deeper qualities of human character. Atheistic efforts must be approached with seriousness and understanding. One sign of our age is that it strives for mutual understanding and sympathy. We sometimes complain about a lack of understanding on the part of the atheistic administration. What, though, have we done toward an understanding of the atheism in our country? It is therefore a matter of analyzing oneself as a Christian and of divorcing from those forms of action, often identified with Christianity, which pay tribute to a past world.

2) Christianity — without reason — is considered as an ideological system which alienates concrete reality. With the Church, the marxists admire and imitate the love of reasoning; but they accuse the Church of abstractionism. For this reason, the Church must show them clearly and incessantly that she is founded on a historical fact, in the personal revelation of the love of God in Christ, and that her doctrine is in accord with the integral reality of man; that it appears as a transcendental fact beyond the variable socio-economic structures. Christianity is a fact and not only a past; a transforming force projected toward the future. It is not a closed doctrinal system. The Christian fact illuminates man insofar as it shows a direction, a goal, and thus engenders confidence in man himself; but the Church must be careful not to give the impression that she can illuminate all the complications of human reality by deducing them from given principles, as if the Church or Christianity is a reasoning mechanism or computer. There are mountains of problems to be approached in humility, openness, sincerity, and a willingness to learn. Among other problems facing the dialogue is the care Christians must take not to reduce the future life to an imaginative translation to heaven. As revelation clearly shows, we must insist on the present transformation here below of the social and cosmic reality in the same way that Christ sanctified his body not by destroying or leaving it, but by transforming it in his resurrection.

Christianity, as the nominal way of life of almost a quarter of mankind, should be leading all men toward an acceptance of everything positive in the world today: all that is born, lives and develops under the impact of the present.

The Council encourages us not to break off the dialogue by our neglect of the art of understanding.

Finally the Council ends this section by giving us the place which Christ holds in the whole universe:

22. a. The truth is that only in the mystery of the Incarnate Word does the mystery of man take on light. For Adam, the first man, was a figure of him who was to come, namely Christ the Lord. Christ, the final Adam, by the revelation of the mystery of the Father and his love, fully reveals man to man himself and makes his supreme calling clear. It is not surprising, then that in him all the aforementioned truths find their root and attain their crown.

b.   He who is "the image of the invisible God" (Col 1:15), is himself the perfect man. To the sons of Adam he restores the divine likeness which had been disfigured from the first sin onward. Since human nature as he assumed it was not annulled, by that very fact it has been raised up to a divine dignity in our respect too. For by his incarnation the Son of God has united himself in some fashion with every man. He worked with human hands, he thought with a human mind, acted by human choice and loved with a human heart. Born of the Virgin Mary, he has truly been made one of us, like us in all things except sin.

c. As an innocent lamb he merited for us life by the free shedding of his own blood. In him God reconciled us to himself and among ourselves; from bondage to the devil and sin he delivered us, so that each one of us can say with the Apostle: The Son of God "loved me and gave himself up for me" (Gal 2:20). By suffering for us he not only provided us with an example for our imitation, he blazed a trail, and if we follow it, life and death are made holy and take on a new meaning.

d. The Christian man, conformed to the likeness of that Son who is the firstborn of many brothers, received "the first-fruits of the Spirit" (Rom 8:23) by which he becomes capable of discharging the new law of love. Through this Spirit, who is the "pledge of our inheritance" (Eph 1:14), the whole man is renewed from within, even to the achievement of "the redemptive of the body" (Rom 8:23): "If the Spirit of him who raised Jesus from the dead dwells in you, then he who raised Jesus Christ from the dead will also bring to life your mortal bodies because of his Spirit who dwells in you" (Rom 8:11). Pressing upon the Christian to be sure, are the need and the duty to battle against evil through manifold tribulations and even to suffer death. But, linked with the paschal mystery and patterned after the dying Christ, he will hasten forward to resurrection in the strength which comes from hope.

e. All this holds true not only for Christians, but for all men of good will in whose hearts grace works in an unseen way. For, since Christ died for all men, and since the ultimate vocation of man is in fact one, and divine, we ought to believe that the Holy Spirit in a manner known only to God offers to every man the possibility of being associated with this paschal mystery.

f. Such is the mystery of man, and it is a great one, as seen by believers in the light of Christian revelation. Through Christ and in Christ, the riddles of sorrow and death grow meaningful. Apart from his Gospel, they overwhelm us. Christ has risen, destroying death by his death; he has lavished life upon us so that, as sons in the Son, we can cry out in the spirit: Abba, Father!

The whole of the Christian vision is both Christo-centric and anthropo-centric. As a matter of fact, one can no longer historically separate (even if we must distinguish) the two, for the simple reason that God has become man. The resurrected Christ is now the Lord of the Universe (22a) in whom and for whom *all* things have been created. Since man has been continuously spoken of as the image of God throughout this section, it was only fitting to end the same section with the Lordship and Kingship of Christ over the entire creation, since man has now been fully incorporated into Christ. The next follows the scriptural developments of the epistles of St. Paul, especially those to the Ephesians and Colossians in which the central place of Christ's Lordship in creation is fully brought out. Thus, the Council says, this place of Christ is valid for all men (22e) and not just for Christians, for "He is the image of the God we cannot see," the New Man, the New Adam, the exemplar according to whom all men have been created and redeemed. There is no other Christ who stands between heaven and earth as the sole mediator and in whom alone man can find harmony and peace with God, with the cosmos, and with each other.

CHAPTER 2

The Community of Mankind

The conciliar document now proceeds to describe the characteristics of the community of mankind in a global and synthetic view. The most salient characteristic of this new world of men is that of socialization which the Council describes as follows:

23. A. One of the salient features of the modern world is the growing interdependence of men one on the other, a development promoted chiefly by modern technical advances. Nevertheless, brotherly dialogue among men does not reach its perfection on the level of technical progress, but on the deeper level of interpersonal relationships. These demand a mutual respect for the full spiritual dignity of the person. Christian revelation contributes greatly to the promotion of this communion between persons, and at the same time leads us to a deeper understanding of the laws of social life which the Creator has written into man's moral and spiritual nature.

b. Since rather recent documents of the Church's teaching authority have dealt at considerable length with Christian doctrine about human society, this Council is merely going to call to mind some of the more basic truths, treating their foundations under the light of revelation. Then it will dwell more at length on certain of their implications having special significance for our day.

First, the documents explain what is meant by this term, "socialization." Pope John XXIII had already dwelt on this aspect at length in his encyclical letter *Mater et Magistra* (see 59, 60-68, 105-109 and *Pacem in Terris,* 65). There he used the term — as is the case here — as sociologists use the term, namely, as a type of global and universal interaction of persons and of things. "One of the salient features of the modern world is the growing interdependence of men one on the other, a development promoted chiefly by modern technical advances" (23a). The concept involves a complicated intertwining of many and varied relationships in the social, economic and technical fields. Since these relationships affect almost all men and nations, men have become more socially dependent on each other in a great number of institutions and associations. This dependency manifests itself in many ways in each of these fields, especially in the economic and industrial complex. There are natural complexifications in each of these fields. Yet, it is noted by our document (23a), that true brotherhood is not brought about by a simple development of these natural institutions. As a matter of fact, socialization, unless directed toward human ends, can lead to a stifling of man and to a limitation of his personal freedom. Therefore, something else must be added in order to create a truly human community: that is, where the human person can find a milieu for his growth and expansion in the economic, social and political orders. It can be done only by an emphasis on the "hierarchy of values" among which are the preaching of fraternity and love given to us in the gospels (23a), and thus, a turning toward those conditions that make human life worthy of man with its corresponding change of mentality of man as he lives and works with his fellows. Since these fundamentals have already been discussed in previous pontifical documents (which we have already seen above), this chapter will simply give their theological foundations and recommend some practical and useful applications (23b). Throughout this section, as is the wont of previous documents, two extremes will be avoided: from one point of view, an extreme individualism which is characteristic of certain social theories of capitalistic vintage and which must be firmly resisted (24) in order to show its falsity. The document illustrates the dependence of men on each other, insofar as they are created in the very image of the Trinity, essentially social, because there is not just one person but three joined as they are by love; forming the most perfect community, the Trinity acts as an exemplar of the human community as well:

24. a. God, who has fatherly concern for everyone, has willed that all men should constitute one family and treat one another in a spirit of brotherhood. For having been created in the image of God, who "from one man has created the whole human race and made them live all over the face of the earth" (Acts 18:26), all men are called to one and the same goal, namely God himself.

b. For this reason, love for God and neighbor is the first and greatest commandment. Sacred Scripture, however, teaches us that the love of God cannot be separated from love of neighbor: "If there is any other commandment, it is summed up in this saying: Thou shalt love thy neighbor as thyself. . . . Love therefore is the fulfillment of the Law" (Rom 13:9; see John 4:20). To men growing daily more dependent on one another, and to a world becoming more unified every day, this truth proves to be of paramount importance.

c. Indeed, the Lord Jesus, when he prayed to the Father, "That all may be one . . . as we are one" (John 17:21, 22) opened up vistas closed to human reason, for he implied a certain likeness between the union of the divine Persons, and the unity of God's sons in truth and charity. This likeness reveals that man, who is the only creature on earth which God willed for itself, cannot fully find himself except through a sincere gift of himself.

This resemblance is further emphasized by appeal to the ontological union of all men in the unique salvation of Christ, the Redeemer (24b, c). Thus, "to men growing daily more dependent on each other," these spiritual motifs give them an excellent exemplar to follow and to realize the fact of what they are ontologically and that they are thus orientated to each other in the spirit of brotherhood. If this is not done, then differences which exist of necessity among men, will be occasions for discord and strife. It must be love that joins men in a common effort for human community (24a). The human person is absolutely in need of his brothers to realize his own vocation. He is, in the traditional terminology of theologians, essentially social by nature. We are therefore at opposite poles from any form of "rugged individualism." This concept will have ramifications throughout the globe as regards what John XXIII called "the universal common good" (see *Pacem*, 132) where the Pope says

> The unity of the human family has always existed, because its members were human beings all equal by virtue of their natural dignity. Hence there will always exist the objective need to promote in sufficient measure the universal common good, that is, the common good of the entire human family.

The Council will deal with each of these aspects in the chapters that follow (24-32). Yet, at the introduction of its exposé, the document reminds men of the example of Christ: that it is only by giving of ourselves that we can hope to find ourselves. The human person is so composed that, in the gospel terms, it is only in losing one's life that one can truly find it. We become ourselves only in complete gift of self to others, and it is only on this basis that a truly human community can be built (24c). It is much like the unity of nature and the plurality of persons in the one God joined in love for a common work. This is man's exemplar in human community since he has been created in the image and the likeness of God himself. Therefore, the source of human community must reside exactly here. Between these two (God and the human person) there is "a certain likeness," since in reality it is the love in the Blessed Trinity that we follow and imitate in building up the human community of man. Pope John had the same idea in *Pacem*. Catholics in particular ought to be cognizant, above all, of the demands of love in the human community, since they and all men (at least in potential and hope) belong to Christ and the Mystical Body of Christ which is the Church. In this relationship, men are joined in real bonds of love and life so intimately and closely that earthly comparison is totally incapable of expressing it. In the Mystical Body, men are truly brothers in Jesus Christ, the Lord. This realization must give impetus to Christians for action in the social order. Man's thirst for justice can find its living water in the well-spring of charity and love in Christ. It will be perfect in the celestial city only, but its effects and partial realization must be felt in the social life of the here below.

> Human society, Venerable Brothers and beloved children, ought to be regarded above all as a spiritual reality: in which men communicate knowledge to each other in the light of truth; in which they can enjoy their rights and fulfill their duties, and are inspired to strive for moral good. Society should enable men to share in and enjoy every legitimate expression of beauty, and encourage them constantly to pass on to others all that is best in themselves, while they strive to make their own the spiritual achievements of others. These are the spiritual values which continuously give life and basic orientations to cultural expressions, economics and social institutions, political movements and forms, laws and all other structures by which society is outwardly established and constantly developed (*Pacem*, 36).

This vision of the Pope for human community is the same as that of our present document. Nothing truly human can escape this sanctifying power of the Word of God; and, consequently, of the Church as well. The objective of the Church will be to orientate and incorporate them into a greater whole in man's *total* vocation. It is with this in mind that the Council develops the next paragraph:

> 25. a. Man's social nature makes it evident that the progress of the human person and the advances of society itself hinge on one another. For the beginning, the subject and the goal of all social institutions is and must be the human person, which for its part and by its very nature stands completely in need

of social life. Since this social life is not something added on to man, through his dealings with others, through reciprocal duties, and through fraternal dialogue he develops all his gifts and is able to rise to his destiny.

b. Among those social ties which man needs for his development some, like the family and political community, relate with greater immediacy to his innermost nature; others originate rather from his free decision. In our era, for various reasons, reciprocal ties and mutual dependencies increase day by day and give rise to a variety of associations and organizations, both public and private. This development, which is called socialization, while certainly not without its dangers, brings with it many advantages with respect to consolidating and increasing the qualities of the human person, and safeguarding his rights.

c. But if by this social life the human person is greatly aided in responding to his destiny, even in its religious dimensions, it cannot be denied that men are often diverted from doing good and spurred toward evil by the social circumstances in which they live and are immersed from their birth. To be sure the disturbances which so frequently occur in the social order result in part from the natural tensions of economic, political and social forms. But at a deeper level they flow from man's pride and selfishness, which contaminate even the social sphere. When the structure of affairs is flawed by the consequences of sin, man, already born with a bent toward evil, finds there new inducements to sin, which cannot be overcome without strenuous efforts and the assistance of grace.

We find here the cardinal principles of all of the Church's social teaching and the ultimate aim of every truly human society: the promotion of the human person (25a). This formed the rock bottom of John XXIII's *Pacem* and *Mater* as well as the total work of Pius XII.

As Christians and as human beings, we must look directly at what social institutions actually do to men and for what motive they are directed and conducted. For the Christian (and for the true human person) there is really one criterion for any enterprise for example, within the context of any economy where it promotes (or not) the human dignity of the men who collaborate within it. This reference to man as person and as incarnate spirit must remain for the theologian a permanent light and final criterion of each historical evolution of the economy, be it moderate socialism, communism, or capitalism. It is instructive, in this respect, that this is exactly what has happened in the papal teachings on private property where the popes have criticized both extremes of denial of private property (communism) as well as that of individualistic capitalism. We have seen that even moderate socialism during the era of Pius XI had made progress along these lines, breaking away from the dogmatic denial of private property by orthodox marxists. Parallel to this evolution there has been a similar one in the teachings of the popes.

This social life of man in society for the promotion of man is not some afterthought on the part of the Church. Man is social by his very nature and he needs his brothers. The Council fathers emphasized this point, since none of what will follow in the entire document can, in any fashion, be fully realized without a strong consciousness of this human (and divine) solidarity among men. It reminds one of the same stress that our Lord gives to the good works of men done for men as, in reality, done for him: "Amen, I say to you, as long as you did it to one of the least of these my brethren, you did it to me" (Matt 25:40).

Then the document gives us a general listing of types of organization necessary for the expansion and development of the human person: some necessary, such as the state and the family; others voluntary, which both come from the right of association for the development of the human person (25b). The Council here underlines this aspect rather forcibly, since it is clear that the mark of a truly free society is the efflorescence of voluntary organization within that society. Pope John XXIII emphasized this aspect of human society in *Mater et Magistra* which he calls "intermediary groups" (11-13, 22, 65, 94). His personalistic view of a balanced and just society is one in which the citizens themselves participate as fully as possible in the social, economic, and political functions of their society. Such participation gives each citizen a feeling of importance and responsibility vis-à-vis society itself; and it makes society more humane and more in conformity with the innate dignity of the human person (see also 55, 94, 112, 118, 154, 161, 182, 197, 205 and *Pacem,* 24, 64, 72, 130, 140, 164). And yet, there is no facile distinction between voluntary and natural associations, since in our complicated and socialized society the two have become more and more interdependent.

It is true that the state and family both correspond in an evident manner to the natural need of man in its most primitive sense; yet, voluntary organization — to the measure that man realizes more and more of what he is and the exigencies of that fact — find their origins and component parts in the natural order. The very reason such voluntary organizations belong to the natural order, is that, by them the human person comes to a fuller expansion and knowledge of who and what he is. One of the most evident types of such voluntary organization in modern times is that of the labor union. Leo XIII gave the working man a special mandate by teaching him that labor unions were a natural right; Pope John XXIII gave this economic and social activity an even more forceful inculcation and justification. He developed the fuller notion of their participation at all levels of industry and in the political organization of the country itself. In any case, as in past pontifical teaching, our document shows itself diametrically opposed to all forms of social individualism at any level of society and gives us a balance between these factors of personalization and social responsibility.

Yet the fundamental difficulty remains in every form of social organization (and this appears throughout our document): that of egoism and selfishness in the affairs of men (25c). The tensions which already exist between the person and the economic and social processes of society are intensified by the spirit of selfish gain and expropriation of some men by other men. Thus, once again, a conversion and change of mentality is needed to overcome this in order to see human society in the sense described above.

26. a. Every day human interdependence tightens and spreads by degrees over the whole world. As a result the common good, that is, the sum of those conditions of social life which allow social groups and their individual members relatively thorough and ready access to their own fulfillment, today takes on an increasingly universal complexion and consequently involves rights and duties with respect to the whole human race. Every social group must take account of the needs and legitimate aspirations of other groups, and even of the general welfare of the entire human family.

b. At the same time, however, there is a growing awareness of the exalted dignity proper to the human person, since he stands above all things, and his rights and duties are universal and inviolable. Therefore, there must be made available to all men everything necessary for leading a life truly human, such as food, clothing, and shelter; the right to choose a state of life freely and to found a family, the right to education, to employment, to a good reputation, to respect, to appreciate information, to activity in accord with the upright norm of one's own conscience, to protection of privacy and to rightful freedom, even in matters religious.

c. Hence, the social order and its development must always work to the benefit of the human person if the disposition of affairs is to be subordinate to the personal realm and not contrariwise, as the Lord indicated when he said that the Sabbath was made for man, not man for the Sabbath.

d. This social order requires constant improvement. It must be founded on truth, built on justice and animated by love; in freedom it should grow every day toward a more humane balance. An improvement in attitudes and numerous changes in society will have to take place if these objectives are to be gained.

e. God's Spirit, who with a marvelous providence directs the unfolding of time and renews the face of the earth, is not absent from this development. The ferment of the gospel too has aroused and continues to arouse in man's heart the irresistible requirements of his dignity.

The document gives a full description of the process of socialization (26a). All this is realized in function of the "common good" which is the very end of human organization of society. This notion has been expanded from the national to the international community where the very process of socialization has contributed greatly in making men one solid community. This common good can be summarized as three basic requisites. The first is the sum total of the riches and services of a particular society which is organized for human needs and expansion. This is the result of the labor and work of all peoples in a society. From this flows the fact that because of human dignity, all men in society have the right to those goods and services necessary for human dignity and without which human dignity is an empty mockery (*Pacem*, 18-22). A strict egalitarian distribution of goods in a particular society is not implied here, but what is meant is that each person has the right to use these goods in sufficient degree to insure the sustaining of his human dignity. To use the maxim of Marx: "From each according to his abilities and to each according to his needs" can have a deeply Christian meaning as well. Man has the right to work because of his originality and irreplaceability; but he also has the obligation to work in order to make his contribution to society and to his fellow men since he is in solidarity with them (see 24-25). All this distribution and redistribution of goods and services must be seen not in the strictly logical and minimal sense, but in the spirit of true brotherhood which binds all men into the solidarity of a true human community. Without this sentiment binding men, we are left with a Hobbsian definition of human community as "a war of all against all" where only by a social contract do men surrender the use of violence for the good of all. These aspects of the common good make the Christian recognize that this notion of the common good is, in reality, an attempt to return to the source of unity and fraternity: the loving Trinitarian existence. Thus the common good is directed to and for the human person, and, for this reason it is economic, social, political and cultural. Any effective social order must take into account that man is an incarnate spirit, composed of body and soul (26b). In a sense, the Council's thought is here very close to that of St. Thomas Aquinas who says that the essence of a community is the suitable disposition of many toward one end. This disposition, explains St. Thomas, consists in many persons living and working together to promote individual and general well-being, but a necessary corollary to this is that these persons also promote the subjective culture or development of each member of that society. Since man becomes richer through his relations with external realities, he must be open to the realities of the world. Therefore, it is only in living the meaning of his relations to the world that man can perfect himself. The end of man in the terrestrial city is that he work in union with others to promote his external culture which further allows the growth of internal culture. St. Thomas saw this when he said that the individual is to society as the part is to the whole. The part is directed to the whole, and as a result, the part profits from the whole.

Thus the common good of society can be considered and studied as the internal end. The health of a person is an intrinsic good. There is also the health of the group, that is, the group's equilibrium which depends both on a material and a formal element. The material element needed for the common good is that the community be comprised of many members, each with his own diversity and originality. Each member must be allowed the free development of his own originality. This places responsibility on both the person and society: the person has the responsibility of developing his tendencies, capacities, talents, and so forth; society must insure favorable conditions for each member to develop his originality. But since acceptance of responsibility by the person and by society is a free act, liberty is primary. The formal element needed for the common good is love (26d). Diversity is ambiguous; it can be the source of disparity or of unity. Love and all the virtues in its services must be present to achieve the common good. Again, this presents a responsibility to the person and to society. The person has the responsibility of developing and cultivating this love. Society, on the other hand, has the responsibility of promoting the community's morality, made up of all the virtues which pertain to the social life; of which, however, liberty comes first.

Christians, then, are to see human society above all as a spiritual reality where brotherhood must flourish. They are to recognize in the evangelical principles of love and justice a driving force which will send them into the city of man to create the conditions of man's social, political, and economic life (26e). This is basically true; since to become flesh and bone, a doctrine must become incarnate within the world, within these fields under pain of remaining a pure abstraction for man, and in the end, meaningless for man. What, one may ask, has the Sermon on the Mount to do with civil rights, urban renewal, nuclear disarmament, the U.S., the economic society, immigration, internal law, peace movements, racism and internationalism? The answer really must be — if Christianity is to be meaningful at all to modern man — everything; for the Church's teachings on these aspects is her vital life-line for the salvation of men of *this* world, at *this* time. In reality, to misunderstand the social teaching and implications of Christianity, is to misunderstand Christianity itself. It must work from within as a ferment and a servant of man, aiding him in his endeavors to become free from the slaveries of the world and slavery from himself. The role of the Church can never be that of a *dominans,* but only that of a *serva* in which she comes to serve man and love man for and in himself, not in an apologetic fashion for "conversion" or for "saving" him, but to be there as his servant and witness of love, with him in his struggles and agonies. Yet, in saying this, we have not as yet solved the problem of confronting this modern mentality and its relation to morality; and, in a sense, to all the problems of the relation of Christianity to the modern world. For it is here that we encounter the *crux problematis* between the believing and unbelieving in the modern world. We must, as we have so far gathered, distinguish (but not separate) Christianity from the autonomy of the political, cultural, social, and economic order ("desacralization"). This, Christianity has done, *grosso modo*, in her documents of the modern church after some terrible setbacks in that abortive period of the 19th century. We simply cannot go back, under the guise of a false neo-sacralism, to the old order (what many authors call the "Constantinian era" from the 4th to the 20th centuries). Nor can we go back to the old relation of "wonder" and "mystery" of the forces of nature (Deism, theophanies and at least to some degree, theodicy, at least of the type that reveals God to us through the mysteries and grandeurs of nature). In this sense, "natural law" as a source of God's direct will for modern man is all but meaningless for him. Indeed, an emphasis on this type of traditional procedure can only lead to superstition as an escape from the real world of desacralization and technology by the Christian.

On the other hand, if we *separate* the Christian reality (not *distinguish*) from the present world and its constructs, we fall into the real heresy of separating faith from the world of man. In such a stance, man attends to his religious duties and simply does not attempt to relate them to the life of faith and its connotations for the life of man in the earthly city of man. In such a case, the technician and scientist fails to see the real relationship between the two in his vision of the world, since science is related to a continuous progress and the scientist does not see where this fits into a unified vision of the world in faith. The whole question of God, then, is entirely outside the whole conspectus of empirical scientific progress. The metaphysician and the priest speak an entirely new (or other) language which he simply does not understand; and which, if he is a man of science, he can only accept "on faith" which is *eo ipso,* a schizophrenic vision of the world and of himself within that world. We have here a very dangerous situation as well as one which is extremely precarious for leading modern men to a correct comprehension of Christianity and its message (which is the whole reason for *aggiornamento* in the modern Church). This explains to a degree the popularity of a Teilhard de Chardin who attempted to bridge this gap and who, because of his expertise on matters both scientific and religious, was in a unique position to do this. That the problem is not realized as critical in the Church is seen by the very rough treatment of De Chardin by many members of the Church, high and low. Teilhard posited — for many, for the first time in modern Christianity — a valid dialogue between the believing and the unbelieving world.

This dialogue must be pursued as so fervently desired by Pope Paul in *Ecclesiam Suam.* But on what basis can it progress? Along the lines of the thought of Teilhard de Chardin, namely, of our mutual confrontation with man himself as man and not as he "relates to nature," or "natural law" which can lead us to incomprehension. It is useless to reduce this to moralisms which appear as platitudinous for modern man no matter how much we speak of "insertion" of Christian principles into the "world" which, in itself, is sterile and unavailing in a dialogue of Christian-unbeliever (atheist). Our truth must be proclaimed in a world which no longer believes and where faith is becoming more and more — not a product of cultural acclimation — but where it must become by force of necessity, a personal and personalizing living response. For today there are more reasons not to believe than to believe, where the whole cultural structure (rural, agricultural, passive, and Christian) and support for the Christian faith (as in the middle ages) have been subverted and which can no longer withstand the invasion of pluralism and atheism. We cease to live in a unified Christian world where faith in God seems so natural and where an unbeliever seems like an obstinate pervert. And for the distant future this is not likely to change. The Church and Christianity must, then, acclimate themselves to living in the diaspora (Karl Rahner). To do this as living witness the Church must establish dialogue with the unbelieving world and she can do this only by the common solicitude, that is, man himself, his freedom and growth. For the Christian, this ought not to be strange since here below the very presence of Christ living in our midst is the brotherly and true love we have for one another. This evidently implies a seeking for our brother what we desire for ourselves: human and civil rights, economic, social, and cultural welfare, freedom from war, and desire for freedom to develop his talents to the greatest degree by education, and so forth. This is all evidently implied in our approach to man as we see, aid and love him.

The document, finally, mentions a summary listing of the rights of man (26c) and it simply restates the essential of what John XXIII had already said in *Pacem* (8-24). Yet, what is to be noticed here is that it is the rights of man which are emphasized above and beyond "things" or goods men might have in society. This does not mean that the institution, for instance, of private property has been eliminated (we shall see this later), only that it is a grave moral aberration to stress property rights (realtors) over human rights or to put them on the same level. Later on, the Council will say the same about work and the instruments of work (67a).

As a consequence of all the above, the Council gives us this evident conclusion:

27. a. Coming down to practical and particularly urgent consequences, this Council lays stress on reverence for man; everyone must consider his every neighbor without exception as another self, taking into account first of all his life and the means necessary to living it with dignity, so as not to imitate the rich man who had no concern for the poor man Lazarus.

b. In our times a special obligation binds us to make ourselves the neighbor of every person without exception, and of actively helping him when he comes across our path, whether he be an old person abandoned by all, a foreign laborer unjustly looked down upon, a refugee, a child born of an unlawful union and wrongly suffering for a sin he did not commit, or a hungry person who disturbs our conscience by recalling the voice of the Lord, "As long as you did it for one of these the least of my brethren, you did it for me" (Matt 25:40).

 c. Furthermore, whatever is opposed to life itself, such as any type of murder, genocide, abortion, euthanasia or willful self-destruction, whatever violates the integrity of the human person, such as mutilation, torments inflicted on body or mind, attempts to coerce the will itself; whatever insults human dignity, such as subhuman living conditions, arbitrary imprisonment, deportation, slavery, prostitution, the selling of women and children; as well as disgraceful working conditions, where men are treated as mere tools for profit, rather than as free and responsible persons; all these things and others of their like are infamies indeed. They poison human society, but they do more harm to those who practice them than those who suffer from the injury. Moreover, they are a supreme dishonor to the Creator.

We are one family by our creation, by our common Father in heaven (Creator), and this was further intensified by the fact of Christ's incarnation and his extension, the Mystical Body of Christ (redemption). Therefore, every man who comes to us is radically our brother regardless of race, color, or creed (27a). Our neighbor is our other self and must be treated as such under pain of separating ourselves by any act of rejection from Christ himself (27b). But above all, as in Pope John's encyclicals, it is not enough to serve our brothers in beautiful words but it must be translated into concrete actions. Here we have a rich theology of Christian action which unites the spiritual and temporal aspects of the Christian vocation on earth. Action for the brothers is here seen as an essential element in the development of Catholic social thought. The document emphasizes that the Christian is not only educated for action but by action. Christian education is no longer enough; it must be supplemented by concrete action on the firing line. The Christian is called upon — in fact is obliged — to become directly engaged in the social and economic activities of the modern world. We have here an intimate interaction of doctrine and action which are both part and parcel of the Christian vocation in, to, and for the terrestrial city of man. Many of the Fathers of the Council insisted rather strongly on this aspect of "every neighbor without exception as another self" and this must be understood in all its stark reality.

Finally (27c), our document gives us a summary list of those things offensive to human dignity taken from various lists of the rights of man (see *Pacem,* 143: "An act of the highest importance performed by the United Nations Organization was the Universal Declaration of the Rights of Man, approved in the General Assembly of December 10, 1948. In the preamble of that Declaration, the recognition of a respect for those rights and respective liberties is proclaimed as an ideal to be pursued by all peoples and all countries"). The list is both general and actual such as that of "brainwashing" ("torments inflicted on body or mind"), torture (Viet Nam), "subhuman living conditions" (slums, favillas, etc.), "arbitrary imprisonment" (South Africa), "slavery" (Saudi Arabia), prostitution (general throughout the globe), "disgraceful working conditions" (Latin America). This section is concluded with a very fine psychological observation; namely, that such evil deeds do more harm to the one performing them than the one on whom they are worked. A man can be a free man even in prison and under force because his spirit is free; the slaveholder is indeed a slave since the basic respect due to a human being is lacking in such a person.

The Council next calls for mutual respect and tolerance for differences of opinion in the public forum. This is the area of civil liberties:

28. a. Respect and love ought to be extended also to those who think or act differently than we do in social, political and

even religious matters. In fact, the more deeply we come to understand their ways of thinking through such courtesy and love, the more easily will we be able to enter into dialogue with them.

b. This love and good will, to be sure, must in no way render us indifferent to truth and goodness. Indeed love itself impels the disciples of Christ to speak the saving truth to all men. But it is necessary to distinguish between error, which always merits repudiation, and the person in error, who never loses the dignity of being a person even when he is flawed by false or inadequate religious notions. God alone is the judge and searcher of hearts; for that reason he forbids us to make judgments about the internal guilt of anyone.

c. The teaching of Christ even requires that we forgive injuries, and extends the law of love to include every enemy, according to the command of the New Law: "You have heard that it was said: Thou shalt love your neighbor and hate your enemy. But I say to you: love your enemies, do good to those who hate you, and pray for those who persecute and calumniate you" (Matt 5:43, 44).

We have here some basic requirements for the dialogue: tolerance (28a), love of the truth and yet respect for the person whom we consider to be in error (28b), and finally a heart free from hatred for injuries done us by our enemies (28c). These conditions of the dialogue would seem to be very stringent and yet the Church being serious in this respect, does indeed approach the dialogue with such an openness of spirit. This problem of the attitude of men in the dialogue will be discussed more at random later in the conciliar development (73, 75). What is recommended here is the acceptance of the fact of a pluralistic society; that is, where there is a diversity of opinions on who and what man is. Mutual tolerance must be the guide here in the actions of men. This cannot (for the Christian) imply any type of indifference as regards the truth. The Christian can never accept the thesis that liberty of conscience means freedom to believe or disbelieve anything one chooses to believe or disbelieve. All men are bound by objective truth revealed once and for all through Christ the Savior. In this sense, a doctrinal error has no objective reality or claim to adherence by anyone. Thus some argue that "error has no rights" and consequently should not be tolerated. But this is to put the whole question in poor perspective. Of course error has no right — and neither does truth. Only persons have rights, even if they hold objectively erroneous views. It is a sound teaching of Catholic theology that although men are bound in the objective order to accept God's revelation as proposed to them by the Church, the formal morality of any action is to be measured entirely in terms of the dictates of conscience at the moment this act is performed. Suffice it to say that a conscience honestly formed — whether it corresponds to objective truth or not — must be followed under penalty of sin. This is not to say that the objective norm (the will of God) is not important. St. Thomas and many Catholic theologians after him have always emphasized the grave moral obligation of all men to form their consciences according to God's objective revelation. Yet, because of various circumstances beyond an individual's control, e.g., birth in another religion, environment, training, he may well be invincibly ignorant of this true objective norm and have thus formed his conscience in an honest and sincere way according to what is objectively incorrect. In such a case, man's conscience must direct all his actions under pain of sin since he has no other way of knowing God's commands.

The document then discusses — as did Pope John — the fundamental distinction to be made between error and the person who errs (28b). The person who errs is always a human person subject to his rights and respect as to his person and opinions. No matter what we may think of his ideas, opinions, he is still and must always remain, the object of infinite respect by all men and by any political community worthy of the name (*Pacem*, 159-160).

Finally (28c), we must note this difference in the present section from the above two; namely, that while the first two

aspects of the problem are intrinsic to the very notion of tolerance, the third — forgiveness of injury — is extrinsic. The Council here directly refers to the gospel, where alone we can find
the reason and strength to overcome what sometimes is an
insurmountable obstacle to mutual understanding among
brothers.

This, of course, is based on the basic equality and dignity of
all men throughout the world:

29. a. Since all men possess a rational soul and are created
in God's likeness, since they have the same nature and origin,
have been redeemed by Christ and enjoy the same divine
calling and destiny, the basic equality of all must receive increasingly greater recognition.

b. True, all men are not alike from the point of view of
varying physical power and the diversity of intellectual and
moral resources. Nevertheless, with respect to the fundamental
rights of the person, every type of discrimination, whether social
or cultural, whether based on sex, race, color, social condition,
languages or religion, is to be overcome and eradicated as contrary to God's intent. For in truth it must still be regretted
that fundamental personal rights are not yet being universally
honored. Such is the case of a woman who is denied the right
to choose a husband freely, to embrace a state of life or to
acquire an education or cultural benefits equal to those recognized for men.

c. Therefore, although rightful differences exist between
men, the equal dignity of persons demands that a more humane
and just condition of life be brought about. For excessive
economic and social differences between the members of the
one human family or population groups cause scandal, and
militate against social justice, equity, the dignity of the human
person, as well as social and international peace.

d. Human institutions, both private and public, must labor
to minister to the dignity and purpose of man. At the same
time let them put up a stubborn fight against any kind of
slavery, whether social or political, and safeguard the basic
rights of man under every political system. Indeed human
institutions themselves must be accommodated by degrees to

the highest of all realities, spiritual ones, even though meanwhile, a long enough time will be required before they arrive at the desired goal.

The document first gives the reasons for this basic equality among men (29a). We have already seen this above. Human equality was a historical realization since this has not always been so. It is only in comparatively recent times that the institution of slavery, for instance, has been eliminated as incompatible with the dignity of man. It took a long time for the gospel ferment of love, justice, and equality to take their roots in the socio-political order in spite of the fact that Christians have lived in these societies. This is known as a historical evolution in the ability to see the consequences of these institutions on the dignity of man, especially in the case of woman (29b). Equal to man, she participates fully in the rights and responsibilities that are hers. In the past, however, she was treated as an inferior or a minor in a male society, even in Christian countries and by Christian thinkers. The modern age will no longer tolerate this inequality. Woman has an originality by the very fact of her sexual existence as a woman; and from this vantage point, the originality of half of the world has barely begun to emerge. But it must emerge because it is woman's right.

Thus, like the Pope in *Pacem,* our document here states very clearly that there is a basic core of humanity which must be respected if peace is to be achieved. It defines this core as the inviolate, inalienable, and universal rights of the human person; these are essential to a sane conception of any present or future national and international order. The function of the state — as we shall see later in more detail — is only to promote, protect, and facilitate the exercise of these rights. Thus, they are called civil rights only insofar as they are guaranteed in laws and constitutions. But fundamentally, they belong to every human being for the reasons given by our document (29a) —

man or woman, black or white, rich or poor, strong or weak —
by the very fact that he possesses human nature. These rights
are not to be violated by government or by other individuals.
Unless men incorporate this basic structure in declarations of
human rights, international laws, and constitutions, men are
simply wasting their time and endangering true peace (*Pacem*,
8-22). Man is made in the image and likeness of God and
therefore must be treated with the respect this entails. Our
document sees — in the final analysis — the dignity of man dependent upon this basic theological theme.

This, of course, does not mean that there can be no inequality in talents, ambition, and so on (29b). This is too
evident for commentary. What it does mean, however, is
that these *accidental* differences be not elevated to absolutes
thus resulting in various forms of exaggerations and discrimination. It can be known as racism, nationalism, ideology, etc. —
but each of these is absolutizing that which is fundamentally an
accident of nature (color, nationality, sex, etc.). This must also
extend itself to the economic sphere where we have the great
disparity between the rich nations and the poor nations (29c).
The document will give long consideration to this aspect of
international life later on in its analysis.

Finally (29c), we note the use of the very controversial term
"social justice" which has long been a source of contention
among Catholic social thinkers. It is used, however, in conjunction with the word "equity" as well as with economic and social
unbalances. Thus, concludes our document, the real damage
here is caused by the excessive disparity between the rich and
the poor and by the rich who do not come to the aid of these
same poor individuals and nations. This leads us to the next
paragraph where the essential conditions of social justice are
enumerated:

30. a. Profound and rapid changes make it more necessary
that no one ignoring the trend of events or drugged by laziness,

content himself with a merely individualistic morality. It becomes increasingly true that the obligations of justice and love
are fulfilled only if each person, contributing to the common
good, according to his own abilities and the needs of others,
also promotes and assists the public and private institutions
dedicated to bettering the conditions of human life. Yet there
are those who, while professing grand and rather noble sentiments, nevertheless, in reality live always as if they cared nothing
for the needs of society. Many in various places even make
light of social laws and precepts, and do not hesitate to resort
to various frauds and deceptions in avoiding just taxes or other
debts due to society. Others think little of certain norms of
social life, for example those designed for the protection of
health, or laws establishing speed limits; they do not even
avert to the fact that by such indifference they imperil their
own life and that of others.

b. Let everyone consider it his sacred obligation to esteem
and observe social necessities as being among the primary
duties of modern man. For the more unified the world becomes, the more plainly do the offices of men extend beyond
particular groups and spread by degrees to the whole world.
But this development cannot occur unless individual men and
their associations cultivate in themselves the moral and social
virtues, and promote them in society; thus, with the needed
help of divine grace men who are truly new and artisans of a
new humanity can be forthcoming.

Today we see more clearly than ever the social dimensions
of our being, and that, to help man, it is no longer sufficient
to meet his needs on an individual basis but also on a social
basis. For better or for worse, man is influenced profoundly by
his social existence for which an "individualistic morality" will
no longer do (30a). Thus a profound social ethic must today
be brought to the consciousness of Christians — which our document tells us, is as yet not fully realized in Christian circles.

There can be no living nor authentic faith in God without
"works of faith" and among these, there is, first of all, that of
caring for others "without distinction of persons": "Thou shalt
love the Lord thy God . . . thou shalt love thy neighbor as thy-

self" (Matt 22:36). To love one's neighbor as oneself is not confined to satisfying, by means of Catholic charities, the most urgent necessities of our neighbor. It means, above all, effectively to desire for him what we desire for ourselves: civil rights, health, education, development, civilization and culture. It means to wage an effective war for him against the evils which we fight for our own advantage, to do our best to eliminate the great economic and social inequalities and the oppression of man by man. Unless priests convey this social message to their people as intrinsic to the Christian message, then we can simply forget about any meaningful *aggiornamento*.

To be a Christian is not purely to serve God but it is also a dynamic social ethic, a service to mankind; it is not merely a theology but also an anthropology. Although Christianity is directed to the "beyond," it nevertheless must influence our actions in the realm of the "here below" by fostering science and promoting civilization. It must give a deeper meaning to our bond with the world and, with their lives centered in Christ, dead and resurrected, at Mass, Christians are the same members who must put the Holy Sacrifice at the center of their lives in the world, among men. They are Christ's true envoys, his ambassadors; they are the spiritual prolongation of Christ's saving liturgical mystery in the midst of their brothers in the world. In virtue of this saving liturgical mystery, they must render the earth more habitable, more humane, more just.

All of the modern revolutions, from a social point of view, have been conceived outside the Church and sometimes in opposition to her. Democracy, religious liberty, the social, the psychological, the scientific revolution, woman suffrage, and finally, the slave problem and civil rights. The charge is grave but can be amply substantiated. The problem for the modern Catholic is to enter into each of these fields and reap what is good and fine in them, bringing the light of charity and faith to bear on them.

The example which our document gives of the blatant failure

of some Christians to recognize their obligations to the commonwealth is that of paying taxes. This can be seen very clearly in Latin America where the tax structures are not only inequitable but where it is actually the poor who do most of the paying. The rich may invest outside the country while failing to reinvest in the future of their own countries. In our own country, the repeal of the equitable income tax would amount to making the rich richer and the poor poorer. The example of speed limits is also a very evident example, since driving an automobile is a double responsibility: one to oneself, and the other to all other members of society who drive on the highway. These laws are moral in nature, since they permit men to live together in harmony, peace, and safety; therefore, the citizen is morally obliged to keep them. These examples are only indications of how citizens are to take seriously their responsibilities for each other in every circumstance of civic and social life. "Let everyone consider it his sacred obligation to esteem and observe social necessities as being among the primary duties of modern man" (30b). It is this type of education, of self-gift and esteem which will assure the promotion of a "new humanity" which is now in the process of being born.

The requirements for this new humanity and its development are, first of all, a very high degree of technical training:

31. a. Individual men, in order to discharge with greater exactness the obligations of their conscience toward themselves and the various groups to which they belong, must be carefully educated to a higher degree of culture through the use of the immense resources available today to the human race. Above all the education of youth from every social background has to be undertaken, so that there can be produced not only men and women of refined talents, but those great-souled persons, who are so desperately required by our times.

b. Now a man can scarcely arrive at the needed sense of responsibility unless his living conditions allow him to become conscious of his dignity and to rise to his destiny by spending himself for God and for others. But human freedom is often

crippled when a man encounters extreme poverty, just as it
withers when he indulges in too many of life's comforts and
imprisons himself in a kind of splendid isolation. Freedom
acquires new strength, by contrast, when a man consents to
the unavoidable requirements of social life, takes on the manifold demands of human partnership, and commits himself to
the service of the human community.

c. Hence, the will to play one's role in common endeavors
should be everywhere encouraged. Praise is due to those national processes which allow the largest possible number of
citizens to participate in public affairs with genuine freedom.
Account must be taken, to be sure, of the actual conditions
of each people and the firmness required by public authority.
If every citizen is to feel inclined to take part in the activities
of the various groups which make up the social body, these
must offer advantages which will attract members and dispose
them to serve others. We can justly consider that the future
of humanity lies in the hands of those who are strong enough
to provide coming generations with reasons for living and hop-
ing.

The theme of responsibility and participation of modern
man in his own destiny are brought out clearly in this paragraph.
Education (31a) given to citizens in proportion to their talents
was also a favorite theme of *Pacem.* The reasons for this are
given by our document. A political democracy as envisioned
in this same paragraph (31c) presupposes an educated citizenry
which can understand issues, since it is the people who assume
responsibility for their own destiny. But more importantly, a
man has a right and an obligation to develop the talents which
God has given him, so that he may make a contribution to
society with his unique genius. This can be accomplished only
by education. Since each man has the right to an education
to develop his talents, the only criterion must be his talents; if
he cannot pay for his education, then the state has a responsibility
to aid him. A man must develop his talents, it is true; but he
will find the perfection of this only when he uses them for the
good of others in a social context. The primary concern, espe-

cially for the Christian, is how to serve man better with what God has given him. The Christian has learned the individual dimension of piety and religious obligation; of his social dimension, however, he has little awareness, and our present document emphasizes this throughout its text.

This theme of responsibility is brought out in 31b where it speaks, in the same line as did John XXIII in *Mater et Magistra,* on both political as well as social democracy (54). In the former, each person participates and contributes according to his talents, abilities, and needs (31c). Each one takes full responsibility as a citizen because political institutions are ultimately directed by the citizen through his representatives. This is a demand today of human nature itself (*Pacem,* 26-27) and thus corresponds to human dignity, because it gives each man a sense of duty and responsibility. Economic society has not as yet such democracy (31b), for no responsibility exists for the promotion of human dignity. Insofar as the direction of an enterprise is concerned, for example, the worker is considered a perpetual minor, a number that can be dismissed or hired according to the "need" determined by market value. He is an automaton to be turned on or off. And this view of man violates all canons of social justice given by the popes as well as by our present document, for the precise reason that an automaton cannot be or develop as a human being. The directives here are given in order to remedy this dehumanizing situation.

The Council gives us some of the elements which are retarding such a humanizing process: the miserable conditions of life of millions of human beings who do not have the sustenance of animals, where millions of them literally starve to death each year and where other countless millions do not have enough to eat; miserable slum conditions found through Asia, Africa, and Latin America which cause them to live as beasts instead of human beings. Responsibility and participation can mean almost nothing to these countless millions. These social conditions must then be alleviated and remedied before we can speak of human dignity here. Our document will return to this aspect in the second part of its text.

Then, finally, the document gives us some light of understanding on the realities of this world: the Incarnate Word.

32. a. As God did not create man for life in isolation, but for the formation of social unity, so also "it has pleased God to make men holy and save them not merely as individuals, without bond or link between them, but by making them into a single people, a people which acknowledges him in truth and serves him in holiness. So from the beginning of salvation history he has chosen men not just as individuals but as members of a certain community. Revealing his mind to them, God called these chosen ones "his people" (Ex 2:7, 12), and even made a covenant with them on Sinai.

b. This communitarian character is developed and consummated in the work of Jesus Christ. For the very Word made flesh willed to share in the human fellowship. He was present at the wedding of Cana, visited the house of Zachaeus, ate with publicans and sinners. He revealed the love of the Father and the sublime vocation of man in terms of the most common of social realities and by making use of the speech and the imagery of plain everyday life. Willingly obeying the laws of his country, he sanctified those human ties, especially family ones, which are the foundation of social structures. He chose to lead the life proper to an artisan of his time and place.

c. In his preaching he clearly taught the sons of God to treat one another as brothers. In his Prayers he pleaded that all his disciples might be "one." Indeed as the Redeemer of all, he offered himself for all even to the point of death. "Greater love than this no one has, that one lay down his life for his friends" (John 15:13). He commanded his apostles to preach to all peoples the gospel's message that the human race was to become the Family of God, in which the fullness of the Law would be love.

d. As the firstborn of many brethren and by the giving of his Spirit, he founded after his death and resurrection a new brotherly community composed of all those who receive him in faith and in love. This he did through his Body, which is the Church. There everyone, as members one of the other, would render mutual service according to the different gifts bestowed on each.

This whole chapter was taken from the Constitution *Lumen Gentium* (9).

> Its end [of the Church] is the Kingdom of God, which has been begun by God himself on earth, and which is to be further extended until it is brought to perfection by him at the end of time. . . .

Our present text is a summary of this whole section except for the fact that the Council here underlines very forcefully the fact that Christ as the Incarnate Word among men shared the social life of all, for all, in solidarity with all men. He did this in order to pass to the new humanity which would be renovated and renewed by his passion, death and Resurrection. His human nature was not destroyed thereby (32a), but in a manner in which we do not fully understand, he sanctified and elevated it to a new order of being. He did this in solidarity with all men in the sense that this same elevation and sanctification would belong to all those who would believe and love him so that they now have become true brothers in the Kingdom of Heaven (32c). They would henceforth, have but one law and that would be one of mutual love.

This whole paragraph serves as the exemplar of the human community on earth for Christians. There is, once again, a relationship between the love and self-sacrifice which Christ had for all men and the same love and sacrifice which Christians must have for each other and for all men in building up the human community on earth. Christ is their exemplar and driving force as they work among men for a more human community.

CHAPTER 3

Man's Activity
Throughout the World

After having considered man as he is in the world, the Council now turns to investigate man as a creating dynamism in the world. From the *homo sapiens* we now progress to man as a *homo faber* as he transforms and constructs the milieu in which he lives:

33. a. Through his labors and his native endowments man has ceaselessly striven to better his life. Today, however, especially with the help of science and technology, he has extended his mastery over nearly the whole of nature and continues to do so. Thanks to increased opportunities for many kinds of social contact among nations, the human family is gradually recognizing that it comprises a single world community and is making itself so. Hence many benefits once looked for, especially from heavenly powers, man has now enterprisingly procured for himself.

b. In the face of these immense efforts which already preoccupy the whole human race, men raise numerous questions among themselves. What is the meaning and value of this feverish activity? How should all these things be used? To the achievement of what goal are the strivings of individuals and societies heading? The Church guards the heritage of God's Word and draws from it moral and religious principles without always having at hand the solution to particular problems. As such she desires to add the light of revealed truth to mankind's store of experience, so that the path which humanity has taken in recent times will not be a dark one.

This transformation of the world by technology has radically changed man's position in the world vis-à-vis this same world. He is no longer the passive agent of its forces and violence but has become more and more the master of his own fate and the director of his own destiny. This has progressed more in the past 100 years than in all previous centuries; hence, theologians have attempted in recent years to give a theology of terrestrial realities and of man's activity in history itself. This same subject matter will be taken up in the second part under "culture," that is, the whole of man's work which he employs to master his milieu and use it for his own perfection.

Culture is a very expansive term. A man who is not cultivated is not a man at all, but a kind of animal in a forest. The "good savage" does not exist, any more than the "Emile" of Jean-Jacques Rousseau. Culture belongs to the essence of the human person. It is not something superfluous which one can do without, but it leads to true and full humanity. It includes, therefore, not only the means for cultivating the land, for improving social and political institutions, but also the artistic expression of the great experiences of man. It has, therefore, a sociological, ethnological aspect; it fulfills itself in history; there is a pluralism of cultures.

This brings us to the heart of the problem raised by the new forms of life: science, critical judgment, psychological discoveries, industrialization, urbanization, etc., which give culture its constantly changing character. Man becomes aware, moreover, of the fact that he is the author of his own culture; for the first time humanity can act on a planetary scale; for example, he realizes he is capable of ending the spectre of misery and of hunger. This is a "new humanism," marked with a sense of responsibility for one's brothers.

By the same token, a new series of problems arise: a conflict between the universal cultural exchanges and the traditional wisdom of peoples: this is the drama of Africa; a conflict between the new and particularly the scientific culture, and the so-called "classical" forms of culture: this is the problem of the humanities; a conflict between the inevitable specialization and the no less necessary synthesis: this is the problem of the universities; a conflict between the increase of cultural riches and the destitution of a whole part of the world: this is the question which one third of the world raises; a conflict between the legitimate autonomy of culture and the religious attitudes of the gift of oneself: this is one of the keys to the problems of atheism.

The Constitution does not claim to answer each of these questions, but only to recall a few principles which are necessary for the true progress of culture. The text recalls, for example, that the obligation of seeking the things of heaven does not diminish, but increases the importance of Christians collaborating in the construction of a better world. In doing so, man fulfills, indeed, the divine order of subjecting the earth to himself and of perfecting creation; at the same time, he fulfills also the great commandment of Christ to devote oneself to one's brothers. Moreover, by the study of history, philosophy, and the exact sciences, and through the fine arts, the human family can be enlightened by a reflection of the eternal wisdom and be better disposed to receive the divine Word, already present in the world, even before the Incarnation. If, therefore, there is in the development of culture, for example, at the level of the exact sciences, a danger of expecting from them the only criterion of the true, there are also in the same scientific research done in common, with patience, objectivity, and forgetfulness of oneself, values, which can be an "evangelical preparation," and which can be informed, enlightened, transfigured by the charity of God.

Moreover, the links between the gospel and culture are many. The diverse forms of culture have always been an essential instrument of the preaching of the gospel; on this the Council recalls that the Church is not bound in an indissoluble way to any form of culture, but it can and ought to assume them, penetrate them with its light, and receive from them in turn the "multiple splendor" of a varied diffusion on the level of language.

Yet our document does not go so far as to give us a whole theology of terrestrial realities. It is satisfied to give the basic questions posed by this new view of man (33b). It is noteworthy here, that, once again, although the Church has moral principles which she draws from the gospel, she has no ready-made solutions for the manifold problems of modern man. In this she can only contribute to such a solution in conjunction with all men of good will in a spirit of true dialogue.

The document now attempts to give us the value and meaning of human activity:

34.   a.   Throughout the course of the centuries, men have labored to better the circumstances of their lives through a monumental amount of individual and collective effort. To believers, this point is settled: considered in itself, this human activity accords with God's will. For man, created to God's image, received a mandate to subject to himself the earth and all it contains, and to govern the world with justice and holiness; a mandate to relate himself and the totality of things to him who was to be acknowledged as the Lord and Creator of all. Thus, by the subjection of all things to man, the name of God would be wonderful in all the earth.

b.   This mandate concerns the whole range of everyday activity as well. For while providing the substance of life for themselves and their families, men and women are performing their activities in a way which appropriately benefits society. They can justly consider that by their labor they are unfolding the Creator's work, consulting the advantages of their brother men, and are contributing by their personal industry to the realization in history of the divine plan.

c.   Thus, far from thinking that works produced by man's own talent and energy are in opposition to God's power, and that the rational creature exists as a kind of rival to the Creator, Christians are convinced that the triumphs of the human race are a sign of God's grace and the flowering of his own mysterious design. For the greater man's power becomes, the further his individual and community responsibility extends. Hence it is clear that men are not deterred by the Christian message from building up the world, or impelled to neglect the welfare of their fellows, but that they are rather more stringently bound to do these very things.

Man has been created in the image of God and thus, like God, he makes progress in history and culture for his own perfection. He is, as we have already seen, God's lieutenant in creation directing and ordering creation for his own good and his own perfection. The Council here follows biblical teaching on the activity of man on earth. God is mingled in human affairs and unless they are built and done under his direction and will, they are nothing (Ps. 126:1-8). With the New Testament, we see a fuller picture of human values considered from the point of view of God's intentions: the Word became flesh (John 1:7) and after his death took his human flesh into heaven with him and it is not to be separated from his person again (Creed). Pain, sickness, and death have been given a redemptive role in the Christian context (Rom 6:58); marriage, the most fundamental of human institutions, is raised to the dignity of a sacrament (Eph 5:22-23); indeed, creation waits for the redemption of man and in the meanwhile is in pain of growth and travail (Rom 8:18): peace, joy, concord, and justice are the fruits of the Spirit and the expected qualities in each Christian life (Gal 5:22); they cannot remain individual or personal, but must first go out to the Mystical Body of Christ (Col 2:17-20) and then to all men if possible (Rom 12:17-18); all human reality falls under the spiritual dichotomy of "flesh-spirit" in the Pauline sense of these words; this means that all men can and must serve Christ or be opposed to him. The epistle to the Ephesians is clearly concerned with a redemption which goes beyond the salvation of individuals (Eph 5:19; Col 1:9; Cor 2:15); it is a Christian anthropology of the whole of creation, inclusive of the world of men and their values. Thus, in capsule form, we see that God, the Lord of History, has given a value to the realities of this world and to man, conferring on them a vital role in the economy of creation and of redemption. The Council in our present text simply points out that there is no simple discontinuity between our everyday activities and the activity in the final kingdom (34b). Each person makes his own personal contribution to the unfolding providential plan of God for and in the world. More than this it is difficult to say and it is a sign of prudence that our text does not go into any real detail on this rather obscure point of theology. In other words, theology has not as yet ripened this question.

Finally, the Council discusses the whole question of how we can unite human activity with the divine purpose as an exercise of love for God and for our brothers (34c).

"I love God in you" is a terribly ambiguous phrase and it runs the added danger of alienation of true love of men one for another. God is not "between" or "in" my brothers. God is my brother, in that loving him, serving him for his own sake, I, by that very fact, love God by the same act. The eruption of divine charity into the world (if we are to believe John the Evangelist) is such that there are not two "agapes" (charities) but only one, and that is the very same love with which and in which I love God *and* my brother.. In Johannine theology (and in Christianity) I cannot have God without my brother nor my brother without God. It is simply impossible to separate them any longer in the present economy of salvation. It is precisely here that we can meet the unbeliever in true and fruitful dialogue without the trappings of a false love and a false apologetic. We encounter, love and meet man for his own sake and in his own right. No falsity, no hypocrisy, no ulterior reasons whatever. God has become, by his incarnation, immanent in man and identified with him. "Amen I say to you that as long as you have done it to one of these the least of my brothers, you have done it to me." The obstacle between men as brothers is utterly broken now and no alienation is possible in such a perspective of man and God. The unbeliever has no reason to suspect Christian motives as ulterior to a particular political, economic, social, or cultural system. There is no such thing as a "perfect" society here below; but there are means and ways to best promote man's dignity and welfare from the slavery of alienation and the forces of unfreedom. There is no such thing as "Catholic" politics or "Catholic" economy or "Catholic" internationalism. There is only man as the supreme value here below and it is man himself who is the middle and essential term in the dialogue between believer and unbeliever. The Christian cannot dislocate man and his faith outside the world which is engaged within the world of concrete men with concrete problems. He cannot escape into a false mysticism or an illusory transcendentalism where the affairs and needs of his brothers are left "here below." Such a view may well be neoplatonic but it certainly is not Christian. Yet, Christian man does look beyond the terrible realities of the here below neither to evade them nor to render them illusory; rather, by loving and serving man, he prepares for his Lord's *parousia* in the very act of love for his brothers. One thereby avoids both pernicious errors against Christianity: disincarnationalism and terrestrial messianism. Social organization indeed has its proper autonomy; it is indeed distinct and independent of the hierarchy of the Church in the exercise of its proper domain; it can never be separated, however, from God and his intent for man. The universal value here below can only be man and it is for him that social organization is created, not man for social organization. As Christians, we are always men, and human dignity and endeavors must always be of supreme importance. In this endeavor and in this sense, there can be no radical division or difference between believer and unbeliever—and this must be kept firmly in mind if there is to be a true dialogue between the two. The Christian religion today — as "sign of the times" to use the famous words of John XXIII — is that we meet God and Christ in the face-to-face encounter with man in the world. All men are the extension of the Body of Christ who became incarnate to be identified with them. How, then, can it be possible not to love the very extension of the body of Christ in the world?

This brings us to another problem within the present document. The problem which expects all things from man's effort alone. The Christian on his part brings a new spirit to bear on the problems of man here below — the spirit of love communicated to him by the Holy Spirit. It animates, informs, and perfects the tendencies of the natural order to a higher level since grace does not destroy nature. On the other hand, the Christian must remember that nature does not destroy grace; he must not fall into a purely natural philanthropy. Even in the midst of the dialogue between the Christian and others, the disciple of Christ knows that what he seeks is beyond just the demands of nature, that his intentions like his actions have entered into the *agape* of Christ. God is not seen by him to be the negator of human activity, but rather that toward him and in him man finds the full expression of his creative dynamism. This (i.e., the former attitude) is one of the fundamental charges made against Christians by atheists and by the new humanism which can be seen to be so utterly false.

These preliminary aspects of the problem were needed before we can fully appreciate the deep crisis which Catholic theology is undergoing in its attempt to become relevant to modern man. In other words, we have been attempting to become relevant, to show how a whole cultural framework must be overcome (flowing from the Graeco-Roman culture in which the present moral theology has developed) and another put in its place if we are to sensibly discuss the problems of today within a cultural context that modern man can comprehend and appreciate. We must see that today's theology evolves from a more or less "objective" morality to a personalistic one. This certainly is not to imply that what has to the present been called "objective" aspects of morality is going to be totally discarded; what it does mean, however, is that today morality will have to be seen as an existential whole, that is, as integrated into man as man, and *his* objective signification with regard to God, other men, the world, and to himself. We start with man and find signification thereby not by some kind of objectified moral system based on the "law of nature" expressing (at least indirectly) the will of God for men. It is man (and not nature) who is created "in the image and likeness of God." If we are to find any real "indirect will of God," it must be in a personalistic dialogue with man. That this is in perfect agreement with divine revelation can amply be seen in the gospel and epistles of John when he discusses the essential neotestamentarian concept of *agape* (which we have already discussed in our own exposé above). The essence of this morality is to love God above all things and our neighbor "as Christ has loved us," that is, as a total gift of self to the needs and sufferings of our neighborhood understood in all of its expansive meaning of the gospels: to wish for him what we wish for ourselves can never mean anything less than the securing for him the economic, social, cultural, and religious freedom with which alone he can live in human dignity and which God certainly wishes for his children.

The Council itself will answer this whole question by saying that "from day to day, in every group or nation, there is an increase in the number of men and women who are conscious that they themselves are the authors and the artisans of the culture of their community" (53a). This increase of responsibility in and for the world on the part of man is within the design of God for the world. It was, as we have already explained it, the original intention of Genesis: man is God's lieutenant in creation, directing and ordering it for the good of himself and his brothers unto the glory of God, his head.

The Council then goes on to analyze that specific human activity called work:

35. a. Human activity, to be sure, takes its significance from its relationship to man. Just as it proceeds from man, so it is

ordered toward man. For when a man works he not only alters things and society, he develops himself as well. He learns much, he cultivates his resources, he goes outside of himself and beyond himself. Rightly understood, this kind of growth is of greater value than any external riches which can be garnered. A man is more precious for what he is than for what he has. Similarly, all that men do to obtain greater justice, wider brotherhood, a more humane ordering of social relationships has greater worth than technical advances. For these advances can supply the material for human progress, but of themselves alone they can never actually bring it about.

b. Hence, the norm of human activity is this: that in accord with the divine plan and will, it harmonize with the genuine good of the human race, and that it allow men as individuals and as members of society to pursue their total vocation and fulfill it.

The essence of the thought here is very simple: man is the end; everything else is a means toward his perfection and never vice versa. Work exists for man, not man for work; property exists for man not man for property. We are brought back to the thought of Pius XI:

For what else is work but the use or exercise of the powers of mind and body on or by means of these gifts of nature? Now, the natural law, or rather, God's will manifested by it, demands that right order be observed in the application of natural resources to human needs; and this order consists in everything having its proper owner. Hence it follows that unless a man applies his labor to his own property, an alliance must be formed between his toil and his neighbor's property; for each is helpless without the other. This is what Leo XIII had in mind when he wrote: "Capital cannot do without labor, nor labor without capital." It is therefore entirely false to ascribe the results of their combined efforts to either capital or labor alone; and it is flagrantly unjust that either should envy the efficacy of the other, and claim all the product.

Capital, however, was long able to appropriate too much to itself; it claimed all the products and profits, and left to the worker the barest minimum necessary to repair his strength and to ensure the continuance of his class. For by an inexorable economic law, it was held, all accumulation of capital falls to the wealthy, while by the same law the workers are doomed to perpetual want or to a very low standard of life. It is indeed true that the course of things did not always and everywhere correspond with this thesis of the so-called Manchester school; but it cannot be denied that the steady pressure of economic and social tendencies was in this direction. That these erroneous opinions and deceitful axioms should have been vehemently assailed, and not merely by those whom they deprived of their innate rights to better their condition, will assuredly surprise no one (*Quadragesimo Anno*, 53-54).

The evident direction of the Pope's reasoning is that the humanization of production demands the participation of all actors, as well as the equal distribution of profit not just to stockholders and owners of capital goods, but to workers, directors, creditors, etc., according to the quantity and quality of their contribution. For owners to say arbitrarily: "Here is a price for labor; here is profit" is a direct dehumanization of the labor process and contrary to the natural law of production. In a primitive economy — without going into the abuses of paternalism — there is no such break, for we have work on a person-to-person basis (craft guilds, even if the major craftsman owned the goods of production); but as the economy becomes more complicated (industrial revolution and its aftermath), it also becomes much more concentrated, and the original and personal division of labor no longer figures in production, except as a simple material result ("work"), a commodity, a price of merchandise to be used for the purpose of profit production, where profit becomes the end for which all else exists, inclusive of the dignity of human labor. No one shares in the work itself, no one really is interested in the work itself, except as a commodity in the process of production to be deducted from final "profit." It becomes the sole property of the capitalist or stockholder, since in such a system work is nothing else than totally recompensed. Therefore, profit becomes the reward of capital itself, independent of all other factors in production of goods.

In classical terms we have here the very definition of capitalism as a profit motive system, vitiating the system itself and morally repugnant to the Christian as well: as economic system in which capital and work are separated, where the law of contract of wages ("the iron law of wages") is the sole meeting between them, and where profit and salary are not only separated, but the latter is actually at the service of the former. Such a system cannot be acceptable to the Christian precisely because of its dehumanizing effects on man's work — his extension in space and time — and such a system has been in fact rejected by John XXIII in *Mater et Magistra*.

Thus it is money and gain which dominate to a very large degree the Western capitalist system, which has broken and dehumanized generation after generation (in this respect, one has only to read a cursory history of the 19th century labor movement and its conditions). This appetite for gain — the biblical *cupiditas*—was always in men as individuals, for there is no reason to suspect that it is any greater today in men than it was in times past; but what modern capitalism has done is to systematize this vice in the cadres of its very economic system *qua* system, and it has become its very reason for being and the law of its institutions, where individuals — inclusive of the individual capitalists themselves — are caught up without remission in this anonymous and dehumanizing violence. The evil is now institutional where its law is profit, and profit alone, and where only institutional and structural reform can make of neocapitalism a truly humanizing system. The system carries within itself a type of vicious circle from which, as it now stands, it cannot escape on its own. Capital produces profit, and profit, in its own turn, produces more capital. Christians — from the earliest times — have always condemned this mode of operation among men, even in the (today) often ridiculed aspect of the Middle Ages where usury was considered an evil. These medieval schoolmen were correct and modern theologians quite wrong, since the former saw very clearly, what many religious defenders of Western capitalism have not seen; namely, that any system of economics which dehumanizes man and his labor, where work (taken here in its broadest meaning) and profit are separated, where man's work as an expression and incarnational extension of himself is treated as a commodity used toward a further end — profit — such a system, these ancients saw clearly, was basically inhuman and unchristian. Money for money's sake, profit for profit's sake, are aberrations from Christianity. Money is for man, not man for money, and it is precisely this vice which infects modern capitalism to its very core, no matter how many laws are passed to curb its abuses. These latter are only paliatives covering its terminal human cancer.

By nature itself, as Pius XI said in the passage quoted above, the riches produced belong by right and by nature to him or to those who participated in their production, the fruit of labor belonging to those who actually labored upon it, directly or indirectly, some more quantitatively, others more qualitatively. Certainly we must admit that a share belongs to the owners of the capital goods themselves, even in a special way, since it is their own labor which has made these goods available for others to work upon. But when the work is that of a community — as is the case with every modern enterprise — produced in consort with proprietor, director and worker, the fruit of that labor belongs to all three categories of man as a community and one cannot morally say (as does the capitalist system today) that one "*pays*" the worker for his work and calls it just, with all the remaining profits accruing to the proprietor and stockholder of capital goods. The reason for this is really quite simple. It flows from the fact that neither a man nor his work is a thing one can pay for and leave aside like other types of property in nature; it is generically different from all other types of property. A man cannot be "*bought*" with money or anything else precisely because he and his work are of infinite value. We therefore do great violence to man by separating him from his work by payment only of a salary or wage.

The document next deals with the autonomy of the temporal and in what way this is to be understood:

36. a. Now many of our contemporaries seem to fear that a closer bond between human activity and religion will work against the independence of men, of societies, or of the sciences.

b. If by the autonomy of earthly affairs we mean that created things and societies themselves enjoy their own laws and values which must be gradually deciphered, put to use, and regulated by men, then it is entirely right to demand that autonomy. This is not merely required by modern man, but harmonizes also with the will of the Creator. For by the very circumstance of their having been created, all things are endowed with their own stability, truth, goodness, proper laws and order. Man must respect these as he isolates them by the appropriate methods of the individual sciences or arts. Therefore if methodical investigation within every branch of learning is carried out in a genuinely scientific manner and in accord with moral norms, it never truly conflicts with faith, for earthly matters and the concerns of faith derive from the same God. Indeed whoever labors to penetrate the secrets of reality with a humble and steady mind, even though he is unaware of the fact, is nevertheless being led by the hand of God, who holds all things in existence, and gives them their identity. Consequently, we cannot but deplore certain habits of mind, which are sometimes found too among Christians, which do not sufficiently attend to the rightful independence of science and which, from the arguments and controversies they spark, lead many minds to conclude that faith and science are mutually opposed.

c. But if the expression, the autonomy of temporal affairs, is taken to mean that created things do not depend on God, and that man can use them without any reference to their Creator, anyone who acknowledges God will see how false such a meaning is. For without the Creator the creature would disappear. For their part, however, all believers of whatever religion always hear his revealing voice in the discourse of creatures. When God is forgotten, however, the creature itself grows unintelligible.

Our document will later go into a detailed explanation of

the forms of autonomy in various fields of human endeavor, e.g., politics and the economic order. Here we are concerned with the whole of human life and activity as understood to have its own autonomy.

A fundamental distinction is made between two distinct types of autonomy. The first is that which flows from the very nature of human sciences, of their own laws and organization as various aspects of existence (36a). Yet, if we speak as if this existence is itself reduced to the single temporal sphere (36b), where existence is simply this monism, then the document views this as a false autonomy. There are two domains — the temporal and the eternal — but we must guard against two extremes in this respect. On the one hand, we can so separate the two that we have either virtually two separate and distinct orders with little or no relationship between the two (in this latter case many will opt for denying one or the other in the concept of "the new humanity"); or, on the other hand, we can reduce the two to a type of concordism where there is danger of the two orders becoming in some way identified. This was one of the dangers in biblical interpretation where science and the bible were seen to buttress each other reciprocally.

Man, in reality, has but one vocation and he must orientate everything under the inspiration and direction of God and his will. Certainly, as our document points out, this cannot deny the legitimate autonomy of the organization and development of science, since it must follow its own ordering principles to be effective. Yet, even these sciences must be given direction *as to their human and ultimate meaning* by the Christian principles of justice and love. For the Christian there is no such thing as a completely autonomous science since man uses these constructs for human ends and purposes and when we say "end" we say with the same breath, morality. We cannot exclude anything from God and dependency on him insofar as he has given all things for our perfection and for leading us to himself. It is this separation which the Council deplores and rejects (36b).

The temporal is not autonomous *as a domain* since it is directed to man's use and God's glory. Its method, its organizing principles are autonomous insofar as divine revelation has nothing to teach us in this respect. But its final use for man — this revelation can and does teach us; and, in this respect, there can be no autonomy. Science gives us a grasp of the real, ordering it for the greater good of man in freedom — freedom from the slaveries of toil, nature and disease; and yet, the freedom of man is such that he uses these products of science — and science itself — to direct himself to an end, a meaning in life and in this respect science finds its fulfillment in man. It is the work of science which is autonomous, not the direction and use of science for human ends.

Yet in all this we must recognize that human activity is colored by sin and egoism:

37. a. Sacred Scripture teaches the human family what the experience of the ages confirms: that while human progress is a great advantage to man, it brings with it a strong temptation. For when the order of values is jumbled and bad is mixed with the good, individuals and groups pay heed solely to their own interests, and not to those of others. Thus it happens that the world ceases to be a place of true brotherhood. In our own day, the magnified power of humanity threatens to destroy the race itself.

b. For a monumental struggle against the powers of darkness pervades the whole history of man. The battle was joined from the very origins of the world and will continue until the last day, as the Lord has attested. Caught in this conflict, man is obliged to wrestle constantly if he is to cling to what is good, nor can he achieve his own integrity without great efforts and the help of God's grace.

c. That is why Christ's Church, trusting in the design of the Creator, acknowledges that human progress can serve man's true happiness, yet she cannot help echoing the Apostle's warning: "Be not conformed to this world" (Rom 12:2). Here by the world is meant that spirit of vanity and malice which transforms into an instrument of sin those human energies intended for the service of God and man.

d. Hence if anyone wants to know how this unhappy situation can be overcome, Christians will tell him that all human activity, constantly imperiled by man's pride and deranged self-love, must be purified and perfected by the power of Christ's Cross and resurrection. For redeemed by Christ and made a new creature in the Holy Spirit, man is able to love the things themselves created by God, and ought to do so. He can receive them from God and respect and reverence them as flowing constantly from the hand of God. Grateful to his Benefactor for these creatures, using and enjoying them in detachment and liberty of spirit, man is led forward into a true possession of them, as having nothing, yet possessing all things. "All are yours, and you are Christ's and Christ is God's" (1 Cor 3:22-23).

As with all of man's creation, it is not without a mixture of good and evil. In other words, man's progress is always ambiguous and this, the Council points out, is all the more momentous today, since man has at his disposition such enormous power for either good or evil. This once again brings us back to the theme of sin and the original fault of man (see 13), which the Council has already developed. It is repeated here in order to emphasize the fact that man in all his works is constantly under the temptation of sin, since he is wounded by the egoism and selfishness of his very nature. This same theme will be repeated when our document speaks of the economic and social order as well (63c).

This temptation of man is described for us in rather somber tones (37b) in the form of the power of darkness and the power of light. It must be noted (as we have done previously) that the Council does not intend to teach any type of dualism in human affairs — only that *within man* there is an imbalance which directs him to seek his own selfish interest rather than consider the total needs of all of his brothers. Because of this, man must constantly be on his guard to recognize this aspect of his nature for fear of letting it overcome him and lead him to destruction. This solemn warning — in spite of the fact that man's progress is in itself good — is a sacred duty of the Church and she would be amiss of her duty if she did not draw man's attention to it (37c). Man must love things and the products of his hands as in the order of means to an end — the end being the perfection of all men unto the glory of God (37d). The document speaks here of "detachment" and "liberty of spirit" since man must use the things of this world in the spirit of service to his brothers. When they are sought for in themselves — whether it be wealth, power, esteem — then we have a perversion of priorities and man becomes a slave to things rather than their master and director. In a sense, the Christian learns to use the goods of this world following the very example of Christ, since he knows that suffering cannot be separated from the task of man here below. He knows that in the final analysis, the goods of the earth are to be used in the spirit of fraternity and service for this end. When man uses them in this fashion, then he knows that he is at once free from any attachment and open to the true meaning of matter, power, and wealth.

Thus we are led to a theology of the activity of man in the world following the example of the Word Incarnate:

38. a. For God's Word, through whom all things were made, was himself made flesh and dwelt on man's earth. Thus he entered the world's history as a perfect man, taking that history up into himself and summarizing it. He himself revealed to us that "God is love" (1 John 4:8) and at the same time taught us that the new command of love was the basic law of human perfection and hence of the world's transformation.

b. To those, therefore, who believe in divine love, he gives assurance that the way to love lies open to men and that the effort to establish a universal brotherhood is not a hopeless one. He cautions them at the same time that this love is not something to be reserved for important matters, but must be pursued chiefly in the ordinary circumstances of life. Undergoing death itself for all of us sinners, he taught us by example that we too must shoulder that cross which the world and the flesh inflict upon those who search after peace and justice.

Appointed Lord by his resurrection and given all power in heaven and on earth, Christ is now at work in the hearts of men through the energy of his Spirit, arousing not only a desire for the age to come, but by that very fact animating, purifying and strengthening those noble longings too by which the human family makes its life more human and strives to render the whole earth submissive to this goal.

c. Now, the gifts of the Spirit are diverse: while he calls some to give clear witness to the desire for a heavenly home and to keep that desire fresh among the human family, he summons others to dedicate themselves to the earthly service of men and to make ready the material of the celestial realm by this ministry of theirs. Yet he frees all of them so that by putting aside love of self and bringing all earthly resources into the service of human life they can devote themselves to that future when humanity itself will become an offering accepted by God.

d. The Lord left behind a pledge of this hope and strength for life's journey in that sacrament of faith where natural elements refined by man are gloriously changed into his body and blood, providing a meal of brotherly solidarity and a fore-taste of the heavenly banquet.

Our paragraph is reminiscent of the words of Pierre Teilhard de Chardin who saw Christ as the Omega point of all creation, of all things on earth and in heaven. Without going this far, our document does see the unfolding of history and of human activity as leading directly to Christ, who, the scripture reminds us, is its origin and end (38a). Sin has tainted all reality (see 37), but sin does not have the final triumph over man or over God's creation. This belongs exclusively to Christ and to him alone. The meaning of all created reality becomes fully evident only in the Incarnate Word (38b) who recapitulates and transforms all creation by his resurrection, communicated to all men who believe and love him and then, by man, to all of the cosmos as well. The destiny of man and of the cosmos is then not a destruction but a transformation which has already begun here below by Christ and the small band of men who believe in him and only to be fully realized in his *parousia*. Meanwhile, Christians are in the intermediary stage of growth toward the fullness of this kingdom and can enter into it only by suffering and by the cross. Thus we have a progressive growth, toward this kingdom, in history. Sin will be defeated only by love — love of God and love of the brethren in the service of each other. Only in this way can the egoism, which is natural in us all, truly die. In this proportion and to a degree which we are ignorant of, humanity slowly but surely progresses toward its culminating point who is Christ and in whom history takes its meaning. Thus the whole of the Christian life (38c) is placed under the aegis of love along with each of its actions. We live by the law of love and the moral life of the Christian must be a continuous unfolding of that love in each of its events. Take one example of this which the Council will deal with at length in its last section: peace.

Now in the nuclear era the vision of witness to peace in a violent world must again emerge from the Christian community as an apologetic motif understood in its deepest meaning.

It is futile to believe that such witness will banish war forever; there is no assurance from divine revelation that war will disappear until, perhaps, there is no viable earth from which it could disappear. After all, Christ, the perfect witness of the Father among men, never succeeded in converting the world — not even a good part of it. But continuous witness he was, even to the "failure" of the cross.

It is perhaps the cross that is in store for those Christians who take the peacemaking vocation seriously, for, given the ideological passions and hatreds currently alive, he can well expect human failure. Yet in his pain and crucifixion from the world (understood in its demonic violence and hatred), the Christian must nonetheless continue to give that witness to peace and brotherhood which will make men again wonder as they did before the miracles of Christ.

Secondly, the Christian must hope that peace is a possibility and he must work for it in optimism. If the Christian were only to hope for what man can do, he would indeed despair. But he has no such right, for "what is impossible to men is possible to God."

In these days of bleak despair and historic inclination to violence and hate — the common philosophy of men in our age — where men really no longer believe in peace, the Christian must become a beacon of hope. Pope John even extended his hope to the communists and did not spurn dialogue with the "enemy." Can we do any better than follow his example? St. Paul has, at second glance at least, a strange text in his epistle to the Romans: "Patience engenders hope" (5:11). It would seem that just the opposite would be true, namely, that it is Christian hope that would give rise to patience. As Father Congar has pointed out so well, those who have not suffered for Christ's cause really do not know how to hope. The man who wishes to enjoy immediately the object of his desire, does not know how to attain his goal. By the patience of their suffering, by the pain and even crucifixion which come to the man of peace from those who do not understand him or who consider him "sentimental" or even traitorous — the Christian discovers he must fling his hope upon him who can make all things new, who can work all things to the peace of mankind, who calls upon his servants to continue the work of reconciliation, bringing peace and forgiveness to man.

Exactly how this transformation will result in a new earth and a new heaven, we simply do not know.

39. a. We do not know the time for the consummation of the earth and of humanity nor do we know how all things will be transformed. As deformed by sin, the shape of this world will pass away, but we are taught that God is preparing a new dwelling place and a new earth where justice will abide and whose blessedness will answer and surpass all the longings for peace which spring up in the human heart. Then, with death overcome, the sons of God will be raised up in Christ,

and what was sown in weakness and corruption will be clothed with incorruptibility. Enduring with charity and its fruits all that creation which God made on man's account will be unchained from the bondage of vanity.

b. Therefore, while we are warned that it profits a man nothing if he gain the whole world and lose himself, the expectation of a new earth must not weaken but rather stimulate our concern for cultivating this one. For here grows the body of a new human family, a body which even now is able to give some kind of foreshadowing of the new age.

c. Hence, while earthly progress must be carefully distinguished from the growth of Christ's Kingdom, to the extent that the former can contribute to the better ordering of human society, it is of vital concern to the kingdom of God.

d. For after we have obeyed the Lord, and in his Spirit nurtured on earth the values of human dignity, brotherhood, and freedom, and indeed all the good fruits of our nature and enterprise, we will find them again, but freed of stain, burnished and transfigured when Christ hands over to the Father: "a kingdom eternal and universal, a kingdom of truth and life, of holiness and grace, of justice, love and peace." On this earth that Kingdom is already present in mystery. When the Lord returns it will be brought into full flower.

The two — the kingdom of God and the city of man — are not coextensive, but this does not mean that they have nothing to do with each other (39c). On the contrary, they are intimately interrelated insofar as the Christian must make the effects of the one — even here below — reflect on the other. The Council did not identify them — since the essence of this transformation is so obscure; yet, the aspects of fraternity, of fraternal communion of freedom, the fruits of our industrious labor will all be returned and purified by Christ when he comes at the *parousia*. This is the object of Christian hope and it is this same hope which gives impetus to these terrestrial activities for the Christian. The works of the industry and history of man are therefore of supreme importance for the Kingdom of God.

CHAPTER 4

The Role of the Church in the Modern World

The result of the first three chapters is now an effective relationship between the Church and the world. In a sense, human activity, human community, and the dignity of the human person are all the ingredients for understanding the profound nature of the relationship between the Church and the world — understood in the above-mentioned sense:

40. a. Everything we have said about the dignity of the human person, and about the human community and the profound meaning of human activity, lays the foundation for the relationship between the Church and the world, and provides the basis for dialogue between them. In this chapter, presupposing everything which has already been said by this Council concerning the mystery of the Church, we must now consider this same Church inasmuch as she exists in the world, living and acting with it.

b. Coming forth from the eternal Father's love, founded in time by Christ the Redeemer and made one in the Holy Spirit, the Church has a saving and an eschatological purpose which can be fully attained only in the future world. But she is already present in this world, and is composed of men, that is, of members of the earthly city who have a call to form the family of God's children during the present history of the human race, and to keep increasing it until the Lord returns. United on behalf of heavenly values and enriched by them, this family has been "constituted and structured as a society in this world" by Christ, and is equipped "by appropriate means for visible and social union." Thus the Church, at once "a visible association and a spiritual community," goes forward together with humanity and experiences the same earthly lot which the world does. She serves as a leaven and as a kind of soul for human society as it is to be renewed in Christ and transformed into God's family.

c. That the earthly and the heavenly city penetrate each other is a fact accessible to faith alone; it remains a mystery of human history, which sin will keep in great disarray until the splendor of God's sons is fully revealed. Pursuing the saving purpose which is proper to her, the Church does not only communicate divine life to men, but in some way casts the reflected light of that life over the entire earth, most of all by its healing and elevating impact on the dignity of the person, by the way in which it strengthens the seams of human society, and imbues the everyday activity of men with a deeper meaning and importance. Thus through her individual members and her whole community, the Church believes she can contribute greatly toward making the family of man and its history more human.

d. In addition, the Catholic Church gladly holds in high esteem the things which other Christian Churches and ecclesial communities have done or are doing cooperatively by way of achieving the same goal. At the same time, she is convinced that she can be abundantly and variously helped by the world in the matter of preparing the ground for the gospel. This help she gains from the talents and industry of individuals and from human society as a whole. The Council now sets forth certain general principles for the proper fostering of this mutual exchange and assistance in concerns which are in some way common to the world and the Church.

The document sees clearly that the Church's interest must be in the total vocation of man which is both celestial and terrestrial, and which here below can and must be distinguished but cannot be separated one from the other. It is God who gives all things their ultimate meaning and it is Christ who makes man realize himself both in his celestial and terrestrial calling. It is Christ, the Lord of heaven and earth as well as Lord of the Church, who alone can make man understand his task on earth; and since the Church is nothing more than his extended body in space and in time, it must, indeed, follow that the Church can and should throw some light on this total vocation of his, which she proposes to do in this paragraph. Once again, the Council strictly avoids all forms of dualism between Christ and the world, since there is only one reality which must be distinguished (secular and sacred) and must also be seen as a whole in the total vocation of man on earth.

The document begins by presupposing everything concerning the mystery of the Church exposed in *Lumen Gentium*. It goes on to give the other dimension of the Church's being — her relationship to and for the world (40a). Her mission is therefore twofold — within the Church itself by constantly reforming and redefining her methods for each new generation. The eternal message of the good news of salvation must, of necessity, remain always as her divine spouse gave it when he founded the Church. There is another dimension of the Church which is taken up in our present document and which is also essential to her being: her relationship to and for the world. It is a presence of the witness of Christ in the midst of men as the "sign raised up among the Gentiles." It is this witness which proclaims Christ's presence among men. This dimension of witness or presence to and for the world is not simply a complementary aspect of the Church's mission on earth; it is a basic dimension of her very nature that is in question here. One is struck by the complementary aspect of these two dimensions of the Church, both in the Church and toward the world: for one exists, in a sense, for the sake of the other. One cannot be understood without the dynamic presence of the other. The Church is the proclamation of Christ and continuation of Christ's salvific mission in space and time. She is the continuing incarnation of Christ among men in this double dimension of within and without the Church. The grace of God in Christ as King and priest is not something superimposed on the world by the

Church. This kingdom of Christ must extend itself day by day in the world during the course of human history by successive generations. Thus, this word of God in Christ exists in time and in human history through the presence of the Church.

The document then gives us a quick resumé of her internal dimensions to God (*Lumen Gentium*) and its connotations for society as a whole (40b). It is important both from a practical as well as a theological point of view to distinguish carefully when we speak of the unique reality which is the Church. Too often have we referred to the "Church" when we really meant the hierarchy who compose an essential dimension of the Church but who are by no means the whole Church. This has been historically understandable, since the latter part of the Middle Ages tended to deny the structural and visible nature of the Church. So in return, the Church had to emphasize that she was a true *societas,* a visible, structuralized institution with some members who ruled while others were ruled. This, of course, was important, for the hierarchical government of the Church pertains to her very nature, but it also has its drawbacks since by emphasizing one aspect of the Church — an essential but not the most important — other aspects of the Church have tended to go either unnoticed or unbalanced by a total view of the whole. More profoundly, the Church, as the order of grace, is the direct creation of the Holy Spirit. This is what we could call the divine element in the Church, since no man, no matter how endowed with supernatural gifts, could possibly perform: the transformation of the sacraments, interior innovation of men by the divine life, the forgiveness of sins. In all this, it is the direct work of God who uses human beings as mere instruments and signs of what He alone can do. Over this aspect of her reality, the Church has only a ministerial power properly speaking. She also has, by divine institution, the proper power of jurisdiction over her own affairs, regulating the cult, even of spiritual punishment for recalcitrant members which is directly exercised by the divinely constituted hierarchy in the Church.

This we might properly call her jurisdictional power and while it has its source in a divine command, it has as its ultimate subject of action the hierarchy itself. It is most important to distinguish between these two kinds of powers and action in the Church.

It is only with such a view that, most profoundly, the Church, properly speaking, is the community of all those who believe and love Jesus Christ, participating in the same divine life, cult, and government as willed by Christ himself. As the Council sees it in *Lumen Gentium*: "The Church has been seen as a people made one with the unity of the Father, the Son and the Holy Spirit" (4).

We see that the hierarchical government of the Church is of divine origin (the bishops considered separately or collegially, and the pope); it is, however, a secondary element in the Church, since it exists as a means to a further end, namely, the salvation and sanctification of the People of God. It is misleading as well as dogmatically incorrect to emphasize the hierarchical element to the point where we use the term "Church" purely and simply to refer to this element in the Church. It is the community in communion with Jesus Christ which is both primary and the end of all else in the Church's mystery of sanctification. Thus the Church is essentially composed of all the *Christi fideles* even though by divine institution these faithful occupy different functions in the Church. Each function, however, in the Church, whether it be hierarchical or lay, is a function of service for the whole body. Each function is a definite charism, that is, a personal gift given to each member of the Church both for his own sanctification as well as for the service and sanctification of all others in the Church as well. We shall see more of this later in our exposé. The New Testament as well as the Church's tradition makes it very clear that no one lives or dies for himself, but for the whole body of the Church. No one is ever alone in the Church for he belongs to an essentially social body which is united by the bonds of faith, love of Christ, and the inscrutable bonds of divine life by the operation of the Holy Spirit in each of the members of the Church.

Once again the document returns to the theme of "compenetration" of one order by the other (40c); but, in reality, this relationship can be understood only in and through faith. The efficacy and the witness of the Church in the world — and thus, in a true sense, the witness of Christ in the world — is a profound mystery, with all its seeming drawbacks and even failures at different periods of the Church's history. Yet, to a person who views the Church as an object of faith, he sees her working among men, sharing their joys and griefs (see 1) and he thus knows that in a mysterious way not entirely seen or understood here below — it is Christ's solicitude for the men of our age which is having its effect on the world here and now through the Church. This does not mean that the Church cannot be seen as a sociological institution (and to a certain degree, can be measured by its method), but that in the final analysis she must be judged by another dimension to be fully understood: the dimension of faith, for the Church is the object of faith for the Christian. And yet, it is here that we also have the greatness and the scandal of the Church even for those who do not as yet believe. Her example and solicitude for man, her love for him must be apparent enough by and through her institutions, her works and finally her faithful, that she will be recognized as an institution which is different from others and will at least be a cause of wonderment to the world — as Christ was for his contemporaries. "See how these Christians love one another" was the witness of the early Church. "By this shall all men know you are my disciples that you have love one for another," is the witness of the gospel. "The Church is a sign elevated among the nations" for all to view and wonder at its love, says Vatican I. All this, of course, is the supreme apologetic of the Church in the world and the only true one. The Church must be seen as the "universal sacrament of salvation" (45a) and there is great scandal when the Church (as an institution or in her individual members both clerical and lay) fails to give such a sign of love and solicitude for men and their problems in the world. In this way, if she is collectively and individually committed to man, she can make a supreme contribution to man in the modern world. In other words, she will become relevant to man and his problems (40c).

This paragraph concludes (40d), as we have already said, by saying that this activity of the Church in the world is not an afterthought or something optional to her being; rather it is part of her very mission for men who are in the world. This, of course, brings us to the whole problem of the relationship between the sacred and the secular, "spiritual," and the temporal and many other applications under which this problem has been seen in the past twenty-five years or so in Catholic theology as well as in the pronouncements of the *magisterium*. Some aspects of this problem were dealt with in Vatican II's *Decree on the Apostolate of the Laity*. We cannot go into a detailed explanation of this important point, but suffice it to say that this remains a problem for the Church in pilgrimage here below. In this final kingdom the seeming dichotomy will be resolved when Christ takes full possession of his kingdom — celestial and terrestrial — which is his by right of creation and redemption. Meanwhile, a distinction must be made — even if we are not permitted to separate them ontologically. The temporal order has its own autonomy (see above, p. 121), but the spiritual must make its effects felt — even here below — in the temporal order in all of its ramifications. Some in the Church will be directed and consecrated more to one than to the other, but this does not mean that either of these diverse functions in the Church are unimportant. The laity will be directed more to the temporal while clergy and religious are directed more to the sacred — without making this an absolute rule since necessity and various cultural patterns are diverse in this specification. What we must avoid here are all forms of absolutism, since in the final analysis both functions are temporary in nature; both laity and clergy have some influence on both orders no matter what their proper functions. Finally, all is done for the perfection of man unto the glory of God. This end is much more important than a strict separation of functions and roles in the Church and in the world. What also must be strictly avoided is any form of dualism where one order has little or nothing to do with the other ("compenetration," says our document). There is one reality over which Christ rules in fact or potentially, and it is the essential role of the Christian to attempt to bring all things under his aegis. In other words, the Church's function in the world is not and cannot be estranged from its function in the world but rather forms part and parcel of the same salvific essential mission to men. The Church is totally for Christ and him alone, but by that very fact, it is for what Christ loves and came into this world: the love of men of every age who can find their full meaning and signification only in Christ. Christ is then the very center of the world and of men.

The Church now goes on to explain the type of aid she wishes to bring to men in the world:

41. a. Modern man is on the road to a more thorough development of his own personality, and to a growing discovery and vindication of his own rights. Since it has been entrusted to the Church to reveal the mystery of God, who is the ultimate goal of man, she opens up to man at the same time the meaning of his own existence, that is, the innermost truth about himself. The Church truly knows that only God, whom she serves, meets the deepest longings of the human heart, which is never fully satisfied by what this world has to offer.

b. She also knows that man is constantly worked upon by God's Spirit, and hence can never be altogether indifferent to the problems of religion. The experience of past ages proves this, as do numerous indications in our own times. For man will always yearn to know, at least in an obscure way, what is the meaning of his life, of his activity, of his death. The very presence of the Church recalls these problems to his mind. But only God, who created man to his own image and ransomed him from sin, provides a fully adequate answer to these questions, and this he does through what he has revealed in Christ his Son, who became man. Whoever follows after Christ, the perfect man, becomes himself more of a man. For by his incarnation the Father's Word assumed, and sanctified through his cross and resurrection, the whole of man, body and soul, and through that totality the whole of nature created by God for man's use.

c. Thanks to this belief, the Church can anchor the dignity of human nature against all tides of opinion, for example those which undervalue the human body or idolize it. By no human law can the personal dignity and liberty of man be so aptly safeguarded as by the gospel of Christ which has been entrusted to the Church. For this gospel announces and proclaims the freedom of the sons of God, and repudiates all the bondage which ultimately results from sin (see Rom 8:14-17); it has a sacred reverence for the dignity of conscience and its freedom of choice, constantly advises that all human talents be employed in God's service and men's, and finally, commends all to the charity of all (see Matt 22:39).

d. This agrees with the basic law of the Christian dispensation. For though the same God is Savior and Creator, Lord of human history as well as of salvation history, in the divine arrangement itself, the rightful autonomy of the creature, and particularly of man is not withdrawn, but is rather reestablished in its own dignity and strengthened in it.

e. The Church, therefore, by virtue of the gospel committed to her, proclaims the rights of man; she acknowledges and greatly esteems the dynamic movements of today by which these rights are everywhere fostered. Yet these movements must be penetrated by the spirit of the gospel and protected against any kind of false autonomy. For we are tempted to think that our personal rights are fully ensured only when we are exempt from every requirement of divine law. But this way lies not the maintenance of the dignity of the human person, but its annihilation.

We have here the unique contribution of the Church. Since man understands himself only in and through Christ (41b), the Church who reveals Christ to the world can make a contribution to the world's progress and full understanding of itself. This aspect of self-understanding coming only through the Incarnate Word was explained earlier. The presence and witness of the Church are a sign, pointing to another. God alone can give a full understanding and meaning to man and this only through Christ, the Incarnate Word. This is so, since in Christ we have an assumption of human nature in its totality by the divine personality of the Second Person of the Trinity, thereby giving significance to the plenitude of the human vocation as it is now willed by God. Christ thus not only sanctified all men, but the entire cosmos as well (41b). That is why only the Church can fully comprehend the dignity of the human body, knowing that it is a sacred thing insofar as it is an indispensable instrument of man within the world and at the same time, a means to a further end, namely, the perfection of the totality of his person. She thus avoids the two extremes of worship of the body as well as the gnostic temptation to despise the body and its works (41c). It is in such a view that the true liberty of the sons of God takes place and is exercised.

Thus the Church aids man to discover his true dignity by avoiding the pitfalls of the extremes of the modern world. His true dignity is guaranteed by the rights of man (41d). She is a constant witness before the world as to these rights and it is here that the Church gives her principal witness to modern man both in season and out of season. This, at one stroke, eliminates all forms of racism, nationalism, and discrimination among men. Man's dignity does not rest on ideology or on wealth or on the accidental contingencies of birth — but on the fact that he is created in the image and likeness of God. It is this "spirit of the gospel" which assures the Church of a rock-bottom foundation to its witness, since it comes not from the fleeting feeling of the times but rather from the very Word of God in revelation (41d). Her message is God's love for man, and consequently that he is a free man in every respect of that word. It is a rock principle in the midst of a rapidly changing world which has no fixed mooring. It is a clear light where so many are blinded by mistrust, power, and other driving forces of the modern world. The Church is slave to none of these but only to this essential and abiding principle. The Church's vision is neither the utopianism of a marxist ideology since she knows that man has no abiding city here below; nor does she profess a cynical pessimism, since she also knows that the effects of the kingdom already present in germ must make some of their effects known in the social order and terrestrial city of man. The Church then holds a middle course knowing that she is yet in a valley of tears, but she is also on the way to the final kingdom and the final *parousia* of Christ, which is coming.

All this assures most firmly the basic rights of man who cannot be reduced to matter or to the slavery of the state or other men — but reveals that it is only man who is the truly absolute here below. It is the gospel and its message of love which keep the Church ever firm to this essential vision. It is herein that the difficulty of the nonbeliever or the atheist resides, namely, that he has no such mooring for his belief in man. This does not mean that there have been no atheists totally dedicated to man and to his good. It simply means that the foundation principle (for him) of this belief does not give him the assurance of firmness as that of the gospel. Why object against torture or abortion? If he justified this objection, then why not sterilization of the unfit and mentally retarded also? And so forth until he is in grave danger of actually denying human dignity. Nor does this mean that the Church herself has always been faithful to the sublime heights of this doctrine; as a matter of fact, she will clearly confess her faults later in paragraph 43. What remains clear, however, is the fact that her message remains firm in spite of the vacillations of her members.

The Council goes on to explain her exact position with regard to the structures of this world. Although her mission of witness is to continue in the city of man, it cannot be a direct partaking of practical answers to practical problems which men must face day by day:

42. a. The union of the human family is greatly fortified and fulfilled by the unity, founded on Christ, of the family of God's sons.

b. Christ, to be sure, gave his Church no proper mission in the political, economic or social order. The purpose which he set before her is a religious one. But out of this religious mission itself come a function, a light and an energy which can serve to structure and consolidate the human community according to the divine law. As a matter of fact, when circumstances of time and place produce the need, she can and indeed should initiate activities on behalf of all men, especially those designed for the needy, such as the works of mercy and similar undertakings.

c. The Church recognizes that worthy elements are found in today's social movements, especially an evolution toward unity, a process of wholesome socialization and of association in civic and economic realms. The promotion of unity belongs to the innermost nature of the Church, for she is, "thanks to her relationship with Christ, a sacramental sign and an instrument of intimate union with God, and of the unity of the whole human race." Thus she shows the world that an authentic union, social and external, results from a union of minds and hearts, namely from that faith and charity by which her own unity is unbreakably rooted in the Holy Spirit. For the force which the Church can inject into the modern society of man consists in that faith and charity put into vital practice, not in any external dominion exercised by merely human means.

d. Moreover, since in virtue of her mission and nature she is bound to no particular form of human culture, nor to any political, economic or social system, the Church by her very universality can be a very close bond between diverse human communities and nations, provided these trust her and truly acknowledge her right to true freedom in fulfilling her mission. For this reason, the Church admonishes her own sons, but also humanity as a whole, to overcome all strife between nations and races in this family spirit of God's children, and in the same way, to give internal strength to human associations which are just.

e. Therefore, this Council regards with great respect all the true, good and just elements inherent in the very wide variety of institutions which the human race has established for itself and constantly continues to establish. The Council affirms, moreover, that the Church is willing to assist and promote all these institutions to the extent that such a service depends on her and can be associated with her mission. She has no fiercer desire than that in pursuit of the welfare of all she may be able to develop herself freely under any kind of government which grants recognition to the basic rights of persons and family, to the demands of the common good and to the free exercise of her own mission.

We have already seen the distinction — but not separation — of the two orders. The Church has been called to save the world but not to direct or control it in any way (42b). Hers is a moral witness to the goodness and solicitude of God for men and the terrestrial city. This does not mean that, in necessity, she cannot be actively engaged in the works of mercy. It simply means that this will not be her normal function in the world. Her principal function in society is to act as a source of unity, recalling to men the brotherhood which they ontologically are (42a), bearing witness to this fraternity by the example of her own life among men. The secular world has, in other words, come into its own possession, into its own right without need of tutelage of the Church. It has become fully secular in the original vocation given to man in Genesis 1:8: "dominate the earth." Henceforth, the basic elements of human society such as physical subsistence, economic structure, cultural and artistic organizations, care of the sick and of the aged, aspirations toward ever more perfect social justice, efforts toward peace and fraternal solidarity among men are fully the right and responsibility of this newly born world. Formerly — for want of anyone else — the Church was forced to do all these things, thus building a whole complex of organization and structures. This phase of her history is now both unnecessary and harmful to her mission to the world in the process of secularization and humanization. All these efforts and aspirations which have been championed by the Church for over a thousand years have become the common patrimony of humanity as such and the content of its fondest hopes throughout the globe in feverish drive toward its fulfillment. Man has become conscious of the laws of his own nature, insofar as he has discovered and continues to discover and exploit the laws of nature itself. Man confronted by nature becomes more human through the growth of science, reason, culture, and society. This secularization of the world by man is a direct development of Christian revelation itself, according to which, as against all pagan religions, the world as God's external creation has been handed over to man, to his experimental science and technical might. This is the clear teaching of the author of the book of Genesis who sees all creation as good because it so comes forth from the omnipotent hand of God and that man, as God's lieutenant, is to continue this act of creation in the world which has been handed over to him. In a very true biblical sense, man's work on the world is a command from God's and as such, man co-operates with God in a secondary but real sense in the continuous act of creation.

That is why the Church has always condemned a certain Gnostic-Manicheism which considers the world and material creation as the work of evil; or the doctrine of those Eastern religions which consider them as "nothing" to be overcome, transcended and absorbed into a state of nirvana. Christianity itself has long been confronted with such a temptation. The first heresy ever condemned by the Church was precisely Gnosticism. The Nicene Creed contains the unambiguous phrase that God is the Creator of all things, "visible and invisible." There is, however, a constant temptation in Christian circles to a type of crypto-Gnosticism, that is, an attitude which considers the material world as well as the tasks within it unworthy of serious consideration by the Christian, and which gives little attention to human activities and temporal realities. Pope John,

let it be said, directly confronted this error in his encyclical
Mater et Magistra. The Pope there emphatically declared that
the material universe and the material labor of mankind are
willed by God. Furthermore, he says, this world which we see
and touch has been re-created by the Incarnation of the Son
of Man. Thus, by reason of his nature man stands on the hori-
zon between matter and spirit. In the beautiful words of St.
Hilary, "he is the bond of friendship uniting and glorifying all
creation." Therefore — and this will have momentous consequences later in our study — Christian man alone is capable
of giving a fully human meaning to the material universe. Pope
John's view of the human city is a daring one: the human
community ought to be, or at least Christians ought to strive to
make it, an imperfect but real reflection of the Kingdom of
Heaven, where justice, peace, freedom, and love are perfect.

This slow maturing of the world which has now come into
its own right has been accomplished, for the most part outside
the Church and her influence, and sometimes in spite of her
opposition. In its early origins, this revolution was even thought
to replace God in a blasphemous manner. According to Feuer-
bach, Marx, and Hegel, a terrestrial messianism would replace
Christian messianism, and man, so long alienated from himself,
would achieve his own kingdom here on earth by building the
city of man and rejecting the false hope of religion, the opium
of the people. These violent episodes were and continue to be
most painful, for these essentially humanistic dynamisms, such
as marxism, contain a great kernel of truth and have acted
as the painful first movements of the birth of the new era for
man and for the Church. To be completely absorbed in condemning the errors therein contained, is to lose sight of the
direction in which such humanism is taking man. It will be the
most sacred duty of the Church to understand fully these movements and aspirations of men and, by entering them, fulfill
them in the process of modern evangelization. Thus her evangelical mission is to create and build up that charity and love

so necessary for human community (42c). Without this, only egoism rules the forces within the community and diversity leads to discord and disruption.

The document then goes on to emphasize the distinction between the Christian message and any particular cultural form in which it is for the moment bound up (42f). Such a confusion has occurred many times in the past and is a danger today as well. As the end of the first session of Vatican II, the essential mission of the Church was formulated by Cardinal Suenens as pointing in two directions. Her mission was within the Church itself by constantly reforming and redefining methods for each new generation of Christians. The eternal message of the good news of salvation must, of necessity, remain always as her Divine Spouse gave it when he founded the Church. The cultural forms into which that message has been poured must continuously come under the scrutiny of the Church to see if it communicates the purity of the Savior's message to her children of this age. If not, then it becomes her solemn duty to embody this message in different cultural forms more in conformity to the mentality and understanding of her children of today. The task is a very delicate one, indeed, and it is the solemn duty of the Church and hers alone to approve of these new forms. But the Council has made one thing very clear; no cultural expression of Christianity, be it Roman, Greek, or Jewish, can ever exhaust the Christian message, much less be the external form in which the good news of the Savior is forever and unalterably entombed. It is this work with which the Council was so diligently concerned. In the words of John XXIII to the assembled Council Fathers:

It is one thing to speak of the substance of ancient doctrine contained in the deposit of faith and another the formulation in which it is vested. We must give great importance to this form and work patiently, if necessary, at its elaboration; we must have recourse to ways of presenting things which correspond better to the teaching authority of the Church which must be, above all, pastoral in nature.

In proof of this, she offers to work under any type of government as long as she receives a minimum amount of freedom, and as long as the basic freedoms and rights of man are safeguarded (42e). This, indeed, is a far cry from "dogmatic democracy" as being the universal vocation for all men as willed by God. It is true that recent popes have spoken very highly of this form of government, but it cannot be said to be the only one under which man's freedom can grow and flourish. The possibility of doing so lies in other types as well. This is the hope, too, for communist regions, and the Church confronts them in the spirit of true dialogue. Human institutions do change in the course of history, and a man is never as good or as bad as the doctrine he teaches. Labels and dogmas do not change, but their underlying meaning is subject to historical evolution as the original condition of these situations change. The revolutionary fervor of Russia, for example, has radically changed from that of 20 to 30 years ago. There has been no radical change in dogma; but the Russians are very interested in peace, so as to safeguard the highly economic and technical society which they have laboriously created over the past twenty years. And so its interests and objectives have changed to a great degree — even if they continue to mouth the same revolutionary clichés. The truth is that all forms of government are subject to the simple law of historical evolution, and that, consequently, there is always hope for even the most totalitarian regimes. Here on earth, there is no absolute or incarnate evil among men.

The document now goes on to give us the actual aid which the Church can bring to human activity in the world — particularly through her laymen who are in the world. There seems to be a sort of parallel between paragraphs 41, 42, and 43 as corresponding to (effectively) Chapters I, II, and III of our first part. In our present paragraph, the Church is content with encouraging Christians to cooperate with all men of good will toward this essential goal. They can take their strength from the fact that Christ is the very end of human history, the point toward which the very desires of history and civilization converge (40b); and that within the world, the Church is a ferment particularly by and through her laymen. They are the instruments of Christ and of the Church whereby this will be brought about in the world. Thus the absolute impossibility of a divorce between faith and life (see 45).

The recommendations of the Council are as follows:

43. a. This Council exhorts Christians, as citizens of two cities, to strive to discharge their earthly duties conscientiously and in response to the gospel spirit. They are mistaken who, knowing that we have here no abiding city but seek one which is to come, think that they may therefore shirk their earthly responsibilities. For they are forgetting that by the faith itself they are more obliged than ever to measure up to these duties, each according to his proper vocation. Nor, on the contrary, are they any less wide of the mark who think that religion consists in acts of worship alone and in the discharge of certain moral obligations, and who imagine they can plunge themselves into earthly affairs in such a way as to imply that these are altogether divorced from the religious life. This split between the faith which many profess and their daily lives deserves to be counted among the more serious errors of our age. Long since, the Prophets of the Old Testament fought vehemently against this scandal and even more so did Jesus Christ himself in the New Testament threaten it with grave punishments. Therefore, let there be no false opposition between professional and social activities on the one part, and religious life on the other. The Christian who neglects his temporal duties, neglects the duties toward his neighbor and even God, and jeopardizes his eternal salvation. Christians should rather rejoice that, following the example of Christ who worked as an artisan, they are free to exercise all their earthly activities by gathering their humane, domestic, professional, social and technical enterprises into one vital synthesis with religious values, under whose supreme direction all things are harmonized unto God's glory.

b. Secular duties and activities belong properly although not exclusively to laymen. Therefore acting as citizens in the world, whether individually or socially, they will observe the laws proper to each discipline, and labor to equip themselves with a genuine expertise in their various fields. They will gladly work with men seeking the same goals. Acknowledging the demands of faith and endowed with its force, they will unhesitatingly devise new enterprises, where they are appropriate, and put them into action. Laymen should also know that it is generally the function of their well-formed Christian conscience to see that the divine law is inscribed in the life of the earthly city; from priests they may look for spiritual light and nourishment. Let the layman not imagine that his pastors are always such experts, that to every problem which arises, however complicated, they can readily give him a concrete solution, or even that such is their mission. Rather, enlightened by Christian wisdom and giving close attention to the teaching authority of the Church let the layman take on his own distinctive role.

c. Often enough the Christian view of things will itself suggest some specific solution in certain circumstances. Yet it happens rather frequently, and legitimately so, that with equal sincerity some of the faithful will disagree with others on a given matter. Even against the intentions of their proponents, however, solutions proposed on one side or another may be easily confused by many people with the gospel message. Hence it is necessary for people to remember that no one is allowed in the aforementioned situations to appropriate the Church's authority for his opinion. They should always try to enlighten one another through honest discussion, preserving mutual charity and caring above all for the common good.

d. Since they have an active role to play in the whole life of the Church, laymen are not only bound to penetrate the world with a Christian spirit, but are also called to be witnesses to Christ in all things in the midst of human society.

e. Bishops, to whom is assigned the task of ruling the Church of God, should, together with their priests, so preach the news of Christ that all the earthly activities of the faithful will be bathed in the light of the gospel. All pastors should remember too that by their daily conduct and concern they are revealing the face of the Church to the world, and men will judge the power and truth of the Christian message thereby. By their lives and speech, in union with Religious and their faithful, may they demonstrate that even now the Church, by her presence alone and by all the gifts which she contains, is an unspent fountain of those virtues which the modern world needs the most.

f. By unremitting study they should fit themselves to do their part in establishing dialogue with the world and with men of all shades of opinion. Above all let them take to heart the words which this Council has spoken: "Since humanity today increasingly moves toward civil, economic and social unity, it is more than ever necessary that priests, with joint concern and energy, and under the guidance of the bishops and the supreme pontiff, erase every cause of division, so that the whole human race may be led to the unity of God's family."

g. Although by the power of the Holy Spirit the Church will remain the faithful spouse of her Lord and will never cease to be the sign of salvation on earth, still she is very well aware that among her members, both clerical and lay, some have been unfaithful to the Spirit of God during the course of many centuries; in the present age, too, it does not escape the Church how great a distance lies between the message she offers and the human failings of those to whom the gospel is entrusted. Whatever be the judgment of history on these defects, we ought to be conscious of them, and struggle against them energetically, lest they inflict harm on the spread of the gospel. The Church also realizes that in working out her relationship with the world she always has great need of the ripening which comes with the experience of the centuries. Led by the Holy Spirit, Mother Church unceasingly exhorts her sons: "to purify and renew themselves so that the Sign of Christ can shine more brightly on the face of the Church."

The document first describes the principal error of our day — especially among Christians: the separation of faith from daily action. It is true as we have already seen, that here below (as long as the Church travels in its pilgrim state), we must distinguish but not separate the creational and the redemptive orders. This, of course, gives us the relative autonomy of the creative order in the way which we have already described (above, p. 121). There can be no such thing as Christian withdrawal from this new condition of humanity. There is both a healthy and an unchristian way of understanding the "secularity" of the world. In one sense, the world has a relative autonomy in following its own methods and discoveries which is further applied to man's social, economic, and temporal good. In this, the constructs of man receive their natural autonomy as well as being directed to man in the manner intended by God. There is another way of understanding the concept of "secularity," so that we attempt to reduce all reality (inclusive of the sacred) to the realm of the secular. There are various types of exaggeration and even error in this regard. There is, first of all, the situation where the sacred dominates the secular, where this latter has no exercise of legitimate autonomy. This happened — to a certain degree — in the high Middle Ages. Secondly, when the secular so dominates the sacred that it no longer recognizes the latter's existence or (a variant of the same, and which our document repudiates in 43a) when the sacred is irrelevant to the world in an excessive dichotomy. There is a real separation of faith and terrestrial activity and, as such, constitutes a very grave error. The fourth way of viewing the problem is where the sacred and the secular are kept distinct but have a unified vision in this same distinction. We must then avoid a certain type of monism, at one extreme, and an excessive dualism at the other.

The Council has been at pains throughout its exposé to point out the various aspects of a theology of secularity. The first element which we have seen is the fact that the secular receives the fullness of its intelligibility only within the context of the sacred and, moreover, only in Christ who sums up within himself both secular and sacred history. A distinction of these two orders, however, does not mean a utopia of any kind. The whole of the created order is still under the influence of sin, and this accounts to a great degree for the ambiguity of the secular order and its constructs. As long as the Church is in pilgrimage here below, she will have to contend with this inevitable fact and warn men against their egoism and sinfulness. This distinction will be kept until the *parousia* where in Christ alone we will see their unity. This distinction "sacred - secular" is therefore fully justified in the present economy of salvation, since we do not understand how this transformation will take place even at the *parousia*. In the present age, we have reached a certain type of autonomous maturity of the secular word, and, as such, the Church's mission in the world can only be one of witness to the essential values of the dignity and rights of man as explained in paragraph 42. Pope John XXIII pointed out this very same phenomenon in *Pacem* (151-153) where he said:

> It is no less clear that today in traditionally Christian nations secular institutions, although demonstrating a high degree of scientific and technical perfection and efficiency in achieving their respective ends, not infrequently are but slightly affected by Christian motivation or inspiration.
>
> It is beyond question that in the creation of those institutions many contributed and continue to contribute who were believed to be and who consider themselves Christians; and without a doubt, at least in part, they were and are. How does one explain this? It is our opinion that the explanation is to be found in an inconsistency in their minds between religious beliefs and their action in the temporal sphere. It is necessary, therefore, that their interior unity be re-established and that, in their temporal activity faith should be present as a beacon to give light, and charity as a force to give life.
>
> It is our opinion, too, that the above-mentioned inconsistency between religious faith in those who believe and their activities in the temporal sphere results — in great part if not entirely — from the lack of a solid Christian education. Indeed, it happens in many quarters and too often there is no preparation between scientific training and religious instruction: the former continues and is extended until it reaches higher degrees, while the latter remains at an elementary level. . . .

To bring knowledge and faith into a proper relationship, the

Christian must see all things as Christ sees them. His proper vocation as a layman is to find Christ's image within things and to consecrate himself to its manifestation. By virtue of creation, all is Christ's *by right;* the great dignity of the lay Christian will be to help make it his *in fact:* to change socio-economic structures so that many can live as men and not as slaves, to humanize penal and labor laws, to guarantee a climate of freedom and tolerance for human beings and respect for property under just laws, to help underdeveloped countries attain the material capacity to live in decency and freedom, to work for peace in international organizations, to do research for better health that men may live their lives comparatively free from mortal danger, to bring out the aspirations of man in art and writing, to fight racial discrimination by legislation and personal example, to work for equitable international trade agreements and tariffs. These are direct works of Christ, and they are but a few in the active litany of work that incorporates every aspect of man's temporal existence. This explains itself in a type of "religious life" for the layman, and he must see it as such in each of these roles. The document explicitly mentions this in 42b. *The Decree on the Apostolate of the Laity* will develop similar themes to an even greater degree. This theology comes out many times in the text:

> Since it is proper to the layman's state in life for him to spend his days in the midst of the world and of secular transactions, he is willed by God to burn with the Spirit of Christ and to exercise his apostolate in the world as a kind of leaven (2). . . .
> This (life with Christ) is to be used by the laity in such a way that while properly fulfilling their secular duties in the ordinary conditions of life, they do not disassociate union with Christ from that life. . . .
> Neither family concerns nor other secular affairs should be excluded from their religious program of life (4). . . .
> Christ's redemptive work while of itself directed toward the salvation of men, involves also the renewal of the whole

temporal order. Hence the mission of the Church is not only to bring to men the message and grace of Christ, but also to penetrate and perfect the temporal sphere with the spirit of the gospel. In fulfilling this mission of the Church, the laity therefore exercise their apostolate both in the Church and in the world, in both the spiritual and the temporal orders (5).

In *Gaudium et Spes* the Council does give us a bit more of a nuance, since it emphasizes that this sphere belongs, principally but not exclusively, to the layman. The distinction between priests and laity is always something relative to time and place. This does not mean that their roles are the same or interchangeable. We have said that the distinction "secular - sacred" would remain here below until the *parousia*. Therefore, there is ample justification for a diversity of roles, all under the aegis of the evangelical witness of love. Yet, necessities and needs vary widely at different places and times; and, therefore, no absolutism is possible here.

Another noteworthy consideration in this paragraph (43f) is the technical competency required for engagement in these various fields by laymen. This is an indirect rejection of any form of clericalism; being a cleric or religious is no assurance of automatic competence in every field. This is evident but perhaps not to a whole segment of the Christian population, and the Council firmly emphasizes this professional competence throughout all its documents. Thus both extremes are avoided here — that of a divorce between the two orders as well as that of identification. Thus the recommendation to both priests and bishops on the necessity for study of the factual situation concerning the various problems of modern man. "By unremitting study they should fit themselves to do their part in establishing dialogue with the world and with men of all shades of opinion" (43f).

On the other hand — and this is important — the Church learns from the world and its own historical evolution:

44. a. Just as it is in the world's interest to acknowledge the

Church as a historical reality, and to recognize her good influence, so the Church herself knows how richly she has profited by the history and development of humanity.

b. The experience of past ages, the progress of the sciences, and the treasures hidden in the various forms of human culture, by all of which the nature of man himself is more clearly revealed and new roads to truth are opened, these profit the Church, too. For, from the beginning of her history she has learned to express the message of Christ with the help of the ideas and terminology of various philosophers, and has tried to clarify it with their wisdom, too. Her purpose has been to adapt the gospel to the grasp of all as well as to the needs of the learned, insofar as such was appropriate. Indeed this accommodate preaching of the revealed Word ought to remain the law of all evangelization. For thus the ability to express Christ's message in its own way is developed in each nation, and at the same time there is fostered a living exchange between the Church and the diverse cultures of people. To promote such exchange, especially in our days, the Church requires the special help of those who live in the world, are versed in different institutions and specialties, and grasp their innermost significance in the eyes of both believers and unbelievers. With the help of the Holy Spirit, it is the task of the entire People of God, especially pastors and theologians, to hear, distinguish and interpret the many voices of our age, and to judge them in the light of the divine Word, so that revealed truth can always be more deeply penetrated, better understood and set forth to greater advantage.

c. Since the Church has a visible and social structure as a sign of her unity in Christ, she can and ought to be enriched by the development of human social life, not that there is any lack in the constitution given her by Christ, but that she can understand it more penetratingly, express it better, and adjust it more successfully to our times. Moreover, she gratefully understands that in her community life no less than in her individual sons, she receives a variety of help from men of every rank and condition, for whoever promotes the human community at the family level, culturally, in its economic, social and political dimensions, both nationally and internationally, such a one, according to God's design, is contributing greatly to the Church as well, to the extent that she depends on things outside herself. Indeed, the Church admits that she has greatly profited and still profits from the antagonism of those who oppose or who persecute her.

Thus, these capacities of the creature, this participation in divine causality are not only given to individuals for their personal benefit and salvation but are, by their very nature, social. They concern man in society insofar as his social life forms part of his very nature. Man is not an individual; he is a person, autonomous, created to follow the laws of his own being. No *a priori* notions of the "nature" of man or "natural law" can be presupposed here; man through reason and his own historical experience is dependent on other men for his personal growth and development. Thus, to take one example from among many, it is not simply a man's work which may reveal material disposed toward grace; a civilization based on man's work presents resources capable of reflecting the Kingdom of God. This "obediential power," this causality of man, has an essential social dimension, and it develops as man develops himself more fully in history. This view of man's social nature in development is of capital importance in the modern world where "socialization" in the above-mentioned sense is the major and universal phenomenon. That is what Origen saw long ago when he said that the Graeco-Roman civilization was an "evangelical preparation." So, too, the values of the modern world: order, justice, human rights, cultural and moral riches — these are considered by Pope John as forerunning signs, and must be so considered by the Church, as predispositions for the diffusion of the gospel in the modern world.

In the actual make-up of mankind in the modern world-wide extension of social, political and cultural values, in the universal consciousness of the rights of man, there are today, just as in the early Roman empire, possible resources in preparation for the gospel — good material for the construction of the kingdom of God in the modern world. This calls for rethinking the traditional structures in which the evangelical message has been carried and for a bold attempt by the Church to reincarnate this message into the new cadres of the modern world.

No doubt these values have been and continue to be ambiguous, contaminated, in fact, by error and sin, it was the same in the time of early Roman civilization where practice of the rights of individuals, families, city life, were equally ambiguous and contaminated with error, and in which, for three centuries, the Church was violently persecuted. Yet, we are in a time of transition where new methods and attempts at accommodation must be made. There will be some mistakes, but what progress has ever been achieved without a willingness to risk some danger of error in proportion to need? And the need for this dynamic *aggiornamento* is urgent in the Church today. It is true to say that, after necessary purification, these values of the modern world are of great importance. For example, the solidarity between men, created by labor organizations and commercial necessity, is an admirable predisposition toward evangelical fraternity; it can become a potent preparation for implementing this evangelical fraternity in the modern world. Furthermore, the anguished aspiration of men and of peoples for peace and for its international advent is a great predisposition toward the hopes of men of good will.

Thus this aid which the Church receives from the world can be narrowed down to three main aspects. First, that she receive the necessary freedom for the fulfillment of her apostolate. This is a precondition for everything else, since where she is persecuted there can be no true dialogue or understanding among men. This primary condition is not farfetched, since there are many areas in the world where her effective activity is so curtailed that we can say that she possesses no freedom. Secondly, the transformation of the world toward freedom, security and promotion of man is a task, willed by God, and, as such, must enter into the economy of salvation as well, since man is saved in the totality of his being and the totality of his vocation on earth. This is accomplished — whether they realize it or not — by believer and unbeliever alike (44b). Finally, we can say that the Church is aided (or hindered) by the type of milieu in which the Church proclaims her doctrine and her witness. Some will be more receptive than others, and the Church must be open to the new cultural forms in which she must translate her doctrine and her message to make them intelligible to modern man. She does not live a disincarnate existence, since she is dependent upon the forms and expressions of various civilizations and cultures and is a solidarity with them (44c). This point is original with *Gaudium et Spes* and is both an aid to her as well as a task for her. She must both learn and be taught in a type of interdependence. She is not and cannot be outside the mainstream of the life of man; rather, her very mission depends on this sort of incarnationalism. She, by her teaching, says to her faithful each day: "The Mass is completed. Go in peace" — in the sense that having learned what love is at its very source, she now sends forth her children to incarnate this love in concrete action in the lives of men.

Thus, liturgy, which is nothing more than dogma prayed, in the phrase of Vatican II, can never be a simple ritual, repeated phrases and readings; but of its very nature it must be viewed as it is: that is, as radically orientated toward daily life. There can never be any disjunction of the two. They are two sides of the same coin of worship, of the Christian life lived in Christ. The Christian's life and practice are a test to see if he has really grasped what God has told him in the liturgical assembly. His life is an extension of the liturgy, a continuous offering, a sort of prolonged and vital liturgy.

We all know very well that worship contains elements of adoration, gratitude, contrition, and petition. But what the Christian community does not seem to understand, to any significant degree, is that worship is also a school for fraternal service. The ancient Greek word expressed this very well: *koinonia,* communion, is both translated as communion with the

Lord in the liturgical assembly, but also a service of the brethren which is only the natural outcome of our mutual commitment to Christ, and, in him, to each other. The great commandments of love of God and of neighbor are indivisible, and worship is the bond which makes them one. The New Testament word of love (agape) is used indiscriminately for both God and man. The Church worships in order to prepare men for God, so that in turn, she may also prepare men for the service of man. The dialogue in the liturgical assembly must not, cannot go on separated from neighbor and from the notion of service. Such a dichotomized view of Christianity is a monstrosity, a monstrosity which goes on today in spite of the frequentation of the sacraments. In a sense, this is the great tragedy of modern Catholicism: too long have we separated worship from the service of the brothers, from our fellow man, without regard to race, color, or creed.

The "good" nineteenth-century Catholic liberals (today: conservatives) practiced their religion well insofar as sacramental frequentation was concerned; but the service of social and economic justice for the brethren wasn't even considered a part of "worship." The same can be said today of our Latin American neighbors. The few rich (all, almost without exception) frequent the sacraments weekly, but obstinately refuse any service of the brethren in just gradual taxation, agrarian reform, investment of capital at home instead of in Switzerland or on Wall Street. Nor must we look across our borders for such a dichotomy. The race problem in the United States is a classic example. How very very many Catholic racists do we have at our communion rails each Sunday (and a few, possibly, in our pulpits). Nor do the aged, the forty-odd million poor of the "other America" seem to cause our consciences much trouble, either in the liturgical community or elsewhere.

The liturgy "makes the Christian" (to use the phrase of the ninth-century French ritual) gives his identification to the city of his celestial calling and his earthly commitment to the city of man. One cannot separate liturgical worship from social action, for together they spell the Christian total commitment. If we emphasize one at the cost of the other we have either "transcendentalism" which has been characteristic of Catholicism of the past 400 years (as well as Eastern Orthodox Christianity). As Peguy once remarked, the reason why many Catholics do not have dirty hands is because they have no hands. The concomitant complement to the liturgy is social action; both together are the fullness of Christian action and commitment.

On the other hand, if we stress social action and justice without the liturgy, we have a type of terrestrial messianism similar to that of marxism. To tell the truth, this is the great temptation of the economically and technically growing world, and most of the blame must be placed on Christians who have been satisfied to go to Mass and the sacraments without realizing the fraternal love in social action as a natural concomitant to liturgical worship.

Once again, the document concludes this chapter — as it has in previous chapters — with Christ at the beginning and at the end of the temporal activity of man. He is the Alpha and Omega of this whole activity of the Church as well as of the world. Much of this has already been exposed in the above-mentioned sections but the Council returns with insistence on this unifying principle of both orders who is Christ, the Incarnate Word. This gives Christians the necessary courage and love to face the titanic tasks of the modern world since the Church has no practical solutions for any of them. What she does have is this rock-bottom principle of comprehension and orientation of both the secular and sacred orders: Christ, the Incarnate Logos:

45. a. While helping the world and receiving many benefits from it, the Church has a single intention: that God's Kingdom may come, and that the salvation of the whole human race may come to pass. For every benefit which the People of God during its earthly pilgrimage can offer to the human family stems from

the fact that the Church is "the universal sacrament of salvation," simultaneously manifesting and exercising the mystery of God's love of man.

b. For God's Word, by whom all things were made, was himself made flesh so that as perfect man he might save all men and sum up all things in himself. The Lord is the goal of human history, the focal point of the longings of history and of civilization, the center of the human race, the joy of every heart and the answer to all its yearnings. He it is whom the Father raised from the dead, lifted on high and stationed at his right hand, making him judge of the living and the dead. Enlivened and united in his Spirit, we journey toward the consummation of human history, one which fully accords with the counsel of God's love: "To re-establish all things in Christ, both those in the heavens and those on the earth" (Eph 11:10).

c. The Lord himself, speaks: "Behold I come quickly! And my reward is with me, to render to each one according to his works. I am the Alpha and the Omega, the first and the last, the beginning and the end" (Apoc 22:12-13).

PART II

PART II

Some Problems of Special Urgency

Our document begins by giving us an introductory paragraph on both the problems of the modern age which the Council will now discuss and the spirit in which they are to be discussed:

46. a. This Council has set forth the dignity of the human persons, and the work which men have been destined to undertake throughout the world both as individuals and as members of society. There are a number of particularly urgent needs characterizing the present age, needs which go to the roots of the human race. To a consideration of these in the light of the gospel and of human experience, the Council would now direct the attention of all.

b. Of the many subjects arousing universal concern today, it may be helpful to concentrate on these: marriage and the family, human progress, life in its economic, social and political dimensions, the bonds between the family of nations, and peace. On each of these may there shine the radiant ideals proclaimed by Christ. By these ideals may Christians be led, and all mankind enlightened, as they search for answers to questions of such complexity.

As we have already seen, these problems should and must be considered by the Church since she possesses the deposit of the evangelical witness. This, of course, gives her no special concrete solutions to these variant and complicated problems, but it does give her the right and obligation to view these problems according to the gospel principles of justice and of love. She has an obligation to apply them to the concrete problems of men; for principles of themselves mean comparatively little unless concretely applied. This second part, taken up again in paragraph 65, deals with concrete problems, by request from many Council Fathers, to be discussed in light of both revelation and concrete human experience. This section is, of its nature, evolutionary in character, since man comes to understand himself ever more perfectly in the light of his historical experience and of his reflection upon it. The aspect of reason was emphasized through this second part in a fashion similar to that of John XXIII in his *Pacem in Terris*. Both documents were addressed to all men of good will, and this was the logical place where they could meet on a common ground. Logically, the first and most important problem facing both the Church and the modern world is that of the family.

CHAPTER 1

Fostering the Nobility of Marriage and the Family

The Council begins this section of *Gaudium et Spes* by citing the dignity of the family and the various problems which it faces today (46). It then proceeds to analyze the entire problem in logical order. First, the family is described in a sociological manner whereby the basic structures of family life as well as its factual situation are given to us (47). Next (48), marriage is described as an institution wherein man and woman in a complete gift of self to each other, promote their love and affectivity. As such, marriage is a stable, and, of itself, a lifelong institution for the couple. In such an institution, for those who believe, the couple encounter Christ in what is known as the sacrament of matrimony whereby their human love is sanctified and elevated to the plane of the divine life itself. Finally, whether it be a sacrament or not, marriage connotes the depth of human love as a reality (49). This finds expression in the mutual gift of the couple in the specificity of their bodies as a sign of this total love and self-gift. This leads logically to a consideration of the family itself (spouses, children), as well as its relationship to external society. The perfection of the totality of human love must here be considered. This implies a training of children in the true meaning of love (as distinct from simple sexuality) (49). Next it should be evident at this point that love between the spouses becomes incarnate in concrete expressions, and children are to be seen as a free expression of that mutual love one for the other. They alone are the judges on just how many children they can bring into the world and on the limits of their responsible love within marriage (50). All this remains true — mutually expressed love and freely accepted children as a gift of love — and yet, the two can come into conflict because of physical, economic, sociological, or psychological reasons of one or both of the partners. There have been various solutions to this conflict which are repugnant to Christian morality (abortion, sterilization, infanticide, and "illicit practices" for the prevention of births). Members of the Church cannot in conscience follow practices which have been condemned by the *Magisterium* of the Church (51). In any case, this path to the perfection of conjugal love is both arduous and difficult and is a work of a lifetime for the couple. On the other hand, society must do all in its power to foster and promote a healthy milieu in which the couple can grow in love and raise their families. In many respects, the natural environment will determine to a great extent how effectively the couple can attain their supernatural end as well (52).

Thus, in logical consequence, the Council gives us a general view of conjugal and family life in society. It begins by discussing the sociological background and difficulties of the family today:

47. a. The well-being of the individual person and of human and Christian society is intimately linked with the healthy condition of that community produced by marriage and family. Hence Christians and all men who hold this community in high esteem sincerely rejoice in the various ways by which men today find help in fostering this community of love and perfecting its life, and by which parents are assisted in their lofty calling. Those who rejoice in such aids look for additional benefits from them and labor to bring them about.

b. Yet the excellence of this institution is not everywhere reflected with equal brilliance, since polygamy, the plague of divorce, so-called free love and other disfigurements, have an obscuring effect. In addition, married love is too often profaned by excessive self-love, the worship of pleasure and illicit practices against human generation. Moreover, serious disturbances are caused in families by modern economic conditions, by influences at once social and psychological, and by the demands of civil society. Finally, in certain parts of the world problems resulting from population growth are generating concern.

c. All these situations have produced anxiety of conscience. Yet, the power and strength of the institution of marriage and family can also be seen in the fact that time and again, despite the difficulties produced, the profound changes in modern society reveal the true character of this institution in one way or another.

d. Therefore, by presenting certain key points of Church doctrine in a clearer light, this Sacred Synod wishes to offer guidance and support to those Christians and other men who are trying to preserve the holiness and to foster the natural dignity of the married state and its superlative value.

We are thus given a sociological survey of the problems and difficulties of the modern family. This is a statement on which all can agree and, in fact, do agree; namely, that it is the health of the family on which the health of the state depends. This was realized by a non-believing country like Russia which began with "free love" and ended with some of the most stringent family codes of any nation on earth (47a). In this section of the paragraph we have an attack on those things which disrupt the dignity of the human family ("self-love, worship of pleasure, and illicit practices against human generation"). In essence, these are the aberrations which attack the family as an institution; namely, the fact that family life is an inter-communion between persons, a seeking after the good of the other. Such practices, in reality, tend to destroy this oblative love of the couple. Thus we see this institution as a "help in fostering this community of love and perfecting its love." In enumerating the practices which endanger the institution of marriage, the Council is careful in citing what is wrong with the familial atmosphere of today. It has avoided two extremes: those who say that nothing is wrong (free love) and the pious literature of those ecclesiastics who carp on and on about the evils of "modern life." The Council's analysis of the modern situation is reserved to a cool, sociological study characterized neither by pious harangues nor by indifferent self-confidence in having "the truth." These difficulties are clear: economic imbalances and conditions, sociological and psychological influences from the milieu in which they live, and finally, the great problem of overpopulation (47b). This leaves men with a sense of anxiety, but our text is not pessimistic. It concludes on a note of confidence, in the sense that men today are once again returning to this institution and viewing those things which influence it as one of the most important problems of our times.

The essence of matrimony is the institution willed by God wherein a man and a woman mutually give each other for life in oblative love. From that moment on — after consent — the institution of marriage is irrevocable by man. The Council now proceeds to describe this aspect in its entirety:

48. a. The intimate partnership of married life and love has been established by the Creator and qualified by his laws, and is rooted in the conjugal covenant of irrevocable personal consent. Hence by that human act whereby spouses mutually bestow and accept each other a relationship arises which by divine will and in the eyes of society too is a lasting one. For the good of the spouses and their offspring as well as of society, the existence of the sacred bond no longer depends on human decisions alone. For God himself is the author of matrimony, endowed as it is with various benefits and purposes. All of these have a very decisive bearing on the continuation of the human race, on the personal development and eternal destiny of the individual members of a family, and on the dignity, stability, peace and prosperity of the family itself and of human society as a whole. By their very nature, the institution of matrimony itself and conjugal love are ordained for the procreation and education of children, and find in them their ultimate crown. Thus a man and a woman, who by their compact of conjugal love "are no longer two, but one flesh"

(Matt 19:6), render mutual help and service to each other through an intimate union of their persons and of their actions. Through this union they experience the meaning of their oneness and attain to it with growing perfection day by day. As a mutual gift of two persons, this intimate union and the good of the children impose total fidelity on the spouses and argue for an unbreakable oneness between them.

b. Christ the Lord abundantly blessed this many-faceted love, welling up as it does from the fountain of divine love and structured as it is on the model of his union with his Church. For as God of old made himself present to his people through a covenant of love and fidelity, so now the Savior of men and and the Spouse of the Church comes into the lives of married Christians through the sacrament of matrimony. He abides with them thereafter so that, just as he loved the Church and handed himself over on her behalf, the spouses may love each other with perpetual fidelity through mutual self-bestowal.

c. Authentic married love is caught up into divine love and is governed and enriched by Christ's redeeming power and the saving activity of the Church, so that this love may lead the spouses to God with powerful effect and may aid and strengthen them in the sublime office of being a father or a mother. For this reason Christian spouses have a special sacrament by which they are fortified and receive a kind of consecration in the duties and dignity of their state. By virtue of this sacrament, as spouses fulfill their conjugal and family obligations, they are penetrated with the spirit of Christ, which suffuses their whole lives with faith, hope and charity. Thus they increasingly advance the perfection of their own personalities, as well as their mutual sanctification, and hence contribute jointly to the glory of God.

d. As a result, with their parents leading the way by example and family prayer, children and indeed everyone gathered around the family hearth will find a readier path to human maturity, salvation and holiness. Graced with the dignity and office of fatherhood and motherhood, parents will energetically acquit themselves of a duty which devolves primarily on them, namely education and especially religious education.

e. As living members of the family, children contribute in their own way to make their parents holy. For they will respond to the kindness of their parents with sentiments of gratitude, with love and trust. They will stand by them as children should when hardships overtake their parents and old age brings its loneliness. Widowhood, accepted bravely as a continuation of the marriage vocation, should be esteemed by all. Families too will share their spiritual riches generously with other families. Thus the Christian family, which springs from marriage as a reflection of the loving covenant uniting Christ with the Church and as a participation in that covenant, will manifest to all men Christ's living presence in the world, and the genuine nature of the Church. This the family will do by the mutual love of the spouses, by their generous fruitfulness, and by the loving way in which all members of the family assist one another.

The Council here emphasizes various influences of the family on every sector of society — on the continuation of the human race, personal and eternal development of the members of the family, etc. All this depends upon the free acceptance of marriage by the couple, but, above all, on the fact that after the consent, marriage as an institution has its own laws as established by God, and is no longer dependent solely upon the will of man. This has been traditional in the marriage thinking and theorizing of the Church. Yet there is a great nuance here (48a); throughout this section, the central fact of marriage as the interpersonal communion of love is stressed and thus is irrevocable because of the total gift of self in oblative love of the couple. As an interpersonal view of marriage, there is not so much of a stress on the strictly juridical aspects of the matter, even if this latter condition is not neglected. Our text manages to incorporate this interpersonal and communitarian vocation into some of the more traditional modes of expression of the past. The couple are one now, not just by a continual consent (which of course, is and remains psychologically true), but by the very institution itself they remain now — and until death — ontologically one, which no force on earth can break. This was clearly seen in the encyclical letter *Casti Connubii* by Pius XI.

Also, traditionally, the text gives us the essential objective of marriage which is "ordained for the procreation and education of children; and find in them their ultimate crown" (48a). It is noteworthy — in spite of the rather strong wishes of some of the Fathers — that the Council did not enter into a discussion or exposition of the traditional concepts of the hierarchy of ends of marriage — one being primary (procreation of children) and the other secondary (mutual love). Our document deliberately refrains from speaking of marriage in this way in its own exposé. It is true — as many theologians have shown in the past — that these formulas can be understood in a legitimate and healthy sense. In this sense, primary means that *only* in the institution of marriage can the procreation of children be fully and completely realized, and that the secondary end can and, in fact, often is realized outside the institution of marriage itself. The traditional terminology, then, is valuable and enlightening, but it remains a fact that much misunderstanding can be read into these formulas: primary and secondary being understood in an order of importance almost to the point where you could have the first without the other, and consequently, a certain "toning down" of the second. Often this has been so in the minds of many of the simple faithful, even if in the minds of most theologians this distinction has never meant "less important" or "non-essential," as would seem to be indicated by the terms "primary" and "secondary." We see today that the attempt to establish the minimum essential for matrimony by the canonist and jurist will simply no longer do. For a total theology of matrimony, one must see and take into complete consideration what we have said above about a man and woman establishing by mutual consent and self-gift an interpersonal communion of love for life. This is certainly not "secondary" in the sense of being unimportant, for it should be evident that the procreation and education of children will depend, to a great degree, on the atmosphere of oblative love of the couple itself. It is an existential situation of mutual interdependence of sexual union which specifically distinguishes this union from every other union of man. It is for life and cannot be retracted by the couple which, of course, makes it generically different from every other type of sexual union on earth among other species of animals. Only men have this power of permanence. They make a total and personal community of mutual and permanent love by which the institution, marriage, becomes the principal object of this same marriage. Upon this will depend the health and love and responsible procreation of children *as willed by the Creator*. Thus marriage must not be seen as a type of "exclusivism" of one aspect by the other, but rather as an intimate interdependence as willed by the Creator who instituted matrimony.

Only in this century have we outgrown the traditional conception in which sexuality is merely the means of procreation. It has been shown with increasing clarity that human sexuality has intrinsically a relational significance, that it is an integral part of the relationship between husband and wife, that it is in fact the basis upon which this relationship is built in love. We have not received our sexuality — that is, the condition of being man or woman — for ourselves. It belongs to our condition of being men and women for each other. It is an invitation to establish a fellowship, an encounter between husband and wife.

"Furthermore, husband and wife are both human persons. So when, at this invitation, they enter into fellowship, they encounter each other as human persons, and their fellowship must fulfill the requirements of all human social relations. The most fundamental demand to this invitation to encounter each other in fellowship by virtue of their sexual diversity, lies in the fact that they are each other's first 'neighbor.' They must practice, in a unique way, love of the neighbor toward each other, with all that this implies both on the human and the Christian level — such as respect and appreciation of the dignity of the other as a person, and the will to promote the good of the other. It follows that the fellowship between a man and woman which we call marriage shall be based first and foremost on love. Each day anew, they must support each other as Christians: conjugal prayer, family prayer, sacramental life, the cultivation of their communal awareness of their tie with God which confirms their sacramental tie with each other. Each day they must grow in love for each other on the human level: consideration, deference, a word of appreciation and encouragement, patience with the other's failings, ability to admit being in the wrong, eliminating failings which displease the partner, cooperation in bringing up the children, disinterested solicitude for the partner's well-being, and so forth (see 1 Cor 13:4-31). Do married people forget too easily that they are each other's first *neighbor?*

"Conjugal love is not a unique form of love of neighbor just because husband and wife live closest to each other, but because it is upheld by a particular *tenderness,* creating an atmosphere of mutual protection, and finds natural expression in signs of affective attachment and in demonstrations of preference for each other.

"This tenderness attaches special significance to the body of the other, giving the married couple a sensibility to *intimacies* and caresses. In this respect, account must be made for individual differences: each married couple must discover for itself the physical intimacies suited to the expression of their conjugal love."[1]

Furthermore, conjugal love includes the desire for sexual relations. Husband and wife express their mutual trust in the fact that they *entrust* their bodies to each other: the giving of self in love goes so far as the giving of their bodies to each other. It was in this sense that St. Paul said that the husband does not rule over his body anymore, but the wife does; and that the wife no longer rules over her body, but the husband does (1 Cor 7:4). A gift is something decisive; one no longer disposes of something one has given to another. Insofar as we give something we *have,* we can divide this possession among several

---

1 L. Janssens, "Moral Problems Involved in Responsible Parenthood," *Louvain Studies,* 1 (Fall, 1966), pp. 4-5.

people. But the husband and wife who give themselves to each other by the gift of their bodies are not giving something they have, but something of what they *are*. The body of each one is an indivisible whole, and therefore the gift is definitive and exclusive. By this very fact, the sexual act is an expression of conjugal love. It is only fitting within marriage, i.e., in the institutionally ratified fellowship wherein a man and a woman have definitively and exclusively given themselves to each other. That is a first reason — later we shall meet another — why we use for the human sexual act the fine expression "marriage act." It is only in place between married persons, for it is in essence an expression and embodiment of married love (or, in F. Leist's words: the language of conjugal love).

"In the past, sexuality was considered solely as a means of procreation, a means which might not be abused as a way of finding enjoyment, nor was it considered in connection with conjugal love, the latter being regarded as a spiritual reality. Now we realize that sexuality, even in its most physical expression, is the basis upon which conjugal love as such is built, and that the immediate and essential sense of the sexual act is precisely to be the expression and embodiment of conjugal love. Conjugal chastity, which demands from the married couple that they respect the sense of their sexuality, obtains in this way a richer content, i.e., their sexual intercourse must never be separated from love; it must rather serve their love and help to increase it."[1]

Then our document goes on to develop the sacramentality of Christian marriage and in what way it is to be seen as a sacrament (48b). It uses the traditional text of St. Paul to the Ephesians, where marriage is to be seen as an interpersonal relationship and community of love. In addition, they base their married love on the type of disinterested love which Christ had for his Church. In this, they imitate Christ in the total oblative

---

1 L. Janssens, *art. cit.*, p. 6.

gift of self and in so doing they encounter Christ himself in their mutual gift. This is the sacrament of Christian marriage which renders Christ himself ever present in the conjugal relationship throughout their married existence. Each partner becomes a symbol and a cause of the presence of Christ in their midst throughout the totality of their married existence in all its joys, pleasures, and agonies. Each of these acts is then sanctified within this total view of the conjugal Christian reality of marriage. This emphasis of the Council on the totality of the presence of Christ in Christian marriage will give a greater depth to the theology of marriage so much alive today (48c). It is this love lived to its fullness in the marriage hearth which is the best example and commentary parents could give on human and divine love (48d). It is also noteworthy that here (48d, e) we have a special insistence by the Council on filial piety on the part of children toward their parents, above all in their old age. This is a keen psychological and Christian insight in the present age of depersonalized social security and old-age institutions (which are, of themselves, a great good), where there is a danger of diminution of this virtue. Children are never excused from one of the fundamental obligations of the commandments: "Honor your mother and your father." This will always remain, even in the modern era of social benefits and welfare agencies.

Widowhood is praised as a "continuation of the marriage vocation" which joins the ancient tradition of the Church holding that it is better to remain always faithful to the one embrace in life and death. This was such a strong tradition that some in the early Church (Tertullian) went so far as to brand as adultery all second marriages. This was certainly an exaggeration, but it does show the reverence of the Church for the unique love-bond of marriage. In an age of perhaps too-easy second marriages, this is a timely reminder of an honorable and ancient tradition in the Church.

Finally, it is by their example of deep Christian living —

their love for all in need and in trouble — that Christian families give their testimony before the world (48e). "By this will all men know that you are my disciples; that you have love for one another." This is an apologetic motif in the world of Christian family living which cannot be exaggerated or overstressed.

The document next goes into a basic description what should constitute conjugal love:

49. a. The biblical Word of God several times urges the betrothed and the married to nourish and develop their wed-lock by pure conjugal love and undivided affection. Many men of our own age also highly regard true love between husband and wife as it manifests itself in a variety of ways depending on the worthy customs of various peoples and times.

b. This love is an eminently human one since it is directed from one person to another through an affection of the will; it involves the good of the whole person, and therefore can enrich the expressions of the body and mind with a unique dignity, ennobling these expressions as special ingredients and signs of the friendship distinctive of marriage. This love God has judged worthy of special gifts, healing, perfecting and exalting gifts of grace and of charity. Such love, merging the human with the divine, leads the spouses to a free and mutual gift of themselves, a gift proving itself by gentle affection and by deed; such love pervades the whole of their lives: indeed by its active generosity it grows better and grows greater. Therefore it far excels mere erotic inclination, which, selfishly pursued, soon enough fades wretchedly away.

c. This love is uniquely expressed and perfected in the special area of matrimony. The actions within marriage by which the couple are united intimately and chastely are noble and worthy ones. Expressed in a manner which is truly human, these actions promote that mutual self-giving by which spouses enrich each other with a joyful and a ready will. Sealed by mutual faithfulness and hallowed above all by Christ's sacra-ment, this love remains steadfastly true in body and in mind, in bright days or dark. It will never be profaned by adultery or divorce. Firmly established by the Lord, the unity of mar-riage will radiate from the equal personal dignity of wife and husband, a dignity acknowledged by mutual and total love.

The constant fulfillment of the duties of this Christian vocation demands notable virtue. For this reason, strengthened by grace for holiness, the couple painstakingly cultivate and pray for steadfastness of love, large-heartedness and the spirit of sacrifice.

d. Authentic conjugal love will be more highly prized, and wholesome public opinion created regarding it, if Christian couples give outstanding witness to faithfulness and harmony in their love, and to their concern for educating their children; also, if they do their part in bringing about the needed cultural, psychological and social renewal on behalf of marriage and the family. Especially in the heart of their own families, young people should be aptly and seasonably instructed in the dignity, duty and work of married love. Trained thus in the cultivation of chastity, they will be able at a suitable age to enter a marriage of their own after an honorable courtship.

Once again our document stresses that which is common between believers and non-believers alike, namely, the constituent element of conjugal love and its promotion in marriage: mutual love and fertility.

"In order to consider fertility in its moral aspects we must take as our starting point the *meaning* of human sexuality. It will always remain true that husband and wife must respect the sense of their sexuality. That principle is immutable. But the knowledge of its *content* can become progressively richer. For centuries people have thought that the only meaning of sexuality lay in its being directed toward the continuation of life. St. Thomas, continuing a long tradition, teaches explicitly that the sexual act in marriage is only morally justifiable if entered upon in order to procreate life, and that a married person who *invites* his partner to sexual relations for any other reason than that of procreation commits at least a venial sin (St. Augustine). This position is perfectly justifiable, if, as was then the opinion, the *only* meaning of sexuality is to be at the service of fertility. That this assertion of St. Thomas causes us now a certain uneasiness is not due to the fact that we start from a different first principle. We accept that husband and wife must remain faithful to the sense of their sexuality. That will always be true. We also accept that sexuality has some connection with fertility. But we can no longer agree, if procreation is presented as the only meaningful factor in human sexuality."[1] At our present level of culture, thanks mainly to progress in the sciences which study man himself — and here we think chiefly of psychology and the medical sciences — we have discovered a richer sense in human sexuality. How then should married people behave in order to live this sense, so far as we can understand it at the moment?

It is this question which must be asked of both believer and unbeliever alike (49a).

The document then goes on to give us an existential description of human love between two human beings (49b). Marriage is distinguished from every other form of friendship by the specificity of sexuality as an external symbol of what has been interiorly given, namely, one's whole self as gift to the other. The Council's statement in this regard is revealing, where it says that love should direct "these expressions as special ingredients and signs of friendship distinctive of marriage." This in itself shows how remote the thinking of the Council is from any type of dualism or Jansenism, in which sexual activity is an ignoble thing in the lives of human beings. This needs little stress in our age, and yet it is noteworthy that any ambiguity has been entirely eliminated by the conciliar document. Nor is marital love platonic, but rather its normal orientation is toward an incarnational and sexual engagement of both body and soul in a totality of self-gift to each other. Sexual expression is an extremely important element in any conjugal relationship whose love is increased and nourished by this mutual self-giving. "These actions promote that mutual self-giving by which spouses enrich each other with a joyful and ready will" (49c). Under the influence of charity, the flesh is a valuable

---

1 L. Janssens, *art. cit.*, p. 3.

aid and instrument in the promotion of conjugal love. It must be prompted by love, however, and a sexual act which is not is a debasement of the human person.

Sexuality is not only orientated toward fertility. It is no less part of its intrinsic sense to be in the service of conjugal love. Even if temporarily or forever a new pregnancy must be excluded, sexual intercourse retains this intrinsic significance. It can even be necessary for saving the most essential values of marriage and family, that is, the trust and harmony required for the task of raising children. If the complete sexual act is not possible in a married couple's situation, cannot even sexual acts of which the physical integrity is not respected still be of positive service to these essential values? Is it not true that sexuality as an expression of the affective relationship is more supple than it is as an instrument of fertility? The realities of life here offer no ground for a rigid codification. May this sphere of the affective relationship and its sexual expression remain under the protection of the general norm of conjugal love? Moreover the distinction here between what is desirable and what is morally obligatory deserves to be respected. More of this in our next section.

We now come to the major question of the fecundity of marriage (50) and the necessity, at times of its limitations (51):

50. a. Marriage and conjugal love are by their nature ordained toward the begetting and educating of children. Children are really the supreme gift of marriage and contribute very substantially to the welfare of their parents. The God himself who said, "It is not good for man to be alone" (Gen 2:18) and "Who made man from the beginning male and female" (Matt 19:4); wishing to share with man a certain special participation in his own creative work, blessed male and female, saying: "Increase and multiply" (Gen 1:28). Hence, while not making the other purposes of matrimony of less account, the true practice of conjugal love, and the whole meaning of the family life which results from it, have this aim: that the couple be ready with stout hearts to cooperate with the love of the

Creator and the Savior, who through them will enlarge and enrich his own family day by day.

b. Parents should regard as their proper mission the task of transmitting human life and educating those to whom it has been transmitted. They should realize that they are thereby cooperators with the love of God the Creator, and are, so to speak, the interpreters of that love. Thus they will fulfill their task with human and Christian responsibility, and, with docile reverence toward God, will make decisions by common counsel and effort. Let them thoughtfully take into account both their own welfare, and that of their children, those already born and those which the future may bring. For this accounting they need to reckon with both the material and the spiritual conditions of the times as well as of their state in life. Finally, they should consult the interests of the family group, of temporal society, and of the Church itself. The parents themselves should ultimately make this judgment in the sight of God. But in their manner of acting, spouses should be aware that they cannot proceed arbitrarily, but must always be governed according to a conscience dutifully conformed to the divine law itself, and should be submissive toward the Church's teaching office, which authentically interprets that law in the light of the gospel. That divine law reveals and protects the integral meaning of conjugal love, and impels it toward a truly human fulfillment. Thus, trusting in divine Providence and refining the spirit of sacrifice, married Christians glorify the Creator and strive toward fulfillment in Christ when with a generous human and Christian sense of responsibility they acquit themselves of the duty to procreate. Among the couples who fulfill their God-given task in this way, those merit special mention who with a gallant heart, and with wise and common deliberation, undertake to bring up suitably even a relatively large family.

c. Marriage to be sure is not instituted solely for procreation; rather, its very nature as an unbreakable compact between persons, and the welfare of the children, both demand that the mutual love of the spouses be embodied in a rightly ordered manner, that it grow and ripen. Therefore, marriage persists as a whole manner and communion of life, and maintains its value and indissolubility, even when, despite the often intense desire of the couple, offspring are lacking.

The document first gives the traditional teaching with regard to children in marriage (50a). They are the fruit of the mutual gift in love of both partners and as such are to be seen as the crown of the conjugal relationship. Normally, fecundity is the fruit of their love in sexual activity. Both texts are to be found in the scripture and are cited here side by side to show that, in reality, they should not and cannot be separated. This courage and aid in the many pains and agonies which are an inevitable part of bringing up a family come from God. The essential virtue here for Christian couples is one of *generosity* and not a certain stinginess of calculation. This is the great principle guiding the Christian couple but like all principles it must come to be specified into the incarnate existence of each individual couple. This is the first principle of what the Council calls "responsible parenthood" and the conditions are laid down for its fulfillment (50b). We can summarize the teaching of the Council, first, by the principle of generosity which we have seen above. Next, a decision of limitation must be made mutually by both partners, as marriage is a sacrament and reality for both, and therefore such a decision cannot be made unilaterally by one or the other party. This consideration must take into account the good of one or another partner (or both), the children already born or to be born (v.g., education, mental retardation), as well as the present and future good of society itself (demographic reasons). Finally, such a decision to limit the number of children for any particular couple is the direct and exclusive responsibility of the couple itself. This is very explicit in a magisterial document and should solve once and for all questions about "getting the confessor's (or the Church's) permission." The means to be morally employed by Christian couples is left to paragraph 51 and is only slightly treated here.

Just as the progress of anthropology and psychology has brought up the problem of the sense of sexuality in marital love as a whole (integration), so the development of the medical sciences — especially since the discoveries of Ogino and Knaus about 1930 — has opened new perspectives for the moral problematic concerning fertility.

"Previously we were unable to check many of the facts connected with the menstrual cycle of the wife. Married couples could not know which sexual acts would lead to pregnancy. When they regularly had intercourse there was only one solution: generously to accept the children born of their conjugal intercourse. In this way there were many families in which births followed in quick succession. We can only look with admiration at the heroism of those fathers and mothers who, in economic conditions far below our own, nobly took on the care of their large families.

"In the meantime science has made progress. In many cases it has made it possible to establish approximately the period of ovulation. By that very fact, fertility becomes more and more a conscious task. Husband and wife can consciously and freely decide whether they will or will not have intercourse on fertile days and thus call forth new life. This, of course, constitutes a significant progress; for it is entirely good that such an important task as the continuation of human life should be less a matter of chance and become ever more *conscious* and *free*, and so be assumed by the married couple in a responsible manner. Hence the expression, which resumes the moral significance of the even much better than 'birth control': *responsible parenthood*."[1]

The question then arises of how married couples are to exercise their responsibility in connection with fertility. The child is the fruit of conjugal love, and for two reasons. It arises out of an act of marriage which, we have said, is by its essence an expression of conjugal love; the desire for physical union, which is part of marital love, becomes concrete reality in the child. But the child is also the fruit of conjugal love in another way, in that the love of husband and wife is the source of their cooperation in bringing up the child. The child is only fully

---

L. Janssens, *art. cit.*, p. 8.

"brought into the world" when it has been brought up by the same love which called it into being and gave it form, and so made it fit to take an adult and independent place in the world. Here we have a second reason for saying that the sexual act is essentially a marriage act. It must be reserved exclusively for marriage, because only the permanent fellowship in life and love of husband and wife forms the cadre, socially ratified as an institution, which can assure and safeguard the children's up-bringing.

"Conjugal love is thus by its essence directed toward the formation of a family. The family is the complete phenomenon from which the measure of fertility and the means to realize a responsible parenthood should be judged. Now, conjugal life and family life bring with them certain values, and thus various duties: (1) there are *all* the demands of conjugal love, as we have described them; (2) there is the orientation toward fertility; and (3) there is the task of bringing up the children. In cases where different values and duties must be assured and safeguarded *at the same time,* conflicts of values and duties are likely to occur. In other words, there can be cases in which limits have to be set to *fertility,* either due to the demands of conjugal *love,* or because of the demands of bringing up the children."[1]

First of all, there are limits by virtue of the demands of love. In this respect the *medical reasons and considerations* are of value. Cases can come up in which the doctor has to forbid pregnancy, either for a time or even forever. Pius XII said that it is a mistake and an injustice (*un errore e un torto*) to advise or impose pregnancy where medical science forbids it. In such a case, it is in fact a question of the health or the life of the woman. For a husband, then, to make his wife pregnant would be a violation of justice, and therefore of love in human relations. In such a case, responsible parenthood demands either the temporary or permanent foregoing of further fertility,

---

1 L. Janssens, *art. cit.,* p. 9.

according to the doctor's advice. Here the regulation of births is not only licit, but an obligation. That is equally the case where the doctor judges that a greater spacing of births is necessary for the physical health or the psychological equilibrium of the wife. How can a husband maintain that he truly loves his wife if he does not take any notice of such medical pronouncements? In particular, the demands made by spacing the births show how real is the moral problem of responsible parenthood. At any rate, the question of spacing births comes up in very many families.

Furthermore, there are the limits imposed by the demands of bringing up the children. The medical indications themselves are connected with these demands, since the life, physical health, and psychological equilibrium of the mother are of the utmost importance for the child and its care. But *economic and social reasons* also come into play. Upbringing includes feeding, clothing, housing, educating, and so forth; all these things cost money and become heavier burdens as the children grow older. It is possible that a married couple is forced to conclude that in their present economic position the birth of another child would be undesirable, and would even pose problems of injustice toward the already existing children, should the latter thereby be deprived of those things necessary for a life proper to human beings. Of course, it is always possible to appeal to sham economic reasons to conceal a fundamental egoism. But this does not alter the fact that in other cases the social and economic indication is really valid and demands the postponement of pregnancy on the grounds of the children's upbringing. The *eugenic reason* is also valid here; for example, the fact that there have been abnormal children, the psychological condition of one of the partners, the fact that after the parents have reached a certain age bringing up the children can pose special problems, and so on.

In recent times there has also been much talk of *demographic reasons*. In this respect, according to the specialists, the problems must now be considered above all regionally. Some countries, particularly in the more highly evolved regions — suffer from an aging of the population (the number of young people is too small in proportion to the number of old people, and but for an increase of fertility this presents a threat to the country's future). On the contrary, in most countries in course of development with a young population, there is such a demographic explosion that the economic and cultural development is hindered. It is, of course, important not to view the demographic indications in too materialistic a light. Here, also, we must take as our starting point the complete phenomenon of the family; each family must be able to find in the wider communities to which they belong the framework and the possibilities which are necessary for a life worthy of human beings.

"In connection with fertility, moral theology will above all emphasize the absolute necessity of having some definite purpose for marriage. Married people must have a genuine disposition, the firm will, and the real intention to arrive, during the course of their married life, at the number of children which is reasonable for their situation. Such a generous disposition is vital as far as morals are concerned. The importance of a responsible purpose in marriage cannot be sufficiently emphasized. Selfishness at this fundamental level is *the sin!* An example: Imagine a newly married couple. The wife has very regular periods, so that it is possible to apply periodic continence without involved long periods of abstinence. The husband and wife reason as follows (whether it is expressed in words or only contained in their intention is immaterial): 'We are going to practice periodic continence systematically so that we never have any children — we are going to make sure we are comfortable, keep what we earn, get around, etc.; and it's all right because we are not doing anything that's not allowed. . . . ' Pius XII said in this respect that the systematic application of periodic continence out of selfish motives is radically opposed to the very meaning of marriage. Moral value is within — in the heart, the Lord said — and in the present case the disposition is fundamentally selfish and thus sinful."[1]

It is therefore clear, that in connection with fertility, some sort of purpose is essential for every marriage. Of course, husband and wife cannot foresee at the beginning how many children will be suitable for their marriage, since they are not to know beforehand which circumstances they will come up against (illness of wife, husband out of work, or unfit for work, economic setbacks, sick or abnormal children, etc.). It follows that their purpose will only be effective to the extent that in the course of their married life, in each new situation, they together answer the question, "What does God desire from us now?" In so doing, they will have to take into account all the objective indications of their own particular case. That their disposition concerning responsible parenthood is sound is to be seen in the fact that in each situation they renew their dialogue in conscience before God. They are then living in accordance with the most fundamental value of conjugal chastity, insofar as they also respect the sense of sexuality in its being orientated toward fertility. Pius XII has explicitly said that the Christian morals of marriage accept a regulation of births, and a regulation within wide limits.

Only in the light of these basic considerations can we properly pose the problem of the means of the regulation of births.

Finally the Council underlines that marriage is not *just* an institution for the purpose of procreation (50c). It is also a mutual exchange of love between two human persons who thereby perfect themselves in such an institution. In this resides a great dignity (49a) which remains even if, in hypothesis, no children are possible in any particular marriage (sterility). Between these two "goods" of matrimony, the Council puts no *hierarchy of values* as did, for instance, Pius XII. Both are essential (at least in spirit) in marriage as God has willed it,

---

1 L. Janssens, *art. cit.*, p. 12.

and, therefore, this placing of a hierarchy between the two is not kept by our document. Its method is more existential and real to the life of marriage of Christian couples. What is stressed above all is their *interdependence*, and, therefore, the Council has given us a more balanced and nuanced document than even former pronouncements of the *magisterium* on marriage.

The document next goes into the all-important question of means to be used to attain the laudable end of responsible parenthood:

51. a. This Council realizes that certain modern conditions often keep couples from arranging their married lives harmoniously, and that they find themselves in circumstances where at least temporarily the size of their families should not be increased. As a result, the faithful exercise of love and the full intimacy of their lives is hard to maintain. But where the intimacy of married life is broken off, its fruitfulness can sometimes be imperiled and its quality of fruitfulness ruined, for then the upbringing of the children and the courage to accept new ones are both endangered.

b. To these problems there are those who presume to offer dishonorable solutions indeed; they do not recoil even from the taking of life. But the Church issues the reminder that a true contradiction cannot exist between the divine laws pertaining to the transmission of life and those pertaining to authentic conjugal love.

c. For God, the Lord of life, has conferred on men the surpassing ministry of safeguarding life in a manner which is worthy of man. Therefore from the moment of its conception life must be guarded with the greatest care. The sexual characteristics of man and the human faculty of reproduction wonderfully exceed the dispositions of lower forms of life. Hence the acts themselves which are proper to conjugal love and which are exercised in accord with genuine human dignity must be honored with great reverence. Hence when there is question of harmonizing conjugal love with the responsible transmission of life, the moral aspect of any procedure does not depend solely on sincere intentions or on an evaluation of motives, but must be determined by objective standards. These, based on the nature of the human person and his acts preserve the full sense of mutual self-giving and human pro-creation in the context of true love. Such a goal cannot be achieved unless the virtue of conjugal chastity is sincerely practiced. Relying on these principles, sons of the Church may not undertake methods of birth regulation which are found blameworthy by the teaching authority of the Church in its unfolding of the divine law.

d. All should be persuaded that human life and the task of transmitting it are not realities bound up with this world alone. Hence they cannot be measured or perceived only in terms of it, but always have a bearing on the eternal destiny of men.

Thus we are confronted with the rather tragic problem of the serious confrontation between the two aspects of marriage and modern life: generosity of procreation and the necessary limitation of the number of children because of modern con-ditions (economic, social and demographic, etc.); between the necessity of an incarnate expression of love through sexual inter-course and the limitation of that fecundity because of the con-ditions of modern life (51a). What is interesting here is the insistence upon that fact that sexual relations cannot be cur-tailed, much less totally abstained from, without serious danger to the marriage itself. This in itself is a very important admission on the part of the official teaching authority of the Church, since this point has not been so clearly made by previous documents of the *magisterium*. This in itself ought to give long and thoughtful pause to those who recommend total abstinence for reasons of prevention of offspring.

The Council then goes on to outline some of the "dis-honorable solutions" to this problem. But what are they? The document is very prudent and circumspect in this regard and it cites only that upon which all would agree: sterilization, abortion and so forth; and as for the contraceptive means of control of birth, the document is satisfied by citing previous condemnations by the popes in its footnote (see 47b as well). Abortion is cited as murder alongside infanticide (51c); conceived life must be safeguarded: "from the moment of its conception life must be guarded with the greatest care." It would seem to imply that the fetus must be considered as a human person from the moment of its conception (it calls its destruction "murder") even if our text does not wish directly to solve the age-old problem of the time of formation of human personality.

Thus we have — at times — a real conflict between procreation and the demands of an incarnate sexual expression of conjugal love. How does the Council go about trying to resolve this great problem (51c)?

We must first go back to how Catholic theology has originally treated this problem.

Is it still legitimate to use the formulas of a past age such as "the law of nature" or even of nature itself to express the present tendency of Catholic morality toward *aggiornamento?* We must carefully define the various senses in which these terms are used today by Catholic moralists.

Where St. Thomas uses the famous phrase *"lex naturae"* he certainly does not mean a reference to *pure biology* or the *physics of nature*. Its essential meaning here is above all within an ethical context. "Law," then, means a command addressed to the conscience to do or not to do something that is seen as good or bad; a practical command to do or not to do something so that my personal action can be morally good or bad. It is a general moral sense within the human heart which says that "good must be done and evil avoided," and the law of conscience governs and directs such actions (see *Summa Theologica*, Suppl. the whole question 65 on this subject). It is the natural light of reason whereby we participate in the eternal law. By this voice of conscience, we humanly participate in the design of God for men and for this universe. In the words of St. Thomas:

> Lumen rationis naturalis, quo discernimus quid sit bonum et quid malum, quod pertinet ad *naturalem legem,* nihil aliud est quam impressio divini luminis in nobis. Unde patet quod lex naturalis aliud est quam participatio legis aeternae in rationali creatur (Ia IIae, q. 91 a. 2).

Or, in other words, man is fully human when he directs, freely and responsibly, his own actions according to the will of the supreme Lawgiver who is God (*"lex aeterna"*) or what St. Thomas calls the *"ratio gubernationis in supremo gubernante"* (I, II, q. 93, a. 3).

It must not be understood as so many principles which, when known, can solve all man's moral problems. This is a deep misunderstanding of the *"lex naturae"* of St. Thomas. It is simply the light of reason itself (whether it be "correct" or "erroneous" is indeed another question) reflecting on the experience of man to determine its rational reference to the sense, meaning, and signification in and by which we can discover God's design for men and the world. Thus, far from removing reason from our more personalistic morality, we are in total agreement with St. Thomas' *"lex naturae"* in making reason the light which must guide us in the discovery of these relationships. Reason does not create its own values (Sartre, Ponty), but by rational elaboration comes to discover the finality of these relationships of man in the world, among men and to God. Man does not "create" his values but simply discovers them by the application of his reason to the facts of his experience.

Yet the term "law of nature" can also have a teleological meaning which is not directly ethical in content. It aims at a signification of the universe and its processes itself. It means the design of God for the universe itself. We find this once again in St. Thomas. *"Naturae nihil aliud est quam ratio cuiusdam artis, menpe divinae, indita rebus, qua ipsae moventur in finem determinatum"* (Phys 1, 14).

It is this sense of "nature" which has caused so much misunderstanding for modern man. We need not go into the whole process of the medieval moral theologian from the 13th to the 17th centuries who elaborated, under the theology on the manifold teleological relationships which they saw everywhere in nature with the implication that therein we find the will of God (indirectly). This forms much of the present-day foundation against birth control based as it is upon teleological considerations of the physical and biological processes of the human reproductive system. Contraception and anovulants are "immoral" because they interfere with the "natural" function of these organs as intended by their Creator. We do not mean to condemn the whole concept of finality because of the abuses of the medieval period, but we do wish to emphasize at this stage (1) that such a view is totally inadequate in our present progress of thought in interpersonal relationships, and that (2) such a process *alone* has, practically speaking, no meaning whatsoever to the modern mind in the sense in which we have already explained.

Finality certainly exists in the universe for man. The theologians of the past were not incorrect in this view of man's situation, since it is plain, for instance, that matter and the material cosmos is at the service of man; that certain organs in man's body are made for a particular function and for no other; among others, that the reproductive system is for the continuation of the human race (but not, certainly, exclusively). Thus, these exist for man and not man at the service of these "natural" orientations and functions. There is a certain hierarchy of values here in which we can see, as did the theologians of past ages, the indirect will of God thereby expressed.

This does not contradict the above notion of "nature" which the modern mind understands. This process of discovery of such a hierarchy of values is not a static concept, but a dynamic one. Man continuously and actively, by reason and experience, sees more clearly the demands of such a hierarchy of values in his universe. Therefore, it is not only a basic fact before which man receives and discovers meaning, but it is also an active task of man where, by the light of reason and reflection of experience, he continuously masters himself ever more perfectly. Thus this continuous moral task of man is a dialogue among the various human sciences of politics, sociology, psychology, as well as moral theology. The earth is at the service of man, but man has the direct responsibility of discovering and mastering farming techniques, irrigation, demography, etc., for a population which is expanding, and which, ultimately, will have to be controlled to rational equation between resources (present and potential) and people (present and future). Moral theology, alone, simply cannot accomplish this tremendous task of man which also implies, in the words of Pope John XXIII, a co-operation with all men of good will. The sexual impulse must also be used for human ends and not for a non-planned (individually and social) blind population growth, "trusting God." God, in the words of St. Thomas, has given men reason to share in the actual governing of this world and the responsibility for this cannot simply be transferred, in falacious reasoning, back to God. Nature and meaning (hierarchy of values, culture) cannot be separated when we speak of man as he exists existentially in the human situation. Man is called not only to humanize the cosmos from a brutal reality to a cultural one, but also to humanize and "culturize" himself as well. For it is only by such a process that man becomes fully himself, in self-realization, that he ever more perfectly reaches the stature which God wishes for him. This self-realization is both individual and social since it is only in social intercourse that man realizes himself as a person. Thus, our "natural law," understood here, combines in perfect harmony the ancient teleological solicitude of theologians with that of modern humanism, in that it is both a fact and a task for man on earth.

There is a third way in which we can speak of the "law of nature" which is neither teleological or ethical as in the above two senses of "natural." It is a type of causal relationship of neutral quality which regulates (in a type of determinism) the world of physical reality. These, of course, can be biological, psychological, sociological, and so forth. Thus we speak of the law of thermodynamics, or the law of gravity. These material and psychic phenomena, we say, are ruled by "natural laws." Included in this is the sexual cycle of ovulation. Modern science's task has been to correlate these empirical phenomena under certain "theories" and "laws" which will explain the effects that will occur when other variables are added or subtracted.

This type of "law" which rules these processes is subject to great elasticity in the sense that it has permitted man to use them and even replace them with the products of his human liberty. We think immediately of heart valves, transplantations, and so forth, in which man — once again in continuation of modern man's orientation to nature — intervenes and uses them for human purposes and signification. Thus physical determinism and human liberty are not at odds here, but by the light of reason, man can, at least to some degree, control and "help" nature attain its end in a human fashion. These presuppose, of course, a certain stability ("laws") in the world about us, and, in this sense, we cannot simply determine values, but are determined by them. Yet this is incomplete, since man can, by his freedom, correct or orientate or modify such processes toward human ends. This is a limitless task and man is the active agent within this process toward humanization of the world, as well as of himself within the world. Man progresses — humanly — by his knowledge and control of these "laws of nature" which he, in turn, uses for a future humanization of the universe and of himself. All this technology, science, and so forth, is morally neutral in that it can be used for good or evil. It is the man who is the free agent here, and there can be no room in such a concept for the Spenserian notion of "continuous progress of goodness." Nuclear energy can be used to power man's machines, to cure his cancers — but it can also be used to exterminate man from the face of the earth.

It is crucial at this point to attempt a unity of these diverse meanings of "nature" and "natural law." We must continuously keep the various meanings intellectually distinct and yet have the ability to synthesize them into a totality at the service of man. This evidently implies a certain hierarchy of ends by which these realities are made for man. Private property, for instance, is one of the basic rights of man for the precise reason that it serves the human end of freedom and individuality. Yet there is a more basic end for which private property exists; it is a means and not an end, namely, that the goods of this world are evidently intended by the Creator for the *use* of all men. Thus, when private property deters from the end of use of material goods for the many to the advantage of the few (Latin America), we have a grave moral aberration, since the hierarchy of human ends has not been respected. I must feed the hungry (moral imperative of brotherly love) but to do this in many economically underdeveloped countries, I must master the "laws of nature" over crops or seeds necessary to increase productivity for this hungry people.

Thus, from all that we have said, we must avoid two extremes in the present elaboration of moral theology. We cannot reject out of hand the teleological aspect of the cosmos, since, otherwise, we run the grave risk of a situational ethic which, even in the context of Christian love, is in grave danger of relativity. Divine revelation simply has not (and did not propose) to answer the thousand different human relationships in which man finds himself each day, e.g., revolutionary war, economic corporatism, agricultural productivity, sexual problems of marriage and population, and so on.

On the other hand (or extreme), we have the greater danger of an "objectified" morality which purports to find morality in the simple (almost biological and physiological) orientations of "nature." This simply will not suffice with the very delicate problem of birth regulation in all of its economic, medical, psychological, sociological and demographic ramifications. To say that "anovulants" are "against nature," while the use of rhythm is in "conformity with nature" is simply to play on words or to use a vulgar sophism, since all the above *together* must be fully taken into consideration before we can make any kind of moral judgment. The moral theologian can no longer make moral judgments arguing solely from the "law of nature." What does he mean when he says: "law of nature"? In which of the three senses is he using the term? If he says, the "moral law," then we have a vicious circle, for he has proven what the problem is, by rephrasing the problem itself. If he answers that in the second case, the possibility of conception is present whereas in the former it is not, then we are also reduced to a contradiction, since the couple using the rhythm have intercourse (at least intentionally and, so far as possible, physically as well), only at sterile periods which are also, of themselves, days when there is no possibility of conception. So we are up against the very same problem in both cases. Or the moral theologian means that the "pill" is against the teleological intention of the very act of intercourse whereas rhythm is not. This makes very little sense, given our deeper notions of human sexuality and of sexual biology (which former generations did not have). Even the *Constitution on the Church in the Modern World* fully recognizes that procreation is not the only end of sexual intercourse. The sexual act in marriage has a complete (even if not an independent) meaning in itself as authentic expression of love which is a basic necessity in well-balanced marriages. Moreover, if the end of each sexual act is procreation (as many of the moralists from the time of St. Augustine thought), then that, in itself, would condemn the rhythm as well.

Finally, the moralist can mean that anovulants are against the laws of biology understood in the third definition of "nature" (ovulatory cycle). Yet, this makes no sense whatsoever since, as we have seen, man is continually intervening and modifying these determinisms for human ends. Man regulates them for "ends" (it is these which must be morally determined), and we simply cannot speak in such a context of acting "against nature."

In what sense are we to understand the moralist when he speaks of "against nature" or "natural law"? It seems that the only sensible way out of this present dilemma of the Church is to discard, to a great degree, what has to the present been called "natural law" *in a non-differentiated sense.* Teleology remains as an important factor in this moral judgment, but all the other factors which we have developed are also an integral part of the moral judgment on the use of the anovulants. Otherwise, the Church is running the very real and grave risk of another Galileo affair in the late 20th century. Thus for the traditional exposé of the problem. What does our present conciliar text say?

We have, first of all, some general principles (generosity, importance of sexual relations in a healthy marriage, objective moral norms covering the use of sexual activity, etc.). This is ruled above all (for the faithful) by the pronouncements of the *magisterium* which has both the right and the duty to pronounce on the various methods.

The principles recalled to mind are generic in tone: there can be no contradiction between divine law and conjugal love; human sexuality is not the same as that of animals because men are persons with freedom and intelligence. No comparison either in end or means of sexuality and its control is possible here; thus, its morality comes from both the subjective intent of the couple *and* objective norms established by God in the conduct of sexual activity and transmission of life. But what are they? What is the end of human sexuality? The Council has said it is not only procreation, but also it must take its significance from the total gift of the couple one to the other.

These thoughts of the Council must inspire moralists to caution in their pronouncements.

The ideal is, of course, that married people should always be able to realize the complete structure of the marriage act. Then it is a *more complete* embodiment of their conjugal love and is also their fundamental desire. That is why it is such an urgent task for the medical sciences to do their best to increase the possibilities of this. But in the meantime the job of the moralist consists essentially in emphasizing that the moral integrity of married people is basically measured both according to the seriousness of their set purpose in marriage as regards conjugal love, and according to the generosity of their purpose for their family concerning their openness toward a responsible parenthood. At the same time, the moral theologian has no right to assert that every incomplete marriage act is an expression of selfishness — and what is sin if not a form of selfishness? Because from the witness borne today by lay people, it is clear that those married couples who are living according to the duty of fertility, in those situations where no better means are at their disposal, certainly do not always resort to incomplete sexual intercouse out of selfishness, but that they frequently only accept it as an emergency solution in order to serve the essential values of their married and family lives — that is, to prevent unchastity, to preserve their mutual trust as also their unity in love and thereby the things required for the task of raising their family.

The term "conflict situation" can give the impression that we have here to do with exceptional cases. This is not so. Such situations can arise at certain moments in any family, and in fact they are numerous. Let us describe more clearly what really happens. For objective reasons, a married couple must give up the idea, either temporarily or forever, of causing a pregnancy. For one reason or another, periodic continence is not practicable, or cannot in their case provide a sufficient guarantee of safety. Regarding the pill they are hesitant. At the same time they realize that both — or one of them, which in effect is the same thing since chastity in marriage is a virtue for two — need sexual relations and the relaxation this provides, because otherwise they would become estranged from each other, or be unable to resist temptation to masturbation, infidelity, or adultery, or run into discord and frictions, which threaten the cooperation in bringing up the children; in short, because sexual intercourse is necessary if they are to safeguard the essential values of their marriage and their family. Since they must avert every risk of insemination, they cannot allow the marriage act to follow its complete structure, and they therefore perform so-called "incomplete sexual acts." In traditional moral theology, which saw human sexuality solely as a means to procreation, such actions were unconditionally condemned as morally unjustifiable. But if it is true that the intrinsic sense of sexuality is to be an expression of conjugal love and therefore to safeguard faithfulness, and since it is the family with its essential values which forms the complete phenomenon from which one must judge the moral worth of behavior, can one then uphold the unconditional condemnation?

Let us conclude with the words of John T. Noonan, writing on "Contraception and the Council":

> The Council, then, has not proposed solutions "directly," as to how conjugal love and parental responsibility may be reconciled. It has, however, set up the main pillars of any solution: procreation and education are insolubly linked goods; conjugal love is in itself a legitimate and laudable purpose of intercourse; embryonic life is to be guarded; the dignity of the person is to provide norms; there is an element of divine law in previous teaching by the Church on contraception; but not all existing law on contraception is immutable. Solutions for the new day are to be found both by discerning what is divine and immutable and by consulting experts and the Christian faithful.[1]

The Council ends this whole section by an exhortation to all Christian couples to live their lives in the light and spirit of the gospels. It is also an appeal to secular authorities to create a milieu favorable to family life (which includes research for

_____
1 *Commonweal*, 83 (March 11, 1966), p 662.

human reproduction so that couples can take full advantage of all scientific information for "responsible parenthood"):

52. a. The family is a kind of school of deeper humanity. But if it is to achieve the full flowering of its life and mission, it needs the kindly communion of minds and the joint deliberation of spouses, as well as the painstaking cooperation of parents in the education of their children. The active presence of the father is highly beneficial to their formation. The children, especially the younger among them, need the care of their mother at home. This domestic role of hers must be safely preserved, though the legitimate social progress of women should not be underrated on that account.

b. Children should be so educated that as adults they can follow their vocation, including a religious one, with a mature sense of responsibility and can choose their state of life; if they marry, they can thereby establish their family in favorable moral, social and economic conditions. Parents or guardians should by prudent advice provide guidance to their young with respect to founding a family, and the young ought to listen gladly. At the same time no pressure, direct or indirect, should be put on the young to make them enter marriage or choose a specific partner.

c. Thus the family, in which the various generations come together and help one another grow wise and harmonize personal rights with the other requirements of social life, is the foundation of society. All those, therefore, who exercise influence over communities and social groups should work effectively for the welfare of marriage and the family. Public authority should regard it as a sacred duty to recognize, protect and promote their authentic nature, to shield public morality and to favor the prosperity of home life. The right of parents to beget and educate their children in the bosom of the family must be safeguarded. Children too who unhappily lack the blessings of a family should be protected by prudent legislation and various undertakings and assisted by the help they need.

d. Christians, redeeming the present time and distinguishing eternal realities from their changing expressions, should actively promote the values of marriage and the family, both by the example of their own lives and by cooperation with other men of good will. Thus when difficulties arise, Christians will provide on behalf of family life those necessities and helps which are suitably modern. To this end the Christian instincts of the faithful, the upright moral consciences of men, and the wisdom and experience of persons versed in the sacred sciences will have much to contribute.

e. Those too who are skilled in other sciences, notably the medical, biological, social and psychological, can considerably advance the welfare of marriage and the family along with peace of conscience if by pooling their efforts they labor to explain more thoroughly the various conditions favoring a proper regulation of births.

f. It devolves on priests duly trained about family matters to nurture the vocation of spouses by a variety of pastoral means, by preaching God's Word, by liturgical worship, and by other spiritual aids to conjugal and family life; to sustain them sympathetically and patiently in difficulties, and to make them courageous through love, so that families which are truly illustrious can be formed.

g. Various organizations, especially family associations should try by their programs of instruction and action to strengthen young people and spouses themselves, particularly those recently wed, and train them for family, social and apostolic life.

h. Finally, let the spouses themselves, made to the image of the living God, and enjoying the authentic dignity of persons, be joined to one another in equal affection, harmony of mind and the work of mutual sanctification. Thus, following Christ who is the principle of life, by the sacrifices and joys of their vocation and through their faithful love, married people can become witnesses of the mystery of love which the Lord revealed to the world by his dying and his rising up to life again.

The presence of the father in the family is an important element in family life (52a). As to mothers, the Council is circumspect in saying simply that when young children are growing up, the presence of the mother is a very important factor as well. No argument against working mothers can be drawn from the text, since this situation is special and must be examined on its own merits. Sexual education should be given in the home, but here again we have only a general principle and not a sociological analysis. There are variant cultures where this is done in a different fashion, and the Council did not wish to make here a blanket recommendation. Nor does it solve the very thorny problem of the not so farfetched hypothesis that many parents fail in this duty at home. Once again, this is a specialized problem that can be solved by an examination of the concrete situation at hand. Finally, the priest has a role to play (e.g., CFM, CANA), as one who encourages and promotes active family life in his parish and community.

CHAPTER 2

The Proper Development
of Culture

Our document now goes on to discuss a rather new subject for the *magisterium*, the problem of culture in the contemporary world. Man is not simply a *homo faber* in the construction of the world, but he is also a *homo artifex*, insofar as he lives not simply a biological life like the rest of the animals but also a cultural life, that is, the fullness of life in conformity to what he is, a spiritually incarnate being:

53. a.   Man comes to a true and full humanity only through culture, that is, through the cultivation of the goods and values of nature. Wherever human life is involved, therefore, nature and culture are quite intimately connected one with the other.

b.   The world "culture" in its general sense indicates everything whereby man develops and perfects his many bodily and spiritual qualities; and strives by his knowledge and his labor, to bring the world itself under his control. He renders social life more human both in the family and the civic community through improvement of customs and institutions. Throughout the course of time he expresses, communicates and conserves in his works, great spiritual experiences and desires, that they might be of advantage to the progress of many, even of the whole human family.

c.   Thence it follows that human culture has necessarily a historical and social aspect and the word "culture" also often assumes a sociological and ethnological sense. According to this sense we speak of a plurality of cultures. Different styles of life and multiple scales of values arise from the diverse manner of doing things, of laboring, of expressing oneself, of practicing religion, of forming customs, of establishing laws and juridical institutions, of cultivating the sciences, the arts and beauty. Thus the customs handed down to it form the patrimony proper to each human community. It is also in this way that there is formed the definite, historical milieu which enfolds the man of every nation and age and from which he draws the values which permit him to promote civilization.

Man expresses his spiritual existence in a thousand different manifestations in books, music, poetry, and in various styles of life and custom. The variant, here, is enough to set him apart from every other type of creation on the face of the earth. He transmits this tradition of his in a thousand different oral and written ways (53b). This includes ways and customs of technology, moral and religious values, family and sexual mores, art and handiwork, and so on. These are social and therefore cultural mores for men.

We may see this as a type of both "objective" and "subjective" culture. Objective culture consists of the objective elements which are realized by human labor and art transforming the world into a human world, that is, art, architecture, painting, writing, technology in all its forms, and so on. Subjective culture is the culture of the person himself, the fact that he perfects himself scientifically, intellectually, morally, and in every way possible to a human being. Obviously, there is a reciprocity here between these two aspects of culture: the very reason objective culture exists is to promote the development of the person's subjective culture, so that he can realize his proper originality. Through this enrichment of each unique person, objective culture is in turn made richer. Work, for instance, is a noble thing, furthering God's creating act, and it is the means of bringing about objective values which men need for the development of subjective culture. The realization of culture is, therefore, a social task in which everyone must make his contribution according to his capacities. Since man becomes richer through his relations with external realities, he must be open to these realities of the world. It is only in living the meaning of his relations to the world that man can perfect himself; he is then a moral creature and he expresses himself by being a cultural creature which is part of his very being. The end of cultural man is that he work in union with others to promote objective culture, which permits the growth of subjective culture. St. Thomas saw this when he said that man, the individual, is to society as the part is to the whole. The part is directed to the whole, and as a result, the part profits the whole.

The Council then goes on to say that nature and culture are intimately related (53a), since we know nature only insofar as it has meaning for man, that is, insofar as nature is culturally acclimated for man. Man, by his work (understood in its most expansive way), renders nature meaningful for himself. We can never perfectly distinguish that which comes from nature and that which comes from man's cultural acclimation in education, customs, etc., that is, what becomes for man a sort of "second nature." Cultural transformation is the only way in which he truly understands nature. Even when dealing with man, one must be very circumspect in claiming that which comes from his "nature" or essence, and that which comes from his cultural acclimation and the influence of this on man's nature itself. Current anthropological studies of both primitive and modern man clearly show us how much of that which was once considered "natural" to man was in reality nothing more than a product of cultural acclimation. Thus one must be very circumspect when speaking of the "essence" of man.

Culture in the conciliar document is taken in its broadest meaning, namely, the manner in which men of any particular place and time express themselves. It is the way in which they organize the totality of their lives in the technical, artistic, religious, and moral spheres, expressed in the day-to-day lives of people of any particular place and time. All this will then result in a vast multiplicity of cultures which our document explicitly recognizes (53c). It follows then that every people on the face of the earth has some type of culture — primitive or modern — in which they express themselves and relate to the world at large. Those who have absorbed and mastered this way of acting are consequently called "cultivated people." This particular culture is bound up ultimately with their proper background and history which is unique to them and transmitted to their children through successive generations, given principally to children in their formative years by education (in all its variant modes of communication in different cultures). This is the process which sociologists call "socialization." Such a culture, however, is not static (outside of very primitive cultures) but rather dynamic and in the constant process of change (54). Particularly is this so in our modern civilization with the increase in socialization, universal transportation, and communication. This has led and continues to lead to some profound changes in the so-called "traditional" societies and can be at the source of much agony and disruption as it transforms itself into a "modern" society (56). This does not mean that all change in cultures is to be rejected out of hand; rather, it must be slowly integrated into a usable form within a particular society. There must be a hierarchy of values as well as a proportion between a strong scientific and technological growth; without a strong moral and religious fiber underlying this order, we are faced with disaster (61). Insofar as the individual is concerned, we have already discussed the concepts of objective and subjective culture by which he can and must integrate himself into the society in which he lives (55, 59). These means of cultural expansion and growth must be brought to his disposal by public authority which plays a great role in this area (60).

The document first gives a general description of the various forms of change which continue to take place in modern society and which have affected the general culture of mankind:

54. The circumstances of the life of modern man have been so profoundly changed in their social and cultural aspect that we can speak of a new age of human history. New ways are open, therefore, for the perfection and the further extension of culture. These ways have been prepared by the enormous growth of natural, human and social sciences, by technical progress, and advances in developing and organizing means whereby men can communicate with one another. Hence the culture of today possesses particular characteristics: sciences which are called exact greatly develop critical judgment; the more recent psychological studies more profoundly explain human activity; historical studies make it much easier to see things in their mutable and evolutionary aspects; customs and usages are becoming more and more uniform; industrialization, urbanization, and other causes which promote community living create a mass-culture from which are born new ways of thinking, acting and making use of leisure. The increase of commerce between the various nations and groups of men opens more widely to all the treasures of different civilizations and thus, little by little, there develops a more universal form of human culture, which better promotes and expresses the unity of the human race to the degree that it preserves that particular aspect of the different civilizations.

55. From day to day, in every group or nation, there is an increase in the number of men and women who are conscious that they themselves are the authors and the artisans of the culture of their community. Throughout the whole world there is a mounting increase in the sense of autonomy as well as of responsibility. This is of paramount importance of the spiritual and moral maturity of the human race. This becomes more clear if we consider the unification of the world and the duty which is imposed upon us, that we build a better world based upon truth and justice. Thus we are witnesses of the birth of a new humanism, one in which man is defined first of all by this responsibility to his brothers and to history.

The Council has already described changes of a scientific and technological nature in the modern world, and we refer the reader to those pages (pars. 5-7, pp. 18-24). A source of confusion in discussing the concept of change and modernization is what is called the process of industrialization. An equation of modernization with industrialization is not completely satisfactory, even if some authors have made it the basic criterion of modernization. It should be obvious, however, that such a factor is very important in the modern world, if for no other reason than that the elites of the developing nations consider this as one of their main objectives in the passing of their societies from a traditional to a modern society in the shortest possible time. In some areas (e.g., Africa), this is used, in turn, for a still further objective, viz: national unity. Yet, industrialization, besides bringing a disruption into these emerging societies, implies a whole concatenation of associated processes which are indispensable to industrialization and which, in their turn, hasten this transition: urbanization, literacy rates, social mobility, exposure to mass media, facilitated transportation, and so on. Our document discusses each of these phenomena in its exposé. These processes cannot but help to change traditional modes of action, thought, creative attitudes toward the world and toward society. It should also be evident that such a concept cannot, does not, exhaust many other aspects of modernization such as that of popular self-determination as well as the development of political parties and structures, which in turn reflect the differentiated needs and specialized interests of various sectors of that society (cf. Chapter IV, Part II, on Politics).

What is noteworthy in our present paragraph (54b) is the emphasis on the concept of "socialization" whose formulization depends heavily on *Mater et Magistra*. We have already discussed this concept (above, pp. 19-20; see also par. 6, p. 20, par. 25, p. 83). It is treated here in a much more profound sense, however, insofar as it examines the very meaning of this vast socio-economic phenomenon. This, of course, guarantees to mankind a more complete mastery over his destiny by controlling those factors over which, in former times, he had no control (55). In other words, it is by these processes of his, that man becomes ever more free and master of himself. It is this aspect of culture which unites all these single elements of man — economic, social, political and technical — into one totality. It is from this vantage point that the Church examines culture.

The document then moves on to examine the various difficulties which face man in this culture of a new humanism. It enumerates them as follows:

56. a. In these conditions, it is no cause of wonder that man, who senses his responsibility for the progress of culture, nourishes a high hope but also looks with anxiety upon many contradictory things which he must resolve.

b. What is to be done to prevent the increased exchanges between cultures, which should lead to a true and fruitful dialogue between groups and nations, from disturbing the life of communities, from destroying the wisdom received from ancestors, or from placing in danger the character proper to each people?

c. How is the dynamism and expansion of a new culture to be fostered without losing a living fidelity to the heritage of tradition? This question is of particular urgency when a culture which arises from the enormous progress of science and technology must be harmonized with a culture nourished by classical studies according to various traditions.

d. How can we quickly and progressively harmonize the proliferation of particular branches of study with the necessity of forming a synthesis of them, and of preserving among men the faculties of contemplation and observation which lead to wisdom?

e. What can be done to make all men partakers of cultural values in the world, when the human culture of those who are more competent is constantly becoming more refined and more complex?

f. Finally how is the autonomy which culture claims for itself to be recognized as legitimate without generating a notion of humanism which is merely terrestrial, and even contrary to religion itself?

g. In the midst of these conflicting requirements, human culture must evolve today in such a way that it can both develop the whole human person and aid man in those duties to whose fulfillment all are called, especially Christians fraternally united in one human family.

The changing aspects of culture have forced these questions on man today. There are various questions here: with the reality of universal socialization, how are we to avoid the uniformity and standardization of the universal culture of man (56b)? There must be dialogue here between the old and the new, but how is this to be done? How safely to traverse from a "traditional" culture to a "modern" one without totally destroying the former (56c)? How can we bridge the knowledge of the elites and that of the simple? What of increasing specialization in all fields and therefore a lack of a synthetic view (56d)? How to avoid the reduction of culture to a simple materialism or to a simple search for the material to the point where it is atheistic and religionless in inspiration (56f)? Finally, (56g) we are given the ultimate criterion to be used in any solution for the above problems in the spirit of the hierarchy of values: the promotion and the dignity of the human person. Man, as he masters his environment, using it for his purposes and perfection, must learn also to master himself as well; since, as we have seen, the imbalances in the world come not from the world or the works of his hands but rather from man, born as he is in a state of sinfulness. This equilibrium between the old and the new is a delicate balance, and one cannot be sacrificed for the purpose of the other. This applies with special force to the underdeveloped areas of the world.

The document now goes on to give some practical implementation to these very general principles cited in Section I:

57. a. Christians, on pilgrimage toward the heavenly city, should seek and think of those things which are above. This duty in no way decreases, rather it increases, the importance of their obligation to work with all men in the building of a more human world. Indeed, the mystery of the Christian faith furnishes them with an excellent stimulus and aid to

fulfill this duty more courageously and especially to uncover the full meaning of this activity, one which gives to human culture its eminent place in the integral vocation of man.

b. When man develops the earth by the work of his hands or with the aid of technology, in order that it might bear fruit and become a dwelling worthy of the whole human family and when he consciously takes part in the life of social groups, he carries out the design of God manifested at the beginning of time, that he should subdue the earth, perfect creation and develop himself. At the same time he obeys the commandment of Christ that he place himself at the service of his brethren.

c. Furthermore, when man gives himself to the various disciplines of philosophy, history and of mathematical and natural science, and when he cultivates the arts, he can do very much to elevate the human family to a more sublime understanding of truth, goodness, and beauty, and to the formation of considered opinions which have universal value. Thus mankind may be more clearly enlightened by that marvelous wisdom which was with God from all eternity, composing all things with him, rejoicing in the earth, delighting in the sons of men.

d. In this way, the human spirit, being less subjected to material things, can be more easily drawn to the worship and contemplation of the Creator. Moreover, by the impulse of grace, he is disposed to acknowledge the Word of God, who before he became flesh in order to save all and to sum up all in himself was already "in the world" as "the true light which enlightens every man" (John 1:9-10).

e. Indeed today's progress in science and technology can foster a certain exclusive emphasis on observable data and an agnosticism about everything else. For the methods of investigation which these sciences use can be wrongly considered as the supreme rule of seeking the whole truth. By virtue of these methods these sciences cannot penetrate to the intimate notion of things. Indeed the danger is present that man, confiding too much in the discoveries of today, may think that he is sufficient unto himself and no longer seek the higher things.

f. These unfortunate results, however, do not necessarily follow from the culture of today, nor should they lead us into the temptation of not acknowledging its positive values. Among these values are included: scientific study and fidelity toward truth in scientific enquiries, the necessity of working together with others in technical groups, a sense of international solidarity, a clearer awareness of the responsibility of experts to aid and even to protect men, the desire to make the conditions of life more favorable for all, especially for those who are poor in culture or who are deprived of the opportunity to exercise responsibility. All of these provide some preparation which can be animated by divine charity through Him Who has come to save the world.

The paragraph begins with the affirmation that because Christians have another homeland (heaven) they need not take interest in the terrestrial city (57a). This is erroneous for a number of reasons, not least of which is the fact that if Christians are to truly love their brothers, they cannot stand by idly in the presence of suffering. Such an indifference is simply incompatible with the Christian message of love (agape). A second reason is that work and man's effort in this regard are in the plan of God who created man "the image of God" or his lieutenant in Creation. We do not know the way this will be purified by God, but we do know that this has a definite reference to the final kingdom of Christ at the *parousia*. This gives us a specific difference between the atheist and the Christian who both work for the good of man here below. Their results may seem to be the same, humanly speaking, but this is not so because man's work — to be fully understood — must be viewed in the light of faith. It does not terminate here below nor with man but, in a sense, receives its full meaning in the light of the final kingdom. In a way we do not fully understand, man's work will continue with him to the beyond. The world and man's work within it are not doomed to total destruction but rather to some sort of purification. The Christian's obligation to work within the world — for its perfection and betterment — ought to be very clear from all this. The Christian, in love, works for his brothers to make shine forth

— at least in an imperfect but real way — the qualities of justice, honor, peace, harmony, which will be fully realized only in the final kingdom of Christ. Thus the love of the Christian is a potent driving force for work within the city of man and is directed toward man himself and for no other reason than love of man himself. He does not work for the "conversion" of man but for *his* perfection and good. Thus when he does this, when the Christian makes a little more love to grow or justice to reign, in reality, he is continuing the very work of Christ himself whose extension the Christian is in the world (57c).

Thus work and research in the earthly city are a true duty for the Christian and not a "basket-weaving" until Christ comes to establish the final kingdom. By subjecting the earth to his technology, man frees himself from the slaveries and caprices of nature with the result that man has more time to develop his spiritual qualities in leisure (57c, d).

The Church has humbly recognized that the above was not always her vision (36), and that she even gravely mistrusted the modern sciences because of some erroneous interpretations of scripture and theology. And yet some warning is necessary even when the Church has fully accepted and justified the general orientation of the technological and scientific universal society, since there is a great danger that society and its culture will be reduced to solely scientific and technological dimensions. This is the major danger of the Eastern-Western blocs as well as of the "third" world in their frenzy for economic development.

What this text (57e) aims at are some aspects of the dehumanization of work. One such attempt to bring the same problem to light was done by John XXIII in a section of *Mater et Magistra*. Furthermore, from a Christian and human point of view, man in the economic sphere (as in all other spheres as well) must be made once again the master and the end of production. This was the objective of John XXIII as well as of our present document. As its objective, the Church is not to give technical solutions to this vast problem, but it is the duty of the Church to keep before man's eyes the fact that man must be the end and the means of any economic system. This implies a return, for instance, from the traditional capitalist system insofar as this system alienates man in the above-mentioned sense. Man is the end and master of property in general and of productive goods in particular. This was what John XXIII meant when he spoke about social responsibility of workers within the enterprise. Such a task can only be performed by connecting his personality with the product of the enterprise. This is the first relationship between man and material goods, namely, that it is his incarnation and extension in space and time, and, as such, coessential to his person, and therefore participant in his personal dignity. To use man for profit is more than materialism; it is a desecration of this incarnate spiritually material being who is man, coexistentially. The evolution of capitalism is one direction of man's relationship with matter and has ended in human failure. As Christians, we cannot and must not see anything eternal or fatalistic about it, flowing, as it were, "from the laws of nature."

This was the profound error of the physiocrats of the 18th century and continues today in those who think that the system in its basic tenets cannot be changed. In fact, with modern socialization, it not only can but must change to meet the absolute need of human society for responsibility. In our efforts at transformation, we must aim at converting the system itself from one of pure profit to a system of work for man. This will, ultimately, entail a new entity different from neo-capitalism. We must occupy the middleground between the two extremes of absolute state collectivism (communism) and the regime of profit-end (neo-capitalism). The popes have situated this humanizing economy and social vision between the two, taking what was most human in both systems in what we call "moderate socialism," where property, capital, and government regulations are guided by one principle, and one principle only: the promotion of the dignity of man, and where everything else, in the final Christian analysis, is a means to this end. This is the view of the popes who contemplate no ideology, no crusade, no "sacred" property rights, no dogmatic state intervention; none of these can be an absolute. They are all relative to human dignity and must be used or not used accordingly. We must not say that we keep an economic institution while keeping the dignity of man (this is a perversion of priorities); but we can say that we keep an institution in order to safeguard and promote human dignity; for we know only too well to what dehumanization of the economy, what depersonalization this profit-motive capitalism has led us for well over a century. It needs reform from its core outward.

We must, with John XXIII, attempt to find and define within the enterprise things which cannot be separated and their mutual interdependence, if we are to have a human system of production: property, instruments of production, direction, work, credit and profit. All rights to the fruits of the common production are founded only on a human presence which, in its turn, gives an enterprise its human and communitarian aspect, making it responsible for production and distribution of fruits. This is so, because the property of an enterprise is unique since it produces goods and services in conjunction with, and not separated from, the infinite dignity of the work of human beings who therefore have a right to share in its effective distribution, profit, and re-investment. It is a type of collective effort and reward, whose appropriations are not given to an exclusive group, but rather determined by a type of qualitative distribution of profit. Of its very nature, this distribution confers on each of the participants in the communitarian enterprise rights which are differential and specific; that of the owner of capital actually engaged in the enterprise over which he has direct responsibility; that of workers whose rewards must respect the qualitative and quantitative variants of each individual's participation in the work of the enterprise; that of the stockholder whose position, humanly speaking, is much more precarious than that of the former two, for capital, as such, has no rights, for it does no work. Yet, it is just for the investor to receive some return, since it is only thanks to his investment that proprietor and worker can produce, sharing together what is the responsibility of all. Thus, this is much more than a simple mathematical distribution of profit, for in the final analysis, it is the communitarian aspect of an enterprise — stockholder, proprietor, director, worker — which establishes and guarantees the rights of persons to the fruit of that enterprise. By it, and by it alone, do we have a true integration of persons within the enterprise itself, where none are alienated, neither from the enterprise nor from its work nor from its profit. Only in such a system will the dualism of "salary payment — capital profit" be effectively healed and integrated within a complete whole. With this synthetic principle, the inhumanity of capitalism is overcome, a system in its economic and spiritual division has ruined these two inseparable poles of human life. The dialectic between the two must once again be established. We shall see more of this when we deal with the economic sphere, properly speaking, in Chapter III.

What we can conclude from this whole section is that there can be no real conflict between scientific knowledge and divine revelation. This is traditional and is enough to cover any temporary struggle between the two. This does not mean that there will be no difficult periods in their relationships, but, as in the past, both will profit by reconsidering their positions with a sincere regard and understanding for each other. This implies research and understanding by and for each other; that research and knowledge are good both for man and for the coming of the kingdom; and that human knowledge is a great good, as God has willed it to be for the expansion and the perfection of man. "All of these provide some preparation for the acceptance of the message of the gospel — a preparation which can be animated by divine charity through him who has come to save the world" (57f).

Now the document goes on to give us the relationship between culture and Christ, the incarnate *Logos*.

58. a. There are many ties between the message of salvation and human culture. For God, revealing himself to his people to the extent of a full manifestation of himself in his incarnate Son, has spoken according to the culture proper to each epoch.

b. Likewise the Church living in various circumstances in the course of time, has used the discoveries of different cultures so that in her preaching she might spread and explain the message of Christ to all nations, that she might examine it and more deeply understand it, that she might give it better expression in liturgical celebration and in the varied life of the community of the faithful.

c. But at the same time, the Church, sent to all peoples of every time and place is not bound exclusively and indissolubly to any race or nation, any particular way of life or any customary pattern of life recent or ancient. Faithful to her own tradition and at the same time conscious of her universal mission, she can enter into communion with the various civilizations, to their enrichment and the enrichment of the Church herself.

d. The gospel of Christ constantly renews the life and culture of fallen men; it combats and removes the errors and evils resulting from the permanent allurement of sin. It never ceases to purify and elevate the morality of peoples. By riches coming from above, it makes fruitful, as it were from within, the spiritual qualities and traditions of every people and of every age. It strengthens, perfects and restores them in Christ. Thus the Church, in the very fulfillment of her own function stimulates and advances human and civic culture; by her action, also by her liturgy, she leads men toward interior liberty.

There are many points which must be noted in this paragraph. The Church herself (58b) uses various cultural modes and expressions in order to communicate her eternal message to men. In the words of Pope John to the Council Fathers, the message of the good news of Christ is the eternal and abiding truth of the Church. This witness to God's word among men by the Church is an essential dimension of her being as given to her by Christ himself. Yet, the cultural embodiments of that message have changed and must continue to change as the history of man continuously changes. This adaptation of Christ's message to new cultural expressions is a continuous task of the Church, the *ecclesia semper reformanda,* whose structures are means in the essential testimonial mission of the Church. This was true in the early centuries of the Church when she adapted the evangelical message first to Graeco-Roman cultural forms and patterns and later to Germanic-Saxon forms. Sporadic attempts were made under Ricci and De Nobile to do this with regard to Eastern cultural patterns. This latter attempt was mostly a failure precisely because many of the authorities in Rome had become convinced of the somehow divinely willed identity of Christianity with Roman Western cultural expressions of the Christian message. This metamorphosis was due not only to a lack of historical perspective but also to a lack of appreciation for the dynamic dialogue of Church-world. The world had become simply a subdivision of the Church, and its autonomy and independence were enslaved by the narrow vision of the concept of the Church in the Middle Ages.

This same struggle continued in the Council chambers of Vatican II. Both the groups of adaptation-dialogue and those of retrenchment-identification were represented, even if the latter constituted a powerful but small minority. The majority of the Fathers, following the thought of John XXIII, saw in the new world of humanism with its secular values, fresh resources which may be likened to preparations of grace, the grace of faith in mystery, the grace of hope in beatitude, and finally, the grace of charity in the common fraternity of all mankind. They saw these new forms not as positive capacities leading inevitably to the accession of grace, but rather as dispositions to receiving it. These openings to grace are, however, more than simply theoretical possibilities. John XXIII saw such dispositions in the world in his encyclical *Peace on Earth,* and he called them "signs of the times" favorable to the evangelization of modern man. Among these, he lists such events as the economic and social advancement of the working class, the entry of women into public life, the equality of peoples, as the first stage in the progress toward a truly human community. These can all be called natural values and Pope John saw them as such. They have become, moreover, the norm in the conduct of the collective life of men. Pope John saw them as open to spiritual values as well, since their ultimate perspective goes further than their immediate realization. All the Fathers of the Church recognize in the grandeur of inanimate nature the *vestigia Dei,* while seeing in the spiritual grandeur of human nature the *imago Dei* itself.

Next, the Church receives this cultural ramification from many and diverse cultures: Graeco-Roman, Byzantine, Russian, Hebrew-Semitic, and many others. The future is wide open to the Church, in this respect, and she is free to accommodate herself in ways of which she is the sole judge. This implies acceptance of new forms of language in which she incorporates her doctrine, new forms of art and architectural expression, and so forth (58b). The Church, on her part, has advantages to bring to existing cultures in the form of respect for human rights to which history itself attests (58d). She protected and prolonged many cultural values in ages past through her monasteries, and so on. The Church also educates peoples as to the worth and value of modernization and scientific accomplishments.

There remain many different values in culture which must be reconciled within a Christian context. It is this problem which our document now investigates:

59. a. For the above reasons, the Church recalls to the mind of all that culture is to be subordinated to the integral perfection of the human person, to the good of the community and of the whole society. Therefore it is necessary to develop the human faculties in such a way that there results a growth of the

faculty of wonder, of intuition, of contemplation, of making personal judgment, of developing a religious, moral and social sense.

b. Cultural because it flows immediately from the spiritual and social character of man, has constant need of a just freedom in order to develop; it needs also the legitimate possibility of exercising its autonomy according to its own principles. It therefore rightly demands respect and enjoys a certain inviolability within the limits of the common good, as long, of course, as it preserves the rights of the individual and the community, whether particular or universal.

c. This Sacred Synod, therefore, recalling the teaching of the first Vatican Council, declares that there are "two orders of knowledge" which are distinct, namely faith and reason; and that the Church does not forbid that "the human arts and disciplines use their own principles and their proper method, each in its own domain"; therefore "acknowledging this just liberty," this Sacred Synod affirms the legitimate autonomy of human culture and especially of the sciences.

d. All this supposes that, within the limits of morality, and the common utility, man can freely search for the truth, express his opinion and publish it; that he can practice any art he chooses; that finally, he can avail himself of accurate information concerning events of a public nature.

e. As for public authority, it is not its function to determine the character of the civilization, but rather to establish the conditions and to use the means which are capable of fostering the life of culture among all even within the minorities of a nation. It is necessary to do everything possible to prevent culture from being turned away from its proper end and made to serve as an instrument of political or economic power.

Like all else here on earth, human culture is subordinate to and for the perfection of the human person (59a). The theme of autonomy of science and culture — for the same reason — has already been discussed in a previous section (cf. pars. 36, 57, pp. 121, 209). It directly refers (59c) to the dogmatic constitution of faith of Vatican I, where this same theme is developed.

All this progress of science and technology must be governed and directed by moral and human ends and concerns. That is why it is so vital for any society not to neglect its moral and religious traditions and growth. It is from this vantage point that the power of the Church can be brought to bear on the whole of the social order and on each of its particular situations. For a fuller development of this see above, pp. 131-136. Catholic faith and morality are so intimately connected, that the Church would be remiss in her duty were she not to take an active and attentive interest in the basic affairs of man in the terrestrial city. It is this sentiment which is outlined for us in this present paragraph (59d). Science must have its legitimate freedom to follow its own methods, but it must be guided by human and moral ends (to which the Church can greatly contribute). If not, it can only lead to the detriment of man. Men of science are discovering this truth more every day (witness the recent uproar over the unwillingness of some U. S. atomic scientists to work exclusively in research for the development of nuclear energy). Out of their concern was born, for instance, the *Bulletin of Atomic Scientists,* a journal dedicated to studying the relationship between nuclear development and ethics.

On the other hand, public authorities cannot arbitrarily impose one culture on a people (59e), but its function must be to encourage the growth of the existing culture while encouraging (by various ways and grants) the access to culture by many or all of its citizens. The state has a positive obligation to see to it that all its citizens enjoy a basic culture by education (reading, writing, medical care, etc.), and that those with talents are given opportunity to develop them in order to contribute to the enrichment of culture (objective). The persecution of cultural minorities is listed as a crime against humanity insofar as it deprives men of the legitimate expression of their personalities. This was dealt with in *Pacem* as well (see 94-97).

The theme of the right of all to a basic culture is again taken up in the following paragraph:

60. a. It is now possible to free most of humanity from the

misery of ignorance. Therefore the duty most consonant with our times, especially for Christians, is that of working diligently for fundamental decisions to be taken in economic and political affairs, both on the national and international level, which will everywhere recognize and satisfy the right of all to a human and social culture in conformity with the dignity of the human person without any discrimination based on race, sex, nation, religion or social condition. Therefore it is necessary to provide all with a sufficient quantity of cultural benefits, especially of those which constitute the so-called basic culture lest very many be prevented from cooperating in the promotion of the common good in a truly human manner because of illiteracy and a lack of responsible activity.

b. We must strive to provide for those men who are gifted, the possibility of pursuing higher studies; and in such a way that, as far as possible, they may occupy in society those duties, offices and services which are in harmony with their natural aptitude and the competence they have acquired. Thus each man and the social groups of every people will be able to attain the full development of their culture in conformity with their qualities and traditions.

c. Everything must be done to make everyone conscious of the right to culture and the duty he has of developing himself culturally and of helping others. Sometimes there exist conditions of life and of work which impede the cultural striving of men and destroy in them the eagerness for culture. This is especially true of farmers and workers. It is necessary to provide for them those working conditions which will not impede their human culture but rather favor it. Women now engage in almost all spheres of activity. It is fitting that they are able to assume their proper role in accordance with their own nature. It is incumbent upon all to acknowledge and favor the proper and necessary participation of women in cultural life.

The document speaks of a "basic culture" which is here taken to mean the basics of education and literacy, in order to prepare citizens for assuming responsibility in the socio-economic and political spheres (60a). This right of education to the greatest extent of human possibilities was also dealt with in

Pacem (13). The reasons for this are numerous. A political democracy presupposes an educated citizenry which can understand issues, since it is the people who assume responsibility for the election of their representatives. A certain minimum of culture is therefore necessary to participate in social life, and the more responsibility that accrues to the people, the more culture and education they must receive. This is particularly true in modern societies where he who has not received this background is considered to be "disadvantaged" or even relegated to the slag heap of unemployables by a technical and modernized society. This, of course, will vary with the condition of each particular society and what is high in one society will be low in another — and vice versa. This will alter with time as well; for what was considered to be a good level in the 19th century is totally inadequate in the second half of the 20th century. Man becomes ever more conscious of his dignity and of the demands this entails with the passing of time and reflection on current conditions. Working conditions which were considered standard in the 19th century are woefully out of date today, because we realize more fully that the dignity of the worker demands more healthful working conditions. This is, of course, very true of the underdeveloped parts of the world where working conditions and living conditions are extremely poor, because the milieu is not as yet very well developed. Thus the great importance of such international organizations as UNESCO, WHO, ILO and FAO to raise the living conditions of these peoples, to permit them to enjoy the minimum of culture with an ever-increasing pace.

The document then goes into a global view of culture taken in its ensemble:

> 61. a. Today it is more difficult to form a synthesis of the various disciplines of knowledge and the arts than it was formerly. For while the mass and the diversity of cultural factors are increasing, there is a decrease in each man's faculty of perceiving and unifying these things, so that the image of

"universal man" is being lost sight of more and more. Nevertheless it remains each man's duty to preserve an understanding of the whole human person in which the values of intellect, will, conscience and fraternity are pre-eminent. These values are all rooted in God the Creator and have been wonderfully restored and elevated in Christ.

b. The family is, as it were, the primary mother and nurse of this education. There the children, in an atmosphere of love, more easily learn the correct order of things, while proper forms of human culture impress themselves in an almost unconscious manner upon the mind of the developing adolescent.

c. Opportunities for the same education are to be found also in the societies of today, due especially to the increased circulation of books and to the new means of cultural and social communication which can foster a universal culture. With the more or less universal reduction of working hours, the leisure time of most men has increased. May this leisure be used properly to relax, to fortify the health of soul and body through spontaneous study and activity, through tourism which refines man's character and enriches him with understanding of others, through sports activity which helps to preserve an equilibrium of spirit even in the community, and to establish fraternal relations among men of all conditions, nations and races. Let Christians cooperate so that the cultural manifestations and collective activity characteristic of our time may be imbued with a human and Christian spirit.

d. All these leisure activities however cannot bring man to a full cultural development unless there is at the same time a profound inquiry into the meaning of culture and science for the human person.

Today, one of the dangers of science is that of specialization, where the view of the ensemble, of part to the whole, is not seen. An expert may be very intelligent in one field and extremely ignorant in the field of moral and religious aspects of culture and society. Many people mistakenly translate a man's great knowledge in, say, nuclear physics, into a trust of an assumed competency, unmerited when he speaks outside his field. This is a great danger today which must be guarded against (61a). Thus human culture forms one whole and man — even before the advent of the scientific age — possessed a wisdom on the ends and means of human life. The Church reminds men once again that scientific and technical life must be directed to, and by, human, rational ends without which there can be no wisdom in life, no matter how much progress is made in many of these areas. Finally, all culture is dependent upon God without Whom there can be only mistrust and discord among men (61a).

Culture also demands the cultivation of the affective life of the individual in society, the first and most important being that of family life (61b). In many respects — as we have seen in Chapter I — this is the most significant element in the cultural formation of any particular society and its culture. That is why our document keeps returning to its importance for society. There are also other elements in society which do and can promote universal culture on a more vast and international scale. Today men have leisure as never before, since cybernation has taken much of the toil of work away affording men more time to consecrate to their total development in the cultural sphere. International sports events can also promote this type of universal culture, toleration and understanding among men (61c). It creates relationships which can be of valuable aid to the participants, for events of socio-political nature later on in life. These create, in a sense, the beginnings of a dialogue among all men of good will where they are introduced to mores, customs, and modes of life different from their own and can prove to be of value in later international relationships.

This paragraph ends with the same question posed throughout our document (61d): who and what is man; for an understanding of man will, in the final analysis, give us the sure key to the understanding of what any one particular culture means.

Lastly in this chapter on culture, the Council seeks to harmonize culture with Christianity itself:

62. a. Although the Church has contributed much to the

development of culture, experience shows that, because of circumstances, it is sometimes difficult to harmonize culture with Christian teaching. These difficulties do not necessarily harm the life of faith, rather they can stimulate the mind to a deeper and more accurate understanding of the faith. The recent studies and findings of science, history and philosophy raise new questions which affect life and which demand new theological investigations. Furthermore, theologians, observing the requirements and methods proper to theology, are invited to seek continually for more suitable ways of communicating doctrine to the men of their times; for the deposit of Faith or the truths are one thing and the manner in which they are enunciated, in the same meaning and understanding, is another. In pastoral care, sufficient use must be made not only of theological principles, but also of the findings of the secular sciences, especially of psychology and sociology, so that the faithful may be brought to a more adequate and mature life of faith.

b. Literature and the arts are also, in their own way, of great importance to the life of the Church. They strive to make known the proper nature of man, his problems and his experiences in trying to know and perfect both himself and the world. They have much to do with revealing man's place in history and in the world; with illustrating the miseries and joys, the needs and strengths of man and with foreshadowing a better life for him. Thus they are able to elevate human life, expressed in manifold forms in various times and places.

c. Efforts must be made so that those who foster these arts feel that the Church recognizes their activity and so that, enjoying orderly freedom, they may initiate more friendly relations with the Christian community. The Church acknowledges also new forms of art which are adapted to our age and are in keeping with the characteristics of various nations and regions. They may be brought into the sanctuary since they raise the mind to God, once the manner of expression is adapted and they are conformed to liturgical requirements.

d. Thus the knowledge of God is better manifested and the preaching of the gospel becomes clearer to human intelligence and shows itself to be relevant to man's actual conditions of life.

e. May the faithful, therefore, live in very close union with the other men of their time, and may they strive to understand perfectly their way of thinking and judging, as expressed in their culture. Let them blend new sciences and theories and the understanding of the most recent discoveries with Christian morality and the teaching of Christian doctrine, so that their religious culture and morality may keep pace with their scientific knowledge and with the constantly progressing technology. Thus they will be able to interpret and evaluate all things in a truly Christian spirit.

f. Let those who teach theology in seminaries and universities strive to collaborate with men versed in the other sciences through a sharing of their resources and points of view. Theological inquiry should pursue a profound understanding of revealed truth; at the same time it should not neglect close contact with its own time that it may be able to help those men skilled in various disciplines to attain to a better understanding of the faith. This common effort will greatly aid the formation of priests, who will be able to present to our contemporaries the doctrine of the Church concerning God, man and the world, in a manner more adapted to them so that they may receive it more willingly. Furthermore, it is to be hoped that many of the laity will receive a sufficient formation in the sacred sciences and that some will dedicate themselves professionally to these studies, developing and deepening them by their own labors. In order that they may fulfill their function, let it be recognized that all the faithful, whether clerics or laity, possess a lawful freedom of inquiry, freedom of thought and of expressing their mind with humility and fortitude in those matters on which they enjoy competence.

It is noteworthy that this last paragraph is not so much a conclusion as a long series of questions. This is not strange, since it is the first time in the Church's history that she, *ex professo*, has dealt with the concept of culture in a conciliar document. It is evident that there remains much theological speculation to be done, and that there are many more questions than answers in this regard. The Church approaches these problems not in a restrictive way but in a way open to the needs and appeals of modern man in the cultural field. It is an attitude, at once receptive and open, as well as sympathetic to the vast changes which many cultures are undergoing today throughout the globe. The Church can here only be of aid and service as this transformation takes place on a global scale. The scientific and technological revolution, for instance, can, indeed, bring about some radical changes in traditional societies, but the Church knows that, in the long run, it is for man's benefit that this revolution should be encouraged and guided. Thus the Church remains as a reminder, guide, and witness to who man is and where he is going. She, in her turn, must accommodate her message to the variant cultures to which she is sent to save (62a). We have already seen this aspect above (see above, p. 145). She must be open to new forms of intellectual and artistic expression in its diverse forms (62b). The Church is a living organism and therefore must progress continuously in this direction.

The Council asks Christians to live and work in close communion with the men of the modern age (62e). It is the principal responsibility of the layman to coordinate and demonstrate the relationship between the tasks of man here below with Christian morals and doctrine. This has been the constant teaching of the Church from the time of Leo XIII (*Rerum Novarum*) up to and including John XXIII (*Pacem in Terris*). This participation extends to all fields of human endeavor: economic, social, political, and cultural, presupposing a dialogue between these expert laymen and Catholic theologians (62f). The day is gone forever when the Catholic theologian can make moral judgments alone. The papal commission presently studying the question of birth control should have been enough to dissipate all ambiguity in this regard. Experts and theologians together must study these urgent problems, since the Spirit speaks to the Church through secular science as well as through sacred science. The concept of dialogue within the Church itself (*Ecclesiam Suam*) necessitates an alteration of attitudes on each side; clerics and laymen are both responsible for the

Church in its further dialogue with the modern world. This will require a change in some of the structures of the Church for normalizing, juridically approving, and promoting contacts and dialogue of this calibre. It is only in harmony with these lay specialists today that the Church can hope to discern the "signs of the times" and attempt to make correct judgments on the agonizing cultural-moral problems of our times. This suggests a climate of open and free debate where these questions can be raised without fear of silence and dogmatic intolerance, both somewhat characteristic of the Church in the past four hundred years.

CHAPTER 3

Economic and Social Life

This chapter of our document is probably the least original of all, for it is nothing more than a summary of the Church's social teaching from Leo XIII (*Rerum Novarum*) to John XXIII (*Mater et Magistra*). It does serve the purpose, however, of putting this doctrine into a fuller context of modern problems and can serve as a *summa* in capsule form of the vast pontifical literature on the social and economic order. The document begins with a general description of economic life:

63. a. In the economic and social realms, too, the dignity and complete vocation of the human person and the welfare of society as a whole are to be respected and promoted. For man is the source, the center, and the purpose of all economic and social life.

b. Like other areas of social life, the economy of today is marked by man's increasing domination over nature, by closer and more intense relationships between citizens, groups, and countries and their mutual dependence, and by the increased intervention of the state. At the same time progress in the methods of production and in the exchange of goods and services has made the economy an instrument capable of better meeting the intensified needs of the human family.

c. Reasons for anxiety, however, are not lacking. Many people, especially in economically advanced areas, seem as it were, to be ruled by economics, so that almost their entire personal and social life is permeated with a certain economic way of thinking. Such is true both of nations that favor a collective economy and of others. At the very time when the development of economic life could mitigate social inequalities (provided that it be guided and coordinated in a reasonable and human way) it is often made to embitter them; or, in some places, it even results in a decline of the social status of the underprivileged and in contempt for the poor. While an immense number of people still lack the absolute necessities of life, some, even in less advanced areas, live in luxury or squander wealth. Extravagance and wretchedness exist side by side. While a few enjoy very great power of choice, the majority are deprived of almost all possibility of acting on their own initiative and responsibility, and often subsist in living and working conditions unworthy of the human person.

d. A similar lack of economic and social balance is to be noticed between agriculture, industry, and the services, and also between different parts of one and the same country. The contrast between the economically more advanced countries and other countries is becoming more serious day by day, and the very peace of the world can be jeopardized thereby.

e. Our contemporaries are coming to feel these inequalities with an ever sharper awareness, since they are thoroughly convinced that the ample technical and economic possibilities which the world of today enjoys can and should correct this unhappy state of affairs. Hence, many reforms in the socioeconomic realm and a change of mentality and attitude are required of all.

f. For this reason the Church down through the centuries and in the light of the gospel has worked out the principles of justice and equity demanded by right reason both for individual and social life as well as for international life, and she has proclaimed them especially in recent times. This Sacred Council intends to strengthen these principles according to the circumstances of this age and to set forth certain guidelines, especially with regard to the requirements of economic development.

What will become very clear throughout this section is that the whole of the economic life is deeply characterized by the social nature of man, which makes all men — and particularly Christians — responsible for each other in their economic and social dignity. Man alone is the end of this life — not profit or wealth (63a). This is emphasized at the beginning of our chapter, in order to show the complete superiority of man over all "property" rights or over all types of economic alienation from his work. Economic activity must respect the dignity of man as well as promote it. It must be a subject of human expansion for each person who is engaged therein as a development and perfection of his personality. All this implies responsibility for himself and for his work. This was a favorite theme of *Mater et Magistra* (see 9, 48, 55, 62-63, 82-84, 90-91, 99, 112, 118, 174, 176-177, 195, etc.) as well as of *Pacem in Terris* (13, 23, 25, 28-30, 34-35, 44, 64, 86-87, 91-92, 120, etc.). As the Pope put it in *Mater:*

> Our Predecessor, Pius XII, remarked that the economic and social function, which every man aspires to fulfill, demands that the activity of each be not completely subjected to the will of others. A humane view of the enterprise ought undoubtedly to safeguard the authority and necessary efficiency associated with unity of direction. It does not follow that those who are daily involved in an enterprise must be reduced to the level of mere silent performers who have no chance to bring their experience into play. They must not be kept entirely passive with regard to the making of decisions that regulate their activity (92).
> Finally, attention must be called to the fact that the desire for a greater exercise of serious responsibility on the part of the workers in various productive units corresponds to lawful demands inherent in human nature. It is also in conformity with progressive historical developments in the economic, social and political fields (93).

The reason for this expanded view of the worker's role, mentioned above, is that man perfects himself by and through his work. In a very special way, his work expresses his personality, and, as such, it ought to be a true expression of himself. This reflection of the worker's personality cannot be achieved except through responsibility, which in turn, cannot be realized without an effective voice in the enterprise in which he works. In his work, a man's actions must be those of a free and responsible human being; and for most men, this is almost impossible without an effective sharing in what they do. A man's humanity is expressed in his economic activity, and if this is not free and responsible, his work lacks human dignity. When a man has the opportunity, which is rightfully his, to perfect his human dignity by and through his daily work, his work then represents, in a true sense, a reflection of his person, which is made in the image of God.

This basic insistence on the worker's full sharing in the industrial structure, a tenet that pervades John XXIII's social thought, may seem to be a fond dream and not an attainable practical end. From one viewpoint, it is a dream, but to be more accurate, it is an ideal that presently does not exist. Yet, such an ideal can be brought into existence in a society which is truly personalistic and where all forms of private property are open to the use and possession of all individuals. The Pope's personalistic vision of society lies between total collectivism and socialistic communism which merges the individual into a sort of amorphous glob, and the tooth and claw *laissez-faire* capitalism which exaggerates the individual. In this Christian social order described by Pope John, man becomes more conscious of his freedom and his responsibility, and thus participates more humanly in the economic and political structures to which he belongs.

From this point of view, Americans are at opposite poles in political democracy and economic democracy. In the former, each American participates and contributes according to his talents, abilities, and needs. He takes full responsibility as a citizen, because political institutions are ultimately directed by him through his representatives. According to *Pacem in Terris* (26-27), this political participation is a basic demand of human nature, and corresponds to human dignity because it gives each man a sense of duty and responsibility. Economic society is not such a democracy, because no responsibility exists for the promotion of human dignity. Insofar as the direction of an enterprise is concerned, the worker is a perpetual minor, a number that can be dismissed or hired according to the *"need,"* determined solely by market demand. His muscles and professional skills are needed, but his opinion and consent are never requested. He is an automaton who is turned on or off. This view of a man violates all canons of social justice given by the Pope, for the precise reason that an automaton cannot be or develop as a human being. In such a view of man, often assumed by Western capitalism, human dignity and human work are a "commodity to be sold," a cynical view condemned over a hundred years ago by Karl Marx. Until this attitude can be corrected by active participation in industry, the worker's human dignity must remain truncated.

The directives in *Mater et Magistra* are meant to remedy this dehumanizing situation. Though the average American factory worker took home a record $125.00 a week in 1966, his gain in human dignity was not commensurate. To Pope John, an industry or an enterprise is not only a profit-making institution, but also a community of persons (93). His understanding of the responsibility of unions to consider the common good (48) and the need for both workers and employers to cooperate in their proper enterprise clearly demonstrate his view of industry as a community:

> We believe further that one must praise in the same way the outstanding endeavors performed in a true Christian spirit by our beloved sons in other professional groups and workers' associations which take their inspiration from natural-law principles and show respect for freedom of conscience (102).

This type of spirit corresponds to the human dignity of workers, because it encourages the development of their sense of responsibility toward the industry itself. Yet this end is impossible to achieve without an effective co-partnership, co-operation, co-ownership. In Catholic social thought, John XXIII has surpassed all other popes in his trust and encouragement of the worker in a free society. The ideal social system is not a socialistic, communistic, or capitalistic system; it is, rather, that system which best promotes human dignity by increasing opportunities for freedom and responsibility in the work to which both worker and employer contribute.

The dignity and personality of the worker are central in paragraphs 82-84 of *Mater et Magistra:*

> Justice is to be observed not only in the distribution of wealth acquired by production, but also with respect to the conditions under which production is achieved. For there is an innate demand in human nature that when men engaged in production they should have the opportunity of exercising responsibility and of perfecting their personalities (82).
>
> It follows that if the organization and operation of an economic system are such as to compromise the human dignity of those who engage in it, or to blunt their sense of responsibility, or to impede the exercise of personal initiative, such an economic system is unjust. And this is so even if, by hypothesis, the wealth produced through such a system reaches a high level and this wealth is distributed according to standards of justice and equity (83).
>
> It is not possible to describe in detail the sort of economic organization which is more conformed to the dignity of man and more suited to developing his sense of responsibility. Nevertheless, our predecessor, Pius XII, opportunely sketches the following directive: small and average-sized undertakings in agriculture, in the arts and crafts in commerce and industry, should be safeguarded and fostered through entry into cooperative unions; in the large concerns, meanwhile, there should be the possibility of modifying the work contract by one of partnership (84).

Obviously, a mere multiplication of economic goods or material benefits does not, of itself, enhance human freedom; both communism and capitalism, therefore, fall under the same censure when their goals are solely concerned with the material advancement of man. In a sense, East and West suffer from different forms of the same cancer: materialism. According to the Pope, that system alone is moral which permits man free initiative and responsibility in his work. The American system has elevated man's material stature, as the communist system may do someday; yet, this does not make him moral or human. A man's dignity is not necessarily increased by the number of autos and gadgets he owns, but by the intellectual, psychological and moral fulfillment of his personality through the work he does. The worker must never be reduced to a passive agent in the production and consumption of goods. The role of a robot, a cog in a consumptive machine, does not correspond to the dignity of man. For the worker, responsibility for production must be added to the consumption of production if we are to attain a human, economic democracy. And since one of the great threats to American society comes from the destruction of personality by impersonal work, the only way to counteract this uniformity of mass production and mass frustration is for man to participate in society through his work.

We have already discussed the concepts of socialization (pp. 19-20). This concept was a favorite one with John XXIII in *Mater*. Thus, the Pope says: *"Socialization is one of the characteristic features of our epoch"* (59). It has been brought about by the application of advanced technology to modern society as well as other factors already cited. Historically, the Industrial Revolution has resulted in the urbanization of the world's population. In 1966, for example, 80% of the American population lived in metropolitan areas; the tendency is also growing rapidly in Asia and Latin America. This characteristic shift from the farm to the city arises from the demands of an industrialized society, demands which range from the concentration of a labor force to the easy access to transportation for raw materials and finished products. Since this complicated interdependency of peoples affects man's powers to work out his own destiny, the natural right of association has become more apparent and necessary. The growth of state power is both an effect and a cause of this natural process, and, as such, the Holy Father recognizes it as an immense good.

> Socialization is, at one and the same time, an effect and a cause of the growing intervention of the state in areas which, since they touch the deepest concerns of the human person, are not without considerable importance nor devoid of danger. Among these are care of health, instruction and education of the young, control of professional careers, methods of care and rehabilitation of those physically or mentally handicapped in any way. Socialization, however, is also the fruit of expression of a natural tendency almost irrepressible in human beings — the tendency to unite for the purpose of obtaining objectives which each ambitions but which are beyond the capacity of individuals.
>
> This sort of tendency has given rise, especially in these latter decades, to a wide range of groups, associations, and institutions having economic, cultural, social, athletic, recreational, professional and political ends. They operate within a single nation and on a world-wide basis (60).

The good which comes from socialization is manifested concretely in the extension and development of man's natural rights in health, education, and welfare (see *Pacem in Terris*, 11-13, 18-22). Grants by the state, scholarships of all kinds, public education, and other educational endeavors help promote the natural right of man to develop his talents. Group insurance, social security, compensations, health insurance, and minimal professional competency have given modern man a sense of security never before enjoyed on the earth. These benefits and others are the result of socialization, which is occurring nationally and internationally.

> [Socialization] makes possible, in fact, the satisfaction of many personal rights, especially those of a socio-economic nature. The right to the indispensable means of human subsistence, to health services, to instruction at a higher level, to

more thorough professional formation, to housing, to employment, to suitable leisure and to decent recreation are typical examples. In addition, through increasing systematization of modern media, of mass communications — press, motion pictures, radio, television — it becomes possible for individuals to participate, as it were, in human events even on a worldwide scale (61).

It is now commonplace to say that the world has become smaller in size, in communication, in trade, and thus it has become interdependent; this growing socialization of society must now indeed be termed international.

Pope John does not deny that there are distinct disadvantages to the process of socialization. The individual's freedom of initiative is restricted, and government interferes in many intimate aspects of a man's life.

At the same time, however, socialization multiplies institutional structures and extends more and more to minute details and juridical control of human relations in every walk of life. As a consequence, it restricts the range of an individual's freedom of action. It uses means, follows methods and creates an atmosphere which make it difficult for one to reach judgments free from external pressures, to work on his own initiative, to exercise responsibility and to assert his personality (62).

The great danger here is depersonalization, the supreme bane of human society. Workers in industry become cogs, welfare recipients become cases, neighbors in housing projects become absolute strangers, social security becomes a number, the government becomes a great bureaucracy which controls and regulates by impersonal laws, liberty of initiative and independence of action become stifled, and each person's responsibility becomes limited. In the United States, certain elements in the population, calling themselves conservative, have sensed these disadvantages and, in reaction to them, have branded any governmental interference as a reduction of freedom. Undoubtedly, the above disadvantages are real and must be carefully con-

sidered in building and planning the social order. Unlike the
so-called conservatives, the Holy Father in this text is fundamentally optimistic about the modern world. He knows that
socialization and stronger governmental powers do not necessarily mean a diminution of freedom and responsibility, because
the advantages of socialization can offset its disadvantages.

> Accordingly, advances in social organization can and should
> be so brought about that the maximum advantages accrue to
> citizens while at the same time disadvantages are averted or
> at least minimized (64).

Since man is a free being, that which he has brought about
in freedom can be controlled; and so any disadvantage which
arises in the social system can be held to a minimum. In a
very real sense, man has, in fact, been freed from the slavery
of fate by socialization. Health insurance and such programs
as Medicare have freed men from the instabilities of health;
Social Security, from the economic infirmities of old age; auto-
mation, from the slavery of back-breaking toil; communications,
from the restrictions of time and space.

The intervention by state authorities, says our document,
will be correspondingly greater as the process of socialization
intensifies (63b). Pope John already pointed out the fact that
because of the vastness, power, and complexity of modern
economy, the state has a positive right to intervene authoritatively for the insurance of justice and a correct distribution of
income in any particular society (*Mater*, 2). The principle is
more fully extended here than it was by Leo XIII and Pius
XI. If the state had the right to intervene in economic and
social matters in 1891, when society was not as complicated and
developed as it is today, this right must apply with even greater
force now. State influence and intervention must necessarily
be more extended, because the economy on a national and an
international scale has become more vast and complicated. In
this respect, we must maintain a balance between two extremes:

those who would deny, as much as possible, any state regulation in economic activity; and those who would permit the government to regulate and control the whole economic process by various types of socialism. For the Pope and our present document, state intervention is not an evil; rather, the state has a positive moral duty to maintain distributive justice in any given society and economy.

Yet, there is reason for anxiety (63c), since men are becoming more materialistic in their pursuit of economic goods. This is true of East and West, and it is a severe critique of both regions where the principal objective of the economic life is profit and gain.

Thus it is money and gain which dominate, to a great degree, the Western Capitalist system, having broken and dehumanized generation after generation (in this respect, one has only to read a cursory history of the 19th century labor movement and its conditions). This appetite for gain — the biblical *cupiditas* — was always in men as individuals; for there is no reason to suspect that it is any greater today than it was in times past. Modern capitalism has systematized this vice in the structures of its very economic system *qua* system. It has become its very reason for being and the law of its institutions, where individuals — inclusive of the individual capitalists themselves — are caught up without remission in this anonymous and dehumanizing violence. The evil is now institutional where its law is profit and profit alone, and where only institutional and structural reform can make of neo-capitalism a truly humanized and humanizing system. The system carries within itself a type of vicious circle from which, as it now stands, it cannot escape on its own. Capital produces profit, and profit, in its own turn, produces more capital. Christians — from the earliest times — have always condemned this mode of operation among men, even in the (today) often ridiculed aspect of the Middle Ages where usury was considered an evil. These medieval schoolmen were correct and modern theologians quite wrong, since the former saw very clearly what many religious defenders of western Capitalism have not seen; namely, that any system of economics which dehumanizes man and his labor, where work (taken here in its broadest meaning) and profit are separated, where man's work as an expression and incarnational extension of himself is treated as a commodity for a further end — profit — such a system, these ancients saw clearly, was basically inhuman and unchristian. Money for money's sake, profit for profit's sake, is an aberration from Christianity. Money is for man, not man for money; and it is precisely this vice which infects modern capitalism to its very core, no matter how many laws are passed to curb its abuses. These latter are only palliatives of a doomed regime.

Today this fundamental abuse is contained in the exclusive attribution to the owner of capital goods of the surplus benefit of production alone. It is not that he (or they) always keep it for personal fortune (even if this is also a fact), but, rather, that in and of itself, the continuous and progressive investment of these riches into new establishments of production from which the human concept of work is rejected, ends by an automatic multiplication of power which cannot be stopped by itself: technology, unavoidably concentrated economic credit, etc. (which are neither good nor bad in themselves, but, rather, simply technical procedures) have now become the instruments of this appropriation of great riches with its above-mentioned vice. This process, then, is truly *"unnatural"* in its most basic meaning, that is, a dehumanization of man as well as of his extension in space and time: his work.

By nature itself, as Pius XI said in the passage quoted above, the riches produced belong by right and by nature to him to those who participated in their production directly or indirectly, some more quantitatively, others more qualitatively. Certainly we must admit that a share belongs to the owner of the capital goods, even in a special way, since it is his own labor which has made these goods available for others to work upon. But when the work is that of a community — as is the case with every modern enterprise — produced in consort with proprietor, director, and worker, the fruit of that labor belongs to all three categories of man as a community.

A man cannot be *"bought"* with money or anything else, precisely because he and his work are of infinite value. We, therefore, do great violence to man by separating him from his work by payment only of a salary or wage. By this act, one has robbed him of his most precious possession: his human dignity. This is exactly what profit-motive neo-capitalism does today — a vice condemnable philosophically as well as theologically, wherein benefits are distributed as if an enterprise were like other types of property (i.e., to be used for further ends, namely, profit) and not, as human dignity demands, a community of labor.

There are other reasons for anxiety as well, says our document, above all, the differences between the rich nations and the poor nations and within these latter countries, working conditions which are unworthy of the human person. The popes have ceaselessly brought out this aspect (see Pius XI, *Quadragesimo Anno*, 66). "Inert matter is ennobled by the artisan while the worker himself is degraded and corrupted" (146) and the blame is to be placed on a small group of men who seek not human dignity by their economic wealth, but simple profit and gain. This is a distortion of the economic community.

Capitalism in Western society based on pure speculation is further based on the profit-motive, not satisfying a social need by an economic good, but engendering a society of people who think only of themselves in a regime of pure profit. This is the age of Wall Street speculators, of share trading; of the up and down points of Dow-Jones averages; panic buying and selling — totally inhuman activity separated from all care of consortium or human product of labor, whose sole function is to make money; entrepreneurs and speculators who are really parasites on the work of other men. Consequently we have an absolute disassociation of direction, capital, and workers of any one or many enterprises. We have here the vast trusts and monopolies of power for evil on an international scale which, since their sole object is pure profit, couldn't care less for the human problems posed in each country, in each particular sector where one or another enterprise is located. Money in this system no longer goes to workers or to stockholders, but is continuously redirected with a closed circle of capital rules only by its own law of profit. All ties with man are broken, and, thereby, capitalism has attained its proper end and moral corruption. When a crop will not bring in correct profits, it is burned, as was done last year on coffee plantations in Colombia, leaving thousands to beg or starve, because the Colombian-American coffee interests and trusts so dictated it. One telephone call from United Fruit headquarters in New York to practically any country in Latin America means profit or indigence for many within that country. The extent of its economic powers on an international scale are simply unknown, but one thing we do know: its own interest becomes its own end before which everything must give way, including the national or even international common good. Such power can destroy a whole political order (as has happened many times in Latin America), engenders insecurity for prices and markets, reduces millions of men to a whim and wish of a few, while preparing a materialistic culture of profit and gain as the first and only law of life. Such a structure is not offended by war itself, since it shares in the great profits made from government contracts in its huge war-machine (Viet Nam). Anti-trust laws are palliatives to curb such a system's more blatant abuses, but the source of its aberration remains within it. Even in the area of palliatives, how very difficult it is to get these enterprises to do something to correct the terrible injustices they inflict on an unsuspecting public, such as water, air, and cultural pollution! What can be done to, once again, progressively humanize this system?

Finally, let us note with the Council, that one of the greatest obstacles to peace in the modern world is the fact that there is such a disparity between the rich and the poor nations. Our document will emphasize this aspect in the last section, when it deals with the question of peace today. Pius XII had said this many times in his Christmas messages and allocutions. But it was John XXIII who saw it most clearly in both *Pacem* and *Mater*. Pope Paul VI made essentially the same plea when he visited India as well as the UN. The paragraph ends by reminding Catholics of the often-proclaimed "social teachings" of the Church with regard to the socio-economic order (63e). If such doctrine were assiduously put into practice, much of the revolutionary fervor presently alive in today's world would not only be attenuated but would also be channeled into the correct means for building up these underdeveloped nations. This teaching is an integral part of the very doctrine of the Church as we have already seen.

The document now goes on to discuss the fact that the economy, in reality, at the service of man and not vice versa:

64. Today more than ever before attention is rightly given to the increase of the production of agricultural and industrial goods and to the rendering of services, for the purpose of making provision for the growth of population and of satisfying the increasing desires of the human race. Therefore, technical progress, an inventive spirit, an eagerness to create and to expand enterprises, the application of methods of production, and the strenuous efforts of all who engage in production — in a word, all the elements making for such development — must be promoted. The fundamental purpose of this production is not the mere increase of products nor profit or control but rather the service of man, and indeed of the whole man with regard for the full range of his material needs and the demand of his intellectual, moral, spiritual, and religious life; this applies to every man whatsoever and to every group of men, of every race and of every part of the world. Con-

sequently, economic activity is to be carried on according to its own methods and laws within the limits of the moral order, so that God's plan for mankind may be realized.

The three areas are explicitly mentioned here, namely, agriculture, industry, and the services rendered in a society. Under the principle of social justice as enunciated by Pope John in *Mater* (73, 128), each of these sections of the economy has the right to share equally with every other sector the higher standard of living on account of increased production. Because of the industrial revolution, however, metropolitan areas have not only become the centers of population and industrialization, but also the principal beneficiaries of economic and social betterment. Rural areas, both in the United States and in other countries, have not kept pace with the growth in the rest of the economy. In fact, because of the agricultural revolution, they have actually fallen behind. This inequity of distribution of wealth is one of the main reasons why agriculture, for instance, has become a depressed area.

In other words, says the Council, the growth and stimulation of the economy is a vast good if it is distributed equitably, and provided that the economy serves man and not just profit. Each has a proper share in what he has contributed to: capitalist, investor, manager, and worker; and each must be rewarded according to the quality and the quantity of his contribution. We have already seen that the economy must become a human and humanizing factor in the lives of men (see pp. 118-121).

The economy, stresses our document, must be in man's control, who uses it for human ends:

65. a. Economic development must remain under man's determination and must not be left to the judgment of a few men or groups possessing too much economic power or of the political community alone or of certain more powerful nations. It is necessary, on the contrary, that at every level the largest possible number of people and, when it is a question of international relations, all nations have an active share in directing that

development. There is need as well of the coordination and fitting and harmonious combination of the spontaneous efforts of individuals and of free groups with the undertakings of public authorities.

b. Growth is not to be left solely to a kind of mechanical course of economic activity of individuals, nor to the authority of government. For this reason, doctrines which obstruct the necessary reforms under the guise of a false liberty, and those which subordinate the basic rights of individual persons and groups to the collective organization of production must be shown to be erroneous.

c. Citizens, on the other hand, should remember that it is their right and duty, which is also to be recognized by the civil authority, to contribute to the true progress of their own community according to their ability. Especially in under-developed areas, where all resources must urgently be employed, those who hold back their unproductive resources or who deprive their community of the material or spiritual aid that it needs — saving the personal right of migration — gravely endanger the common good.

What our document is saying is that the best system for economic freedom and expansion of personality in the economic sphere is a diffusion of ownership by all who participate in the actual production of economic goods. Pope John had already underlined this aspect in *Mater et Magistra*.

In that document, he was very cognizant of precisely this problem and suggested various ways in which this inhuman situation of the worker could be ameliorated. Labor, he insists, must concern itself not only with its private interests, but also with interests which affect the whole social body.

If we turn our attention to the social field, we see the following developments: the formation of systems of social insurance and, in some more economically advanced states, the introduction of comprehensive social security systems; in labor unions the formation of, and increasing stress on, an attitude of responsibility toward major socio-economic problems; progressive improvement of basic education; an ever wider distribution of welfare benefits; increased social mobility with a consequent lessening of class distinctions; a greater interest in world events on the part of those with an average education (*Mater,* 48).

Modern times have seen a widespread increase in worker associations organized with juridical status in many countries and across national lines. They no longer unite workers for the sake of conflict but rather for joint effort — principally in the field of collective bargaining. But we cannot fail to emphasize how imperative or at least highly opportune it is that the workers should be able freely to make their voices heard, and listened to, beyond the confines of their individual productive units and at every level of society (*Mater,* 97).

The Pope approves such participation, and in expanding his suggestions in paragraphs 97-103, he presents the most dynamic, as well as the most daring, part of the encyclical. His suggestions pass beyond "bread and butter" issues, and strike at the very heart of industrial organization. In the words of Pope John, the workers must proceed from a work contract ("bread and butter" issues such as just wages, vacations, health conditions, insurance and so on), to a contract of open participation. In paragraph 32, he explains that Leo XIII believed in such power for the worker and he assumes this power in the present encyclical. For Pope John, worker participation should ultimately end in a contract of partnership through such instruments as cooperatives, profit-sharing, shares, and stocks in the company. In *Quadragesimo Anno,* Pope Pius XI had previously mentioned similar cooperation in industrial organization, and here Pope John gives the concept added emphasis. Following the established principle of Pius XII, Pope John does not claim that this kind of participation is a natural right. But he observes that Pius XI had strongly urged such worker participation and, in paragraph 75 of *Mater et Magistra,* he suggests ways to implement this principle through self-financing by industry and workers, participation by shares, credits, and various other means of active direction and cooperation in the industry itself. Making the thought of Pius XI his own, Pope John insists that the prod-

uct of any industry is never the achievement of one or the other
party alone: it is the fruit of both the employer's and the
employee's labor. When these aspects of the Pope's theology of
work are considered, the concept of *laissez-faire* capitalism is
directly condemned, as is the theory that only the profit motive
regulates industry. Because the workers are co-producers of the
product, they are entitled to a greater profit for their labor; it
must not all accrue to the owners of industry.

> In this connection, we must recall the principle proposed
> by our predecessor Pius XI in *Quadragesimo Anno:* "It is
> totally false to ascribe to capital alone or to labor alone that
> which is obtained by the joint effort of the one and the other.
> And it is flagrantly unjust that either should deny the efficacy
> of the other and seize all the profits" (76).
> Experience suggests that this demand of justice can be met
> in many ways. One of these, and among the most desirable,
> is to see to it that the workers, in the manner most suitable,
> are able to participate in the ownership of the enterprise itself.
> For today, more than in the times of our predecessor, "every
> effort . . . must be made that at least in the future a just share
> only of the fruits of production be permitted to accumulate in
> the hands of the wealthy, and that a sufficiently ample share
> be supplied to the workingmen" (77).

The Pope says this sharing "is a demand of justice" in our
day, and a matter of strict justice, not a concession by the corporation, since it is more than probable that the worker's labor
has gone into the wealth allotted to further productivity and
expansion. It is another way in which the Pope sees a more
widely diffused ownership of private property in modern society.
And while suggestions on how this is to be accomplished are
contingent, the concept of co-partnership is not; and, because
it is not, it "is a demand of justice."

Since there are many ways of actively sharing in industrial
and economic profit, the Pope does not attempt to give specific
means of accomplishing this end. The question of profit-sharing
becomes more complex when it is observed that each industry

reinvests a portion of the profits in a renovation of machinery, new construction, expansion of plants, and so on. All this necessary reinvestment is done with the profit which was earned by both industry and labor; and while it is obvious that all of the profit cannot be shared directly, part of the dividends and capital investment can be shared by such means as stocks and bonds. The workers' participation in the actual property of the concern is not merely an act of generosity or efficiency (for instance, a further incentive for more and better production), but desirable in itself as a title of justice (see paragraph 32 for the same idea). In the Pope's mind, the corporation is to become closer to what its name implies: a corporation of both workers and employers who share a mutual responsibility and dignity that proceed from the ownership of the one and same concern. Corporation, in this sense, is a true and concrete application of what the Pope means by "socialization," one of the main themes of the letter.

One of the biggest tasks in this field today is to attempt to bridge the difference between the very rich and the very poor:

66. a. To satisfy the demands of justice and equity, strenuous efforts must be made, without disregarding the rights of persons or the natural qualities of each country, to remove as quickly as possible the immense economic inequalities, which now exist and in many cases are growing and which are connected with individual and social discrimination. Likewise, in many areas, in view of the special difficulties of agriculture relative to the raising and selling of produce, country people must be helped both to increase and to market what they produce, and to introduce the necessary development and renewal and also obtain a fair income. Otherwise, as too often happens, they will remain in the condition of lower-class citizens. Let farmers themselves, especially young ones, apply themselves to perfecting their professional skill, for without it, there can be no agricultural advance.

b. Justice and equity likewise require that the mobility, which is necessary in a developing economy, be regulated in such a way as to keep the life of individuals and their families from becoming insecure and precarious. When workers come from another country or district and contribute to the economic advancement of a nation or region by their labor, all discrimination as regards wages and working conditions must be carefully avoided. All the people, moreover, above all the public authorities, must treat them not as mere tools of production but as persons, and must help them to bring their families to live with them and to provide themselves with a decent dwelling; they must also see to it that these workers are incorporated into the social life of the country or region that receives them. Employment opportunities, however, should be created in their own areas as far as possible.

    c. In economic affairs which today are subject to change, as in the new forms of industrial society in which automation, for example, is advancing, care must be taken that sufficient and suitable work and the possibility of the appropriate technical and professional formation are furnished. The livelihood and the human dignity especially of those who are in very difficult conditions because of illness or old age must be guaranteed.

This condition is too well known and was exposed by Pope John XXIII in *Mater et Magistra* (155-163). The wretched condition that exists in these poor countries cannot be over-emphasized. The statistics are familiar, and yet these impersonal lists and charts often obscure the fact that each member of each symbol represents a living, suffering, individual human being. One must visit, or at least make a strenuous empathetic leap to, the crowded streets of Bombay or the favelas of Rio de Janeiro to experience the deep feelings which this document evinces in its plea for justice. Two-thirds of the world's people are ill-fed, ill-clothed, and ill-housed. According to the most recent figures of FAO, thirty-five million people die each year from lack of food. In Pakistan alone, over 60 percent of the children die before they reach the age of three years. This whole effort is, of course, based on the equality of men and the fact that they are brothers. Since the whole of the human race is a true family under the Fatherhood of God (and this has never been seen as a simple metaphor by the Church or the popes), individual men and individual nations have a serious moral obligation to come to the economic aid of those who are less fortunate or less developed. The world's goods and resources — as we shall see more fully later — have been created for all men, and not for any particular nation; thus the patrimony of the whole human race is the sum total of all the wealth of individual nations (*Mater*, 157). Our text adds very forcefully that this elimination of poverty must come about "as quickly as possible." As for the special difficulties of the agricultural sector of society mentioned here by our document, one may consult with profit what John XXIII exposed in this regard in *Mater et Magistra* (137-148).

The document next treats of the conditions of work as well as those of leisure.

67.   a.   Human labor which is expended in the production and exchange of goods or in the performance of economic services is superior to the other elements of economic life, for the latter have only the nature of tools.

b.   This labor, whether it is engaged in independently or hired by someone else, comes immediately from the person, who as it were, stamps the things of nature with his seal and subdues them to his will. By his labor a man ordinarily supports himself and his family, is joined to his fellow men and serves them, and can exercise genuine charity and be a partner in the work of bringing divine creation to perfection. Indeed, we hold that through labor offered to God man is associated with the redemptive work of Jesus Christ, who conferred an eminent dignity on labor when at Nazareth he worked with his own hands. From this there follows for every man the duty of working faithfully and also the right to work. It is the duty of society, moreover, according to the circumstances prevailing in it, and in keeping with its role, to help the citizens to find sufficient employment. Finally, remuneration for labor is to be such that man may be furnished the means to cultivate worthily his own material, social, cultural and spiritual life and that of his dependents, in view of the function and productiveness of each one, the conditions of the factory or workshop, and the common good.

c. Since economic activity for the most part implies the associated work of human beings, any way of organizing and directing it which might be detrimental to any working men and women would be wrong and inhuman. It happens too often, however, even in our days, that workers are reduced to the level of being slaves to their own work. This is by no means justified by the so-called economic laws. The entire process of productive work, therefore, must be adapted to the needs of the person and to his way of life, above all to his domestic life, especially in respect to mothers of families always with due regard for sex and age. The opportunity, moreover, should be granted to workers to unfold their own abilities and personality through the performance of their work. Applying their time and strength to their employment with a due sense of responsibility, they should also all enjoy sufficient rest and leisure to cultivate their familial, cultural, social and religious life. They should also have the opportunity freely to develop the energies and potentialities which perhaps they cannot bring to much fruition in their professional work.

Thus the priority of work over everything else (67a). Work is an extension of man himself and, his incarnation in space and time, as it were, has a dignity of its own, superior to that of any other economic or productive goods. For our discussion of work see pp. 117-120. One thing must be added here (67b) in the generalized concept of work and that is the professional services which were expanded by John XXIII in *Mater et Magistra*.

The Pope's argument to expand the concept of private property results from his keen understanding of the new conditions in modern, economic society. Until comparatively recent times, most people lived on farms. For them, the normal means to security was a patrimony of stable capital goods which could be depended upon to provide food and shelter. Today, a man provides security for himself and his family through such things as health, survivor and old-age insurance. Above all, however, a man no longer makes his livelihood by his work on a farm; he does so by virtue of his professional skill. Over 70 percent of the people in modern Western society live in metropolitan areas and derive their livelihood directly from their professional skills. This demand for professional skill is becoming so prevalent that in the next five to ten years students without technical training, or "dropouts," will have no possibility of finding work.

This shift from the dependence on capital goods to professional skills is an important effect of socialization (see the Pope's discussion in paragraphs 59-62), and as such, is to be considered a step forward. By its very nature, socialization has been both the cause and the effect of the complexity and the enrichment of our modern civilization. Since the process of socialization has been intensified through the increasing interrelationships of professional and technical skills, these skills must now be an integral part of any consideration of modern civilization. Through these complex interrelationships, the objective culture of mankind has been enriched; that is, the objective elements such as art, architecture, painting, writing, and technology.

Finally, the Council focuses upon five points in the worthy conditions of work for the human person (67c): adaptation of work to worker; work ought not to be the subject for alienation of the worker but rather for his expansion and perfection; the conditions and organization of work ought to be accommodated to the needs of the worker insofar as this is possible — especially for family life, to the sex and age of the workers themselves. The document insists on the conditions of work for mothers of families since this is on the increase in modern society. The Council is prudent in this regard, since diverse cultures have different roles for women in the accomplishment of their tasks. Nor is it proven sociologically, that at least some work outside the home by mothers is detrimental to home life. On the contrary, it would seem that such occupations can give many mothers in modern society an expansion of their personalities and talents. Fourthly, the work itself must lead to the expansion of the personality of the worker himself, (see above, pp. 128-129). And lastly, workers need periods of rest not only to recuperate physically but mentally, spiritually, and morally as well. This is an extremely important part of the worthy conditions of work, and thus, in the words of our document, "a demand of the human person." This poses the whole problem of the proper use of leisure which our document does not develop.

The document next deals with the actual participation in the enterprise by the workers themselves:

68. a. In economic enterprises it is persons who are joined together, that is, free and independent human beings created to the image of God. Therefore, taking account of the prerogatives of each — owners or employers, management or labor — and without doing harm to the necessary unity of management, the active sharing of all in the administration and profits of these enterprises in ways to be properly determined should be promoted. Since more often, however, decisions concerning economics and social conditions, on which the future lot of the workers and of their children depends, are made not within the business itself but by institutions on a higher level, the workers themselves should have a share also in determining these conditions — in person or through freely elected delegates.

b. Among the basic rights of the human person is to be numbered the right of freely founding unions for working people. These should be able truly to represent them and to contribute to the organizing of economic life in the right way. Included is the right of freely taking part in the activity of these unions without risk of reprisal. Through this orderly participation joined to progressive economic and social formation, all will grow day by day in the awareness of their own function and responsibility, and thus they will be brought to feel that they are comrades in the whole task of economic development and in the attainment of the universal common good according to their capacities and aptitudes.

c. When, however, socio-economic disputes arise, efforts must be made to come to a peaceful settlement. Although recourse must always be had first to a sincere dialogue between the parties, the strike, nevertheless, can remain even in present-day circumstances a necessary, though ultimate, means for the defense of the workers' own rights and the fulfillment of their just desires. As soon as possible, however, ways should be sought to resume negotiations and discussions leading toward reconciliation.

We have already spoken of this in the development of the thought of *Mater et Magistra* (above, pp. 108-129). We refer the reader to that section of the commentary. What the Council insists on here is that such participation be the affair of all who contribute to the enterprise and not just of a few (v.g., investors, capitalists). It must include managers and workers as well (68a). It states the general principle and leaves the practical implementation to the ingenuity of each particular culture (v.g., profit-sharing motifs, stocks in the company, etc.). The document makes special mention of the unity of direction of the enterprise in which each takes personal responsibility for what is done in that enterprise.

As regards the traditional right of workers to form a union (68b), this is a continuation of the social teaching from Leo XIII to John XXIII. Since the natural right of such union organization has been a part of Catholic social thought, the principal means for achieving a more humanized society is for citizens to organize into small, personal groups. One of the clearest examples of individuals organizing for effective responsible action is the labor union. With the benefits of modern technology and socialization, the worker has become more cognizant of his rights as a citizen and, therefore, of his responsibilities to the total society in which he lives. Because society has an extensive influence on the worker, he must also have the power, as well as the right, to make his voice felt in its formation.

Finally, the doctrine on the right to strike after all other avenues have been closed is upheld by our document (68c). This is classical in the Church — even if she has never before spelled it out so clearly. In Spain, for instance, the strike is still illegal, so that it is timely to repeat this fundamental right of the worker. It would seem that our document strongly insists on a work by contract, and that, without it, the worker may legitimately proceed to a strike.

Next comes the teaching that the goods of this world are made for all — an indirect appeal to the rich to come to the aid of the poor. It is noteworthy that this paragraph precedes the treatment of the right to private property, because in the hierarchy of values this is the more important:

69. a. God intended the earth with everything contained in it for the use of all human beings and peoples. Thus, under the guidance of justice together with charity, created goods should be in abundance for all in an equitable manner. Whatever the forms of property may be, as adapted to the legitimate institutions of peoples, according to diverse and changeable circumstances, attention must always be paid to this universal goal of earthly goods. In using them, therefore, man should regard the external things that he legitimately possesses not only as his own but also as common in the sense that they should be able to benefit not only him but also others as well. On the other hand, the right of having a share of earthly goods sufficient for oneself and one's family belongs to everyone. The Fathers and Doctors of the Church held this opinion, teaching that men are obliged to come to the relief of the poor and to do so not merely out of their superfluous goods. If one is in extreme necessity, he has the right to procure for himself what he needs out of the riches of others. Since there are so many people prostrate with hunger in the world, this Sacred Council urges all, both individuals and governments to remember the aphorism of the Fathers, "Feed the man dying of hunger, because if you have not fed him, you have killed him," and really to share and use their earthly goods, according to the ability of each, especially by supporting individuals or peoples with the aid by which they may be able to help and develop themselves.

b. In economically less advanced societies the common destination of earthly goods is partly satisfied by means of the customs and traditions proper to the community, by which the absolute essentials are furnished to each member. An effort must be made, however, to avoid regarding certain customs as altogether unchangeable, if they no longer answer the new needs of this age. On the other hand, imprudent action should not be taken against respectable customs which, provided they are suitably adapted to present-day circumstances, do not cease to be very useful. Similarly in highly developed nations a body of social institutions dealing with protection and security can, for its own part, bring to reality the common destination of earthly goods. Family and social services, especially those that provide for culture and education, should be further promoted. When all these things are being organized, vigilance is necessary to prevent the citizens from being led into a certain inertia vis-à-vis society or from rejecting the burden of taking up office or from refusing to serve.

We have here the ancient distinction between the right of usage and the right of property. To understand Pope John's reconsideration of the concept of private property, it must be made clear that the right of usage is prior to and conditions the right to private property. God has created man as a body and a soul, an incarnate being, and as such, man has a natural right to use the world's goods for the conservation of his life, the fruition of his talents, and the protection of his health. This right precedes the right of property, and in traditional Catholic social thought, the right to property is a derivative, or a concretization, of the right of usage. In other words, the right to use material goods is fundamental and primary, while the right to own material goods is secondary and derived. The right to property exists so that an order might be established by which the right of usage is assured and guaranteed.

The right of property is a means to an end, and it is therefore subordinate to the right of usage, the end itself. Since every means is relative, the doctrine of the absolute right of private property is a grave social aberration. Clearly, then, private property must ultimately promote the right of usage. For example, large landholdings in the hands of a few Latin Americans represent a serious disorder because the right of usage is denied to the many. To correct this disorder, agrarian reform is a pressing need of social justice in many of these Latin American countries. Property is thus a social responsibility, and it must be used to promote the general welfare. The social responsibility which accrues to the right of private property is a fundamental concept in the social thought of recent popes (43). This paragraph is a clear development of the idea of Pius XII's radio message of 1941. In this message the Holy Father stated:

> Every man, as a living being gifted with reason, has in fact from nature the fundamental right to make use of the material goods of the earth, while it is left to the will of man . . . to regulate in greater detail the actuation of this right. This individual right cannot in any way be suppressed, even by other clear and undisputed rights over material goods. Undoubtedly, the natural order, deriving from God, demands also private property. . . . But all this remains subordinate to the natural scope of material goods and cannot emancipate itself from the first and fundamental right which concedes their use to all men. (On the anniversary of *Rerum Novarum*)

The words of Pius XII are clear and Pope John simply makes them his own. This concept of the right of usage is further emphasized in *Pacem in Terris:*

> The right to private property, even of production goods, also derives from the nature of man. This right, as we have elsewhere declared, is an effective aid in safeguarding the dignity of the human person and the free exercise of responsibility in all fields of endeavor. Finally, it strengthens the stability and tranquility of family life, thus contributing to the peace and prosperity of the commonwealth (21).
>
> However, it is opportune to point out that there is a social duty essentially inherent in the right of private property. This principle of social philosophy allows for such necessities in modern social life as agrarian reform, the nationalization of basic industries in case of true public need, the right of eminent domain, and civil rights legislation, which demands equal public accommodations for all citizens (22).

All of these considerations on the rights of usage do not

change or supplant the natural right to own private property, though some persons have made such a conclusion after a rapid reading of the encyclical. A closer examination, however, will show that this interpretation is not correct. On the contrary, the right to private property is more important today than ever before, and though Pope John wants to expand the concept of private property to include recent developments, his argument rests solely on traditional thought. In short, the Pope wants to show that private property is a relative right and not absolute, as the 19th century Manchesterian liberals maintained.

The Council then goes on briefly to speak about investments:

> 70. Investments, for their part, must be directed toward providing employment and sufficient income for the people both now and in the future. Whoever make decisions concerning these investments and the planning of the economy — whether they be individuals or groups or public authorities — are bound to keep these objectives in mind and to recognize their serious obligation of making sure, on the one hand, that provision be made for the necessities required for a decent life both of individuals and of the whole community and, on the other, of looking out for the future and of establishing a proper balance between the needs of present day consumption, both individual and collective, and the demands of investing for the generation to come. They should also always bear in mind the urgent needs of underdeveloped countries or regions. In monetary matters they should beware of hurting the welfare of their own country or of other countries. Care should also be taken lest the economically weak countries unjustly suffer any loss from a change in the value of money.

The riches of any economy are determined by the amount of money which is reinvested in the industry for development and expansion. This is important, but since these investments belong to individuals, there is no one to look out for public investments (parks, forests, roads, bridges, orphanages, etc.). The public authority has the sacred obligation to see to it that the public sector of investment does not suffer but rather expands to the extent of need. It is here as well that we have charity practiced on a public level where reinvestment means health and welfare for many in society. This is, above all, true of Latin America where real charity would exist, if the rich were to reinvest their money in building up their own countries instead of banking it on Wall Street. The public authority, moreover, has the obligation to provide from strict reforms to improve, protect, and facilitate such investments.

Yet the concept of private property for all is still a basic right of man:

71. a. Since property and other forms of private ownership of external goods contribute to the expression of the personality and since, moreover, they furnish one an occasion to exercise his function in society and in the economy, it is very important that the access of both individuals and communities to some ownership of external goods be fostered.

b. Private property or some ownership of external goods confers on everyone a sphere wholly necessary for the autonomy of the person and the family, and it should be regarded as an extension of human freedom. Lastly, since it adds incentives for carrying on one's function and duty, it constitutes one of the conditions for civil liberties.

c. The forms of such ownership of property are varied today and are becoming increasingly diversified. They all remain, however, a cause of security not to be underestimated, in spite of social funds, rights, and services provided by society. This is true not only of material goods but also of intangible goods such as professional skills.

d. The right of private ownership, however, is not opposed to the right inherent in various forms of public property. Goods can be transferred to the public domain only by the competent authority, according to the demands and within the limits of the common good, and with fair compensation. Furthermore, it is the right of public authority to prevent anyone from misusing his private property to the detriment of the common good.

e. By its very nature private property has a social quality

which is based on the law of the common destination of earthly goods. If this social quality is overlooked, property often becomes an occasion of a passionate desire for wealth and serious disturbances, so that a pretext is given to those who attack private property for calling the right itself into question.

f. In many underdeveloped regions there are large or even extensive rural estates which are only slightly cultivated or lie completely idle for the sake of profit, while the majority of the people either are without land or have only very small fields, and, on the other hand, it is evidently urgent to increase the productivity of the fields. Not infrequently those who are hired to work for the landowners or who till a portion of the land as tenants receive a wage or income unworthy of a human being, lack decent housing and are exploited by middlemen. Deprived of all security, they live under such personal servitude that almost every opportunity of acting on their own initiative and responsibility is denied to them and all advancement in human culture and all sharing in social and political life is forbidden to them. According to different circumstances, therefore, reforms are necessary: that income may grow, working conditions should be improved, security in employment increased, and an incentive to working on one's own initiative given. Indeed, insufficiently cultivated estates should be distributed to those who can make these lands fruitful; in this case, the necessary ways and means, especially educational aids and the right facilities for cooperative organization, must be supplied. Whenever, nevertheless, the common good requires expropriation compensation must be reckoned in equity after all the circumstances have been weighed.

Thus while the right to private property is not only subordinate to the right of usage of this world's goods, it can never be held superior to a man's right to life and the corresponding means necessary to insure that right. Yet, the right to private property — as is evidenced here — remains unchanged (see *Mater et Magistra,* 111). The essential reason for this right is always the same: it permits the expansion of the human personality in the pursuit of a stable and concrete good. The error of the nineteenth century was that the right to private property was believed to be absolute. The popes and our document insist on the social character of private property and do so in order to assure that, always and everywhere, it will serve the community in the fulfillment of the personalities of all its citizens (71a).

Our document also observes (71b) that private property guarantees human freedom and autonomy. Since it is dangerous for a man to remain totally dependent on the contemporary state which is characterized by impersonality and complex socialization, private property acts as a buffer to the all-consuming power of the state which it can have over the individual. Through private property, man has initiated his personal development and provided for his security; and "without it the fundamental manifestations of freedom are suppressed or stifled" (*Mater et Magistra*, 109). Private property is thus the clear manifestation of the individual's priority over state; and since the individual is always prior to the state by natural law, any truly free society cannot and will not unnecessarily restrict this right.

Furthermore, without this right, man is reduced to economic and personal slavery (71d). To lack freedom is not necessarily to be locked in jail; slavery is also that condition in which a man has no security for the future, and in such a condition, he cannot live in peace of mind. The right of private property is, in other words, a guarantee of freedom.

Our document also discusses other means of security in our day (71c). Since both private property and social securities conform to man's nature, both must be considered in any understanding of social justice. It is no longer possible to say that the regime of private property as traditionally expressed is *the* ideal toward which society must evolve. *De facto,* society has evolved differently, and our document takes note of this new situation: social security and public insurances are not necessarily worth less, less desirable, than private property, and vice versa.

Our document finally concludes this chapter with an attempt to relate the socio-economic activity of man with the kingdom of Christ.

72. a. Christians who take an active part in present-day socio-economic development and fight for justice and charity should be convinced that they can make a great contribution to the prosperity of mankind and to the peace of the world. In these activities let them, either as individuals or as members of groups, give a shining example. Having acquired the skills and experience which are absolutely necessary, they should observe the right order in their earthly activities in faithfulness to Christ and his gospel. Thus their whole life, both individual and social, will be permeated with the spirit of the beatitudes, notably with a spirit of poverty.

b. Whoever in obedience to Christ seeks first the Kingdom of God, takes therefrom a stronger and purer love for helping all his brethren and for perfecting the work of justice under the inspiration of charity.

Once again we return to the privileged area of the apostolate of the layman where he must bring the principles of justice and charity to bear on the social order, both collectively and individually. Laymen can thus contribute to fraternal love in a very true — and in our day — in a very important manner. In this way, they can also make a contribution to the peace of the world. The Council explicitly cites the evangelical texts in this regard: Luke 3:11, 10:30, 16:1-3; Matt 5:3, 6:34; Mark 8:66, 12:29; Jer 5:1; Phil 4:25; 2 Cor 8:13; 1 Tim 6:8. All these texts are concerned with the love of our brothers realized in concrete actions of giving to the poor of what we have. In today's world, Christians exercise this charity both as individuals and as a collectivity, working in the public forum to achieve justice and therefore love of the brothers. The whole of the economic life must be permeated by this spirit of fraternal, Christian love.

CHAPTER 4

The Life of the Political Community

Christians cannot afford to be disinterested in the political life. "All Christians must take account of their own special vocation in the political community; they must present an example by developing in themselves a sense of responsibility for, and dedication to, the common good." The Constitution also recommends that "those who are, or can become, adapted to the service of the political art, which is so difficult, but at the same time so noble, should prepare themselves and be ready to exercise it without regard to their own interests or material benefits" (75e).

The Christian is therefore called to assume political responsibility according to his capabilities and his availability. It is a duty which, if he is in any way capable, he must not shirk. This political activity must not be guided by personal ambition, by the pursuit of success at all costs, or by the thirst for power and gain; since for the Christ, politics is a service and, as Pope Pius XI said, "the field of the greatest charity, the political charity." But he will, of course, bring to the field of politics passion and enthusiasm, cultural and professional preparation, and moral dedication, without dousing his own aspirations — a good measure of ambition is necessary, and without a desire for success, one cannot make politics a life vocation. He must, however, purify this ambition in the fires of charity.

Our document begins with a general description of the political life today:

73. a. In our day, profound changes are apparent also in the structure and institutions of peoples. These result from their cultural, economic and social evolution. Such changes have a great influence on the life of the political community, especially regarding the rights and duties of all in the exercise of civil freedom and in the attainment of the common good, and in organizing the relations of citizens among themselves and with respect to public authority.

b. The present keener sense of human dignity has given rise in many parts of the world to attempts to bring about a politico-juridical order which will give better protection to the rights of the person in public life. These include the right freely to meet and form associations, the right to express one's own opinions and to profess one's religion both publicly and privately. The protection of rights of a person is indeed a necessary condition so that citizens, individually or collectively, can take an active part in the life and government of the state.

c. Along with cultural, economic and social development, there is a growing desire among many people to play a greater part in organizing the life of the political community. In the conscience of many there arises an increasing concern that the rights of minorities be recognized, without any neglect for their duties toward the political community. In addition, there is a steady growing respect for men of other opinions or other religions. At the same time, there is wider cooperation to guarantee the actual exercise of personal rights to all citizens, and not only to a few privileged individuals.

d. However, those political systems, prevailing in some parts of the world are to be reproved which hamper civic or religious freedom, victimize large numbers through avarice and political crimes, and divert the exercise of authority from the service of the common good to the interests of one or another faction or of the rulers themselves.

e. There is no better way to establish political life on a truly human basis than by fostering an inward sense of justice and kindliness, and of service to the common good, and by strengthening basic convictions as to the true nature of the political community and the purpose, right exercise, and sphere of action of public authority.

Pope John already analyzed the relationship of citizens to each other (Part I, *Pacem in Terris*) and to the state (Part II). Both of these are covered in 73b and 73c, respectively. The essential order of peace in the civil community is one of guarantee of civil and human rights of which men of our day are becoming increasingly aware. The second is characterized by a greater participation by all citizens in the decision-making process of government. This guarantee of civil liberties is "a necessary condition so that citizens, individually and collectively, can take an active part in the life and government of the state" (73b). This was emphasized in *Pacem* (73-74):

> It is in keeping with their dignity as persons that human beings should take an active part in government although the manner in which they share in it will depend on the level of development of the political community to which they belong.

The essential function of government is to promote and protect the civil rights of its citizens (73b). To understand this personalistic concept of man's rights, the nature of these rights must be examined closely. It is evident that the subject of these rights is the human person himself, because he has intelligence and free will making him capable of and responsible for the realization of his moral destiny. They are *universal* because they belong to all citizens; they are not arbitrary "gifts" of the state but rather pertain to what man essentially is, and to his fulfillment as a human person. They are *inviolate* and *inalienable*, because each person has a destiny which no one else can fulfill for him; and if each man must fulfill his destiny, he must have the means, ensured by his fundamental rights, to do so. It is, therefore, only the individual person who is subject of these rights, and the law and the state exist only to promote and to safeguard these rights in the city of man. Our document gives us a partial list of these rights — free association, freedom of speech and publication, and so on. A more complete list can be found in *Pacem,* 11-34. *The Declaration on Religious Liberty* of Vatican II dealt more particularly with the freedom of conscience and religion as did *Pacem* before it. Thus in paragraph 2 the *Declaration* says:

> This Synod . . . declares that the right to religious freedom has its foundation in the very dignity of the human person, as this dignity is known through the revealed Word of God and by reason itself. This right of the human person to religious freedom is to be recognized in the constitutional law whereby society is governed. Thus it is to become a civil right.

Participation in civil life is to be encouraged (73c) and promoted not only from above by civil authorities but also from below by intermediary and voluntary organizations of the citizens. Pope John dealt with this as a chief characteristic of the free society. This would include organizations such as labor unions which make their voice and interest felt even in government; free political parties would promote various programs for the common good, and so on. Among these are a participation in the political community as such, concern over the rights of minorities, respect for and toleration of differing opinions in the pluralistic society which is a characteristic of the present day. This would imply an active participation and engagement in the affairs of the political community and not simply a passive acquiescence, which results, in reality, from an indifference to the political process. This is, indeed, unworthy of the Christian.

"Pluralistic society" is used as a term by the document itself (76) and is presupposed to be the general rule today and a condition in which Christians must exercise their apostolate. We shall see more of this later when the document deals *ex professo* with this question.

As to the rights of minorities, the encyclical *Pacem in Terris* gave a good section to the question:

> The demands of justice are admirably observed by those

civil authorities who promote the general welfare of those citizens belonging to a smaller ethnic group, particularly as regards their language, the development of their natural gifts, their ancestral customs, and their accomplishments and endeavors in the economic order (96; also 94-95; 97).

Our present text also stresses the duties of minority groups, as well, since they can make exaggerated demands of those same authorities which would seriously endanger the common good. They have a tendency to exaggerate their qualities as a gesture of self-defense and this ought to be guarded against. It is the right and duty of the public authority to harmonize (not uniformize) all for the greater common good of the civil body. Minor groups must prevent all closing in upon themselves and must recognize certain fundamental, universal, common values which must be brought into harmony with their own particular values. As a matter of fact, with the close and rapid interchange of customs and ideas on an international plane, this assimilation of various cultural aspects and customs can lead to a further enrichment of minority groups. Thus, toleration and communication are the chief characteristics of various ethnic and cultural groups on a national and international scale.

Finally (73e), we have mention of the two characteristics which will best promote the political community of any society: a sense of justice and "kindliness" (*benevolentia*). This latter term comes from the tolerance and respect which citizens have one for another and which therefore results in harmony and peace despite differences on a civic (or other) level. This is not merely a "tolerance" from a negative point of view but proceeds further to a respect for the dignity of the sacred personality of those who differ from us, either politically, socially, or even religiously.

The Council now turns its attention to the very nature and end of the political community:

74. a. Men, families and the various groups which make up

the civil community are aware that they cannot achieve a truly human life by their own unaided efforts. They see the need for a wider community, within which each one makes his specific contribution every day toward an ever broader realization of the common good. For this purpose they set up a political community which takes various forms. The political community exists, consequently, for the sake for the common good, in which it finds its full justification and significance, and the source of its inherent legitimacy. Indeed, the common good embraces the sum of those conditions of the social life whereby men, families and associations more adequately and readily may attain their own perfection.

b. Yet the people who come together in the political community are many and diverse, and they have every right to prefer divergent solutions. If the political community is not to be torn apart while everyone follows his own opinion, there must be an authority to direct the energies of all citizens toward the common good, not in a mechanical or despotic fashion, but by acting above all as a moral force which appeals to each one's freedom and sense of responsibility.

c. It is clear, therefore, that the political community and public authority are founded on human nature and hence belong to the order designed by God, even though the choice of a political regime and the appointment of rulers are left to the free will of citizens.

d. It follows also that political authority, both in the community as such and in the representative bodies of the state, must always be exercised within the limits of the moral order and directed toward the common good — with a dynamic concept of that good — according to the juridical order legitimately established or which should be established. When authority is so exercised, citizens are bound in conscience to obey. Accordingly, the responsibility, dignity and importance of leaders are indeed clear.

e. But where citizens are oppressed by a public authority overstepping its competence, they should not protest against those things which are objectively required for the common good; but it is legitimate for them to defend their own rights and the rights of their fellow citizens against the abuse of this authority, while keeping within those limits drawn by the natural law and the gospels.

f. According to the character of different peoples and this historic development, the political community can, however, adopt a variety of concrete solutions in its structures and the organization of public authority. For the benefit of the whole human family, these solutions must always contribute to the formation of a type of man who will be cultivated, peace-loving and well-disposed towards all his fellow men.

The first observation (74a) is that government is not a product of sin or war of all against all, but a demand of human nature in order for man to reach his perfection in society. This follows the teaching in *Pacem,* 46-52. There the Pope taught that authority is a good because man, *being* social by nature, needs to have his rights coordinated, protected, and promoted. The Pope rejected the theory which regards government and political authority as something sinister or at least a necessary evil. Authority is not a social convention or contract in the Rousseau-sense of the word; it originates in the moral order and is a necessary element in any human society. This is the Thomistic tradition and is taken up here by our document — *homo non se sufficit.* It finds its full justification in and for the common good of the citizens in the manner of an instrument. It cannot supplant the citizen; it can only aid him to attain his end and facilitate his becoming more humanly perfect by the development and the exercise of his originality. A person then, in government, has authority inasmuch as he is a mediator between people and the exigencies of the ends which these people must attain. In other words, every organ of authority is at the service of others. That is why the heads of government are called ministers. Christ gave the perfect definition of authority when he said: "I have come not to be ministered to, but to minister. Whoever wishes to be first among you must be the servant of all" (Mark 10:44-45). The priest has his ministry, the government has its ministers, and all institutions have their administrations. Therefore, in reality, it is the sense of justice and love which is the driving force behind the vast machinery of government, and not force. The citizens who see this, obey from a sense of moral obligation. What is forced cannot be a virtue. The essence of this common good is above all the guarantee and promotion of the rights and the freedoms of its citizens. *Pacem* was most emphatic on this point. The government must guarantee and sometimes limit and coordinate these rights for the good of all.

Men of good will in the same society may well differ in the solutions brought to various problems facing the political community (74b). It will be the function of the public authority to reconcile and coordinate all to a common end or good. This present distinction of the decision-making process by the authority, comes after the discussion of the broader concept of the community which is much larger and is logically anterior to state authority. Authority exists as a means to an end — in this case, to *serve* and coordinate the larger community where men find their fullest development. Thus as we have explained, it is a "moral force" in the affairs of men and not simply " a force." The end of authority determines the competence and limits of authority, and the persons who are to obtain this end determine the amount of authority which must be used. Those under authority must act on their own initiative. The organ of authority must never crush personal initiative but should always be in the service of it. There are, therefore, certain principles which the organ of authority is to remember: it must respect the personal initiative of others; it must supplement initiative when necessary; it must orientate initiative when it deviates from the right course; and it must use force if necessary, but only as a last resort. He who exercises authority is therefore the mediator between what this person or community wishes to, or must, realize. In this light (74d), authority is moral in nature and citizens are bound in conscience to obey its legitimate directives. Pope John was able to write in *Pacem:*

> When the authority uses as its only or its chief means either threats and fear of punishment or promises of rewards, it cannot effectively move men to promote the common good of all.

Even if it did so move them, this would be altogether opposed to their dignity as men, endowed with reason and free will. As authority is chiefly concerned with moral force, it follows that civil authority must appeal primarily to the conscience of individual citizens . . . (48).

This authority proceeds from a demand of human nature (74c) and not simply from a contract instituted among men. Its appeal to conscience is willed by God. One cannot find here the least approval of that totalitarian and dictatorial power which finds its moral force solely in the will of the leader or chief of state. He is but a minister of the common good and must base his decisions not on what he wants, but on what is objectively demanded by the common good. One must, therefore, be very careful in the use of "all authority is from God." The question of resistance to tyrannical government will be treated in the following paragraph and such a discussion is rather rare in ecclesiastical documents. We now proceed to the actual collaboration of citizens in public life:

75. a. It is in full conformity with human nature that there should be juridico-political structures providing all citizens in an ever better fashion and without any discrimination the practical possibility of freely and actively taking part in the establishment of the juridical foundations of the political community and in the direction of public affairs, in fixing the terms of reference of the various public bodies and in the election of political leaders. All citizens, therefore, should be mindful of the right and also the duty to use their free vote to further the common good. The Church praises and esteems the work of these who for the good of men devote themselves to the service of the state and take on the burdens of this office.

b. If the citizens' responsible cooperation is to produce the good results which may be expected in the normal course of political life, there must be a statute of positive law providing for a suitable division of the functions and bodies of authority and an efficient and independent system for the protection of rights. The rights of all persons, families and groups, and their practical application, must be recognized, respected and furthered, together with the duties binding on all citizens. Among the latter, it will be well to recall the duty of rendering the political community such material and personal services as are required by the common good. Rulers must be careful not to hamper the development of family, social or cultural groups, nor that of intermediate bodies or organizations, and not to deprive them of opportunities for legitimate and constructive activity; they should willingly seek rather to promote the orderly pursuit of such activity. Citizens, for their part, either individually or collectively, must be careful not to attribute excessive power to public authority, not to make exaggerated and untimely demands upon it in their own interests, lessening in this way the responsible role of persons, families and social groups.

c. The complex circumstances of our day make it necessary for public authority to intervene more often in social, economic and cultural matters in order to bring about favorable conditions which will give more effective help to the citizens and groups in their free pursuit of man's total well-being. The relations, however, between socialization and the autonomy and development of the person can be understood in different ways according to various regions and the evolution of peoples. But when the exercise of rights is restricted temporarily for the common good, freedom should be restored immediately upon change of circumstances. Moreover, it is inhuman for public authority to fall back on dictatorial systems or totalitarian methods which violate the rights of the person or social group.

d. Citizens must cultivate a generous and loyal spirit of patriotism, but without being narrow-minded. This means that they will always direct their attention to the good of the whole human family, united by the different ties which bind together races, peoples and nations.

e. All Christians must be aware of their own specific vocation within the political community. It is for them to give an example by their sense of responsibility and their service of the common good. In this way they are to demonstrate concretely how authority can be compatible with freedom, personal initiative with the solidarity of the whole social organism, and the advantages of unity with fruitful diversity. They must recognize the legitimacy of different opinions with regard to temporal solutions, and respect citizens who, even as a group, defend their points of view by honest methods. Political parties,

for their part, must promote those things which in their judgment are required for the common good; it is never allowable
to give their interests priority over the common good.

f. Great care must be taken with regard to civic and
political formation, which is of the utmost necessity today for
the population as a whole, and especially for youth, so that all
citizens can play their part in the life of the political community. Those who are suited or can become suited should
prepare themselves for the difficult, but at the same time, the
very noble art of politics and should seek to practice this art
without regard for their own interests or for material advantages.
With integrity and wisdom, they must take action against any
form of injustice and tyranny, against arbitrary domination
by an individual or a political party, and any intolerance. They
should dedicate themselves to the services of all with sincerity
and fairness, indeed, with the charity and fortitude demanded
by political life.

The document is clear: all citizens have the *obligation* to
participate in public life (75a). The text actually demands institutions which will promote participation on the part of all
its citizens. Its justification comes from human nature itself.
The reason for this is clear: when citizens participate, authority
becomes less an external force and more of a personal engagement of the citizen in his own destiny, which, indeed, is a moral
obligation of the human person. In this way, power becomes
more human and more responsible for the individual citizen.
Our submission to the political order is, in a sense, a yielding to
a greater good than our individual selves — but it can never be
to a greater good which would be foreign to ourselves. No
alienation is possible here, since we ourselves are engaged in
the very political act. The common good is our good, and
society also exists for our personal perfection.

The Council next opts for the same as did Pope John in
Pacem concerning the division of powers (75b). Pope John
was very emphatic in this respect.

We consider, however, that it is in keeping with the innate
demands of human nature that the state should take a form

which embodies the threefold division of powers corresponding to the three principal functions of public authority . . . this in itself affords protection to the citizens both in the enjoyment of their rights and in the fulfillment of their duties (68).

For the first time, such praise for the democratic process has been incorporated in a Church document as authoritative as an encyclical. Our document follows suit here. Thus democratic form of government — along with its division of powers — is explicitly accepted by our text. The threefold division of governmental powers — legislative, executive, and judicial — is a modern form dating from the eighteenth century, that found expression in France in Montesquieu, and earlier in the English tradition. In this concept, the limits of the public authority are generally written into laws, constitutions, bills of rights, and other public documents to insure the rights of all citizens more effectively. Officials are not to overstep the bounds set by these limiting ordinances (*Pacem*, 76). In the division of power, the Pope saw a protection against abuses by public officials and a surer guarantee of the rights of the citizen. In the Western tradition of democratic government, each division acts as a check and a balance to the others, thus preventing any one division from usurping complete power. "A government by laws, and not by men" went the old adage of the "far West."

In a most discreet way (75c) our document tries to take into account the non-Western traditional method by which the public authority can and should intervene in the affairs of the community at large. Thus the way is open to a more or less greater opportunity for intervention by the state (see our discussion of this on pp. 238-239). There must be as much freedom as possible (the general rule) with as much intervention as is truly compatible with the common good. Two extremes must be avoided in this regard: totalitarianism (the state runs everything), and liberalism (private interest groups rule all) — to the detriment of the general good of the citizens.

Then we have outlined for us the obligations of the Christian in the political order. History has shown that they — more than other men — have been most intolerant on both a political as well as on a religious plane (75d, e).

But once the Christian has pledged himself to the political life, what sort of politics is he to make? A "Christian" politics? Evidently, a Christian cannot make politics that are not in accord with his own Christian commitment. But what does this commitment mean in terms of political activity, and in which sense can we still speak of "Christian" or "evangelical" politics?

Some facts must be cleared first: a Christian who makes politics does not act as a fiduciary of the Church in a religious society, nor is he a deputy of such a one; he is not a spokesman of the Church, here to protect her interests, neither the material ones nor the spiritual ones. He has not received any mandate whatsoever from the Church since she is not in a position to give a political "mandate." He acts only in his own name and in his political actions pledges only himself and must follow his own conscience. It is true that the Church plays a great and decisive role in the formation of his conscience through her social teachings, and through the moral judgments which she gives about matters concerning the political order. Thus, in his political actions, the Christian can never ignore these teachings and cannot absent himself from moral judgments. The social doctrine of the Church and her moral judgments which she delivers in the political order do not refer to the technical aspects of the political, social, or economic problems, since the Church has no competence in political technique and concrete choices. In such cases the Christian is independent of the Church and must follow solely his own conscience. It is evident that he must keep the social teachings of the Church and her moral judgments in mind while acting in the political sphere, but the application of these teachings and moral judgments to concrete cases is his task, and he must follow the dictates of his own conscience on the one hand, and the dictates of his professional competence, on the other. Being independent in his political choices, the Christian must attain inspiration for his actions from the social doctrine of the Church and from her moral judgments, and attempt to effect and actuate the political life according to them.

The document concludes by emphasizing the seriousness with which the political vocation must be taken by all citizens of society (74f). These directives are not simply intended for the rulers of a society but for all its citizens, who are principally responsible for their own political destinies. Included in this is the fight against injustice, discrimination, oppression, absolutism, and intolerance; included also is the struggle for personal and professional integrity, sincerity, generosity, charity and political courage. All these qualities, of course, are needed to an even greater degree by him who would exercise the function of public official.

Finally, we come to the relationship between the political authority and the Church:

76. a. It is very important, especially where a pluralistic society prevails, that there be a correct notion of the relationship between the political community and the Church, and a clear distinction between the tasks which Christians undertake, individually or as a group, on their own responsibility as citizens guided by the dictates of a Christian conscience, and the activities which, in union with their pastors, they carry out in the name of the Church.

b. The Church, by reason of her role and competence, is not identified in any way with the political community nor bound to any political system. She is at once a sign and a safeguard of the transcendent character of the human person.

c. The Church and the political community in their own fields are autonomous and independent from each other. Yet both, under different titles, are devoted to the personal and social vocation of the same men. The more that both foster healthier cooperation between themselves with due consideration for the circumstances of time and place, the more effectively will their service be exercised for the good of all. For man's horizons are not limited only to the temporal order; while living in the context of human history, he preserves intact his eternal vocation. The Church, for her part, founded on the love of the Redeemer, contributes toward the reign of justice and charity within the borders of a nation and between nations. By preaching the truths of the gospel, and bringing to bear on all fields of human endeavor the light of her doctrine and of a Christian witness, she respects and fosters the political freedom and responsibility of citizens.

d. The Apostles, their successors and those who cooperate with them, are sent to announce to mankind Christ, the Savior. Their apostolate is based on the power of God, who very often shows forth the strength of the gospel in the weakness of its witnesses. All those dedicated to the ministry of God's Word must use the ways and means proper to the gospel which in a great many respects differ from the means proper to the earthly city.

e. There are, indeed, close links between earthly things and those elements of man's condition which transcend the world. The Church herself makes use of temporal things insofar as her own mission requires it. She, for her part, does not place her trust in the privileges offered by civil authority. She will even give up the exercise of certain rights which have been legitimately acquired, if it becomes clear that their use will cast doubt on the sincerity of her witness or that new ways of life demand new methods. It is only right, however, that all times and in all places, the Church should have true freedom to preach the faith, to teach her social doctrine, to exercise her role freely among men, and also to pass moral judgment in those matters which concern public order when the fundamental rights of a person or the salvation of souls require it. In this she makes use of all the means — but only those — which accord with the gospel and which correspond to the general good with due regard to the diverse circumstances of time and place.

f. While faithfully adhering to the gospel and fulfilling her mission to the world, the Church, whose duty it is to foster and elevate all that is found to be true, good and beautiful in the human community, strengthens peace among men for the glory of God.

Here we have two distinct problems: the relationship between Church and state (a very old problem indeed); and, as we have explained above, the distinction which ought to exist between a Christian's actions in his own name and those performed in the name of the Church. In the former, the Christian is free to propose various and even differing solutions to the concrete and practical problems of the civic order. Here, as we have said, what is needed above all in a pluralistic society (76a) is the virtue of tolerance and respect for the personalities of others. And yet, the Christian must take inspiration from his faith.

He must not aim at a certain type of integration. The intention of "Christian politics" can no longer be the establishment of a *civitas christiana* or a *civitas Dei*; that is the construction of a "Christian" order, somehow imposed from above, where everything would conform to the dictates of Christian faith and morals, in the laws and institutions as well as in practical life. The act of faith is, in fact, free, and Christian morals bring with them needs which are unacceptable to the non-Christian. It is impossible to impose a social and political order, in harmony with Christian faith and morals, upon a world which does not accept Christianity. On the other hand, the state and politics are secular, terrestrial, and lay realities which have as an end the temporal common good, not the attainment of a supernatural goal of man; they must not be opposed to the reaching of this goal and they should even, to some extent, favor. Their direct goal, however, is not the propagation of faith and the advancement of Christian morals. What then, is the aim of Christian politics? It is the creation of a human social and political order which is able to safeguard the dignity of the person and at the same time advance its development by being open to the supernatural. In order to explain the meaning of this "opening to the supernatural," we may recall what was said in *Pacem in Terris,* where Christians are urged to "prepare themselves in the light of faith and with the force of love, so that institutions of economic, social, cultural, and political nature should not create any obstacles, but rather facilitate, or render less difficult, perfection for all people, in the natural order as well as in the supernatural one" (147). Further on, the same encyclical notes that "in national communities of Christian tradition, the institutions of the temporal order, though they surround themselves with a high degree of scientific-technological perfection and with great efficiency with respect to their respective aims, are often characterized by the paucity of ferment and Christian accents" (152). Therefore, it will be the task of Christian politicians to make an effort to inject into political life and political realizations this "ferment and Christian accents."

The Church, however, can never be identified with any one particular political system (76b), and yet this does not mean she is indifferent to the character of the various regimes. Her doctrine, it is evident, is not and cannot be compatible with every political regime (totalitarianism). She encourages, from a positive point of view, active and free participation by the citizens in the political affairs of their own destiny; and papal documents make it clear how much compatibility there is between Christian teaching and any truly democratic regime (see *Pacem*, 52). Her principal function in the political order is to bear continuous witness to the essential dignity of the human person.

Then we have, once again, the general principle of the independence of Church and state (76c) with the point of interdependence being stressed as well. There must be cooperation between them, since it is the same human person who is both citizen and Christian; and, as we have seen, there can be no conflict between these two roles as one should inspire the other in the spirit of justice and of love. The natural development of a man does not exclude but, on the contrary, calls for the supernatural expansion of the human person in the totality of his vocation as willed by God. In the present economy of salvation, these two are aspects of the very reality of the unique vocation of man by God. Hence, there is an interdependence between the two (politics and Christianity), in the way we have exposed this above (pp. 277-278). The Church does not pronounce on any "ideal" situation normalizing this relationship (v.g., concordats, separation, union). There can be no ideal here (contrary to what many canonists thought until very recently), but it must be left to proper circumstances and times. What is good for one country will not be for another "with due consideration for the circumstances of place and time." This has given the Church more freedom than any other period of her history (see opening talk of John XXIII to the Council Fathers, October 11, 1962).

The document then shows clearly how different are the ways of accomplishing her tasks by the Church from those of the political order (76d). She bears witness to the dignity and the divine vocation of man in a completely nonviolent and free way — in the manner of the gospels. Christ appeals there by signs, by example, by service, and by poverty; he constrained man in no way whatsoever. It is essentially this very same type of witness which the Church uses toward the world and the political order. She must continuously bear witness by her example to the complete gift of self in love, in disinterested love, to the needs of the person of modern man, irrespective, as the document stated earlier, of race, color, creed and national origin. She does this for her own children by a correct formation of conscience regarding service they must bring to the political order *for the love of men.*

CHAPTER 5

The Fostering of Peace and the Promotion of a Community of Nations

It is, perhaps this chapter of the Constitution which was awaited with the greatest anticipation by the whole world. Thus, in a sense, the expectations of the world, both Catholic and non-Catholic, were too great for any Council to fulfill. The reason is clear: the Council in any ecclesiastical document cannot give men a ready-made blueprint for their manifold ills. The most it can do is give some general principles, encouragement, and an intense hope that in these tasks and agonies of men, Christians will cooperate to the fullest extent of their power. That is why the Council, in its very first paragraph of this chapter, was able to say that it "wishes passionately to summon Christians to cooperate, under the help of Christ, the author of peace, with all men in securing among themselves a peace based on justice and love and in setting up the instruments of peace" (77b). This entire chapter will be such an encouragement on the part of the Catholic Church.

At the Council itself, there was a strong division among the Fathers on how to formulate our text. It was a touchy problem, indeed, since many of the Fathers were of the opinion that the traditional theory of the "just war" was dead-letter for the modern world — not in the sense that it was no longer applicable, at least in its general contours, but in the sense that there hasn't yet been a war in which this limitation of violence has been applied. The only limitation to violence in war, thus far, has been the judgment of the less scrupulous party who was quickly followed by his adversary. The Council itself recognized this feeling of many bishops when it bluntly said after examination of the facts of modern war: "All these considerations compel us to undertake an evaluation of war with an entirely new attitude" (80b). It was among these Fathers that we find a strong desire for a prophetical text for this chapter; that is, that mankind has now reached the moral consensus, that given these facts of history, the methods of modern war and the willingness of men of the great powers to use them, man has made war an absurdity with the result that the Council should solemnly proscribe and anathematize all wars. They took very seriously the words of John XXIII in *Pacem in Terris:* "It is humanly impossible to think that war can be — in an atomic age — the adequate means for restoring violated rights" (127).

Another group of Fathers wanted a more practical pastoral text which would examine the world as it is and after such a realistic analysis, proceed by degrees to the ideal on which all of the Fathers were agreed upon, namely, the proscription of all wars in the affairs of men. This group argued that "anathemas" would really accomplish nothing and give men no practical orientations during this dangerous period when "the whole human family faces an hour of supreme crisis in its advance toward maturity" (77a). Moreover, the intention of both John XXIII and Paul VI in summoning the Council was precisely to avoid all forms of condemnation, but rather to bring healing and practical suggestions for the actual accomplishment of this goal: peace. Besides, condemnations will accomplish nothing, leaving men of good will without any positive orientation from the Church on the concrete problems which they must face in the world *such as it exists.* We have here a type of practical and politico-religious realism which, in fact, is reflected in our present text. Not that the prophetical has been

entirely eliminated, for we shall see that many of their animad-
versions were incorporated into our present text (praise of non-
violence, conscientious objection, condemnation of all forms of
total war, etc.). In the final analysis, however, our present document has chosen to confront the world as it is, to attempt to
limit its present violence, and by small gradations to move
toward the ideal which both groups agree should be the final
object of this section: love and justice giving rise to true peace
with a total proscription of war as a fit means of restoring
violated rights (international agreements on prisoners and non-
combatants, international organizations leading to stronger international political authority, and above all, eliminating the
causes of war such as poverty and misery — to which the whole
last third of this chapter is dedicated). It was this type of moral
persuasion which the Council Fathers hoped to accomplish with
the present chapter and, to a great degree, it is reminiscent of
the momentous talk of Paul VI before the UN on October 4,
1965, where the Pope outlined the same paradoxes contained in
our document: anxiety and hope, the futility of war and the
right of a nation to self-defense, the poverty of millions which
directly threatens the peace, and the enormous sums spent on
arms and means of destruction. Thus in the words of the Pope:

> You are a network of relations between states. We would
> almost say that your chief characteristic is a reflection, as it
> were, in the temporal field, of what our Catholic Church
> aspires to be in the spiritual field: unique and universal. In
> the ideological construction of mankind, there is on the natural
> level nothing superior to this. Your vocation is to make
> brothers not only of some, but of all peoples. A difficult under-
> taking, indeed; but this it is, your most noble undertaking.
> Is there anyone who does not see the necessity of coming thus
> progressively to the establishment of a world authority, able
> to act effectively on the political and juridical levels?
>
> . . . .
>
> Many words are not needed to proclaim this loftiest aim
> of your institution. It suffices to remember that the blood of

millions of men, that numberless and unheard of sufferings, useless slaughter and frightful ruin are the sanction of the pact which unites you, with an oath which must change the future history of the world. No more war, war never again. Peace, it is peace which must guide the destinies of people and of all mankind.

.   .   .   .

Peace, as you know, is not built up only by means of politics, by the balance of forces and of interests. It is constructed with the mind, with ideas, with the works of peace. You labor in this great construction. But you are still at the beginning. Will the world ever succeed in changing that selfish and bellicose mentality which, up to now, has been interwoven in so much of its history? It is hard to foresee; but it is easy to affirm that it is toward that new history, a peaceful, truly human history, as promised by God to all men of good will, that we must absolutely march. The roads thereto are already well-marked out for you; and the first is that of disarmament. If you wish to be brothers, let the arms fall from your hands. One cannot love while holding offensive arms. Those armaments, especially those terrible arms which modern science has given you, long before they produce victims and ruins, nourish bad feelings, create nightmares, distrust, and somber resolutions; they demand enormous expenditures; they obstruct projects of union and useful collaboration; they falsify the psychology of peoples.

As long as man remains that weak, changeable and even wicked being that he often shows himself to be, defensive arms will, unfortunately, be necessary. You, however, in your courage and valiance, are studying the ways of guaranteeing the security of international life, without having recourse to arms.

It is remarkable how our present text has taken each of these themes and woven them into this fifth section and it is in the spirit of this talk of the Pope before the UN — practical but at once tending toward the ideal of elimination of all wars from the affairs of men — that this section is orientated. Practical and workable steps toward the ideal of total and universal peace. The mentality of men must change as a precondition of a sound peace, and it is toward this goal that the energies of all men of good will, but especially of Christians, must be directed. Too often in the past, Catholic moral theology has been overly concerned with a limitation of violence (a good thing in itself which remains in our present document), but not preoccupied with the constructions and progressive methods toward peace. It is this change of mentality and orientation which the present document hopes to accomplish by its moral persuasion. Thus it begins the chapter:

> 77. a. In our generation when men continue to be afflicted by acute hardships and anxieties arising from the ravages of war or the threat of it, the whole human family faces an hour of supreme crisis in its advance toward maturity. Moving gradually together and everywhere more conscious already of its unity, this family cannot accomplish its task of constructing for all men everywhere a world more genuinely human unless each person devotes himself to the cause of peace with renewed vigor. Thus it happens that the gospel message, which is in harmony with the loftier strivings and aspirations of the human race, takes on a new luster in our day as it declares that the artisans of peace are blessed "because they will be called the sons of God" (Matt 5:9).
>
> b. Consequently, as it points out the authentic and noble meaning of peace and condemns the frightfulness of war, the Council wishes passionately to summon Christians to cooperate, under the help of Christ, the author of peace, with all men in securing among themselves a peace based on justice and love and in setting up the instruments of peace.

This solicitude for peace at an international level has been emphasized time and again by the Popes over the past 50 years, from Benedict XV, and above all by Pope John XXIII in his encyclical on peace, *Pacem in Terris*. The reason is quite simple: mankind has come to a turning point in its history; it has reached a real crisis, since men and nations are becoming and have already become interdependent on an international level economically, socially, culturally, and even politically by that process which Pope John called "socialization" (*Mater et*

Magistra, 18), and which was outlined by our document in many other sections of its exposition of the modern situation (see 6e, 25b, 42c, 54). We have already seen this important concept in our introduction and elsewhere (cf. pp. 19-20). We have said that this concept embraces a global and universal interaction of persons and things, a complicated intertwining of many and varied relationships in the economic, social, political, and technological fields. Since these relationships affect all nations and peoples, men have been more universally and socially dependent on each other in a way undreamed of in past history. This phenomenon seems to be permanent and irreversible and that is what the Council refers to when it speaks of humanity's "advance toward maturity" (*in suae maturitatis processu*). Men have come to that point harmonization of the globe which is no longer a dream but a fact, and with it have come the concomitant dangers of total ruin and destruction by weapons which this same science and technology have given us. Thus, once again, the terrible ambiguities of modern times and the necessity of a new attitude, of a new mentality on how to solve the differences between nations on an international level other than war. Another war will and can only mean total obliteration of victor and vanquished alike. As John Kennedy once said, victory will only be "ashes in our mouth." That is why the Council "passionately" wishes to turn men from the traditional mentality of redress of grievances by war and violence toward a whole new concept of international morality in the relationship between nations. It is in this way that we can see today more than ever before in man's history the deeper connotations of the evangelical message of peace emphasized by Christ in the beatitudes, and so long neglected by the Christian community itself. In our day, the Christian — whether politician, lawmaker, Peace Corps worker, or individual citizen — will be recognized as another Christ to the proportion that he strives — in his own way — toward peace. "Blessed are the peacemakers, for they shall be called sons of God."

The Council then goes on to give us the constituent elements of peace (positive) and what peace is not (negative). It is noteworthy that the Council's definition of peace is different from the traditional Augustinian definition as the "tranquility of order." The reason is quite easy to understand, namely, the fact of the established disorder throughout the globe. That is, despotic, totalitarian regimes which rule vast areas of the world, indeed have order of a sort, but not an order which respects true peace: the dignity and rights of man, political, social, and economic freedom, etc. (the communist countries, Iran, Taiwan, South Vietnam, Spain, and many Latin dictatorships). In order to avoid this sort of ambiguity, the concept of peace as to its constituent parts is simply an order of justice and love. So our document defines it:

78. a. Peace is not merely the absence of war; nor can it be reduced solely to the maintenance of a balance of power between enemies; nor is it brought about by dictatorship. Instead it is rightly and appropriately called an enterprise of justice (Isa 32:7). Peace results from that order structured into human society by its divine Founder, and actualized by man as they thirst after ever greater justice. The common good of humanity finds its ultimate meaning in the eternal law. But since the concrete demands of this common good are constantly changing as time goes on, peace is never attained once and for all, but must be built up ceaselessly. Moreover, since the human will is unsteady and wounded by sin, the achievement of peace requires a constant mastering of passions and the vigilance of lawful authority.

b. But this is not enough. This peace on earth cannot be obtained unless personal well-being is safeguarded and men freely and trustingly share with one another the riches of their inner spirits and their talents. A firm determination to respect other men and peoples and their dignity, as well as the studied practice of brotherhood are absolutely necessary for their establishment of peace. Hence peace is likewise the fruit of love, which goes beyond what justice can provide.

c. That earthly peace which arises from love of neighbor symbolizes and results from the peace of Christ which radiates from God the Father. For by the Cross the Incarnate Son, the Prince of Peace reconciled all men with God. By thus restoring all men to the unity of one people and one body, he slew hatred in his own flesh; and, after being lifted on high by his resurrection, he poured forth the spirit of love into the hearts of men.

d. For this reason, all Christians are urgently summoned to do in love what the truth requires (Eph 4:15), and to join with all true peacemakers in pleading for peace and bringing it about.

e. Motivated by this same spirit, we cannot fail to praise those who renounce the use of violence in the vindication of their rights and who resort to methods of defense, which are otherwise available to weaker parties too, provided this can be done without injury to the rights and duties of others or of the community itself.

The Council starts on what peace is not. It is neither the absence of war as the cold war clearly shows with all its suspicion, fear, and mutual hate which endanger the very foundation of true peace. It is not a balance of forces or terror which the document will go into later in its discussion (81a, b). Nor can the order of peace be imposed from without by any type of despotism since — as the document was at pains to show throughout the first four chapters — men must freely take upon themselves their own responsibility for their destiny. Peace is the order of love and of justice. 78a and 78b are both an equilibrium explaining the role of each in the attainment of peace. First, justice. Chapter III of Part II was consecrated to this objective. Men are not means of profit or tools of the state. Man's dignity demands that he be freed from the slaveries of poverty and destitution from which almost two-thirds of the world's population suffers. This is an international problem of justice and one of the greatest threats to peace in the world. That is why it is not strange that the document consecrates the whole last part of this chapter to the "causes of war," among the greatest being poverty, disease, underdevelopment on an international scale. Peace is an empty mockery as long as these conditions are allowed to exist in the world. It demands that we eliminate racism and nationalism as well, and look upon all men and nations in the brotherhood of the human family. This task is not accomplished once and for all, but remains a continuous task, a dynamic concept of justice for all men. Each individual, each nation must continuously re-evaluate his actions to eliminate therefrom all forms of selfishness, racism, and egoism which affect all human actions and dealings. This demands a continuous victory over individual and national passion and egoism. Thus the concept of justice is viewed in a dynamic rather than a static way, as something which will never be fully achieved as well as an ideal for men to continuously strive for. As Reinhold Niebuhr put it: "Patriotism transmutes individual unselfishness into national egoism," and it is this danger which the Christian must be continuously on his guard against.

Yet, this is not enough to accomplish the work of peace in today's world. Justice has been defined as the minimum of respect of the human person, his rights, and originality. This applies on the international level as well, since one nation which seeks to dominate another culturally, economically, or politically, cannot exercise love at an international level which is also required by the natural law. Love implies the will of promotion of the other both individually and socially. That is why the last third of this chapter is spent on the means necessary to help the underdeveloped nations. Love is thus raised to an international level. Economic cooperation between nations must be seen in the light of this love. All this, of course, is beyond the moralistic concept of "rights" of a nation "to strict justice," but rather, one of openness and goodness as well as mercy on the part of those who "have" toward those who "have not." Somehow, a real fraternity must be created at an international as well as on an individual level. Only in this way can the nations of the world slowly but surely come to know and trust each other.

It is this "new mentality" of which our document speaks which must become ever more dominant in international relations.

Our document sees this love communicated by the Holy Spirit working in the world even among those who do not explicitly recognize him. The document sees a relationship once again between the peace of heaven and the peace on earth. Much in the same spirit of John XXIII in *Pacem in Terris*, there is an intrinsic relationship between the two, with the result that they are not two but one. In the Pope's mind, peace is not merely the absence of war, a negative concept; rather, it is a positive concept whose component parts are "an order founded on truth, built according to justice, verified, and integrated by charity, and put into practice" (167). Thus, peace is attainable in this world. Terrestrial peace is an imperfect but real participation in the one and unique peace which is God's. In this concept of peace, the absence of war is a result — not the definition — of peace. Peace is not man reconciled with himself as the marxists would have it; it is not an optimistic self-evolution of humanity, as the eighteenth and nineteenth centuries thought; it is not a pseudo-Christian escape into a happy indifferentism which has no effect in the world; it is not the evasive illusion of some oriental religions. It is rather an order of justice and love that is animated by a true disinterested love of all men on both an individual and international level. Our present text adds the texts from scripture (78c) where Christ reconciles all things to himself, destroying hatred and sin by his death and resurrection. No longer is there distinction of Jew or Gentile, rich or poor, ignorant or intelligent, black or white, man or woman, American or Japanese — but Christ in all, reconciling all men in a true and deep bond of fraternity. This celestial peace must have its effect on the earthly city of man. In the measure that men are penetrated with this Spirit of this same love which truly unites them into a true family, a true community which they ontologically are, they will put to death the selfishness, egoism, and sin which are at the root of violence and war among men. It is this fear of each other, this mutual distrust which spirals the arms race, which causes each side to spend fortunes on war and a pittance for the works of peace and development. Catholic thought along the above lines can make a great contribution toward this type of international morality. This implies a going beyond the limits of "just war," or balance of terror (a "trap" says our document) to create cooperation and communication between all men. The rest of this chapter will be dedicated to some concrete proposals on how this can be accomplished in the modern age.

Finally (78e), for the first time in an official ecclesiastical document, we find explicit praise and approval for the use of the method of non-violence in the attainment of just goals and rights. The Council is thinking of such examples as Nobel Prize winner, Rev. Martin Luther King. This method has now found a place in Catholic theology, insofar as the person who practices such a method follows the example of the cross of Christ ("motivated by this same spirit") which was, then and now, a "stupidity" to those men who lack faith in God's ways among men. In a sense, these men and women who practice such a method from this motive have attained the height of moral perfection which other men — inclusive of many Christians — have not yet reached, either because of fear or ignorance or malice in all three. Christ accomplished the works of God by absolute non-violence and this remains our ideal in human affairs as well. And yet, this world and men within it being sinful and imperfect, as they are, this method of "non-violence" cannot in fact be practiced everywhere "without injury to the rights and duties of others or of the community itself" (see 79d, where the Council says that "war has not been rooted out of human affairs").

We might also mention a note of self-accusation on the part of the Church herself who in her past history has used violence to accomplish goals here on earth (Inquisition, Crusades, recourse to the "secular arm of the state," etc.). We have evolved in our religious communities to the moral consciousness of the utter futility and even blasphemy of trying to impose faith or spiritual goals by the use of violence (see the whole of the document on *Religious Freedom*). Men must not evolve to a similar moral standard with regard to the secular order as well, given the futility and utter blasphemy of total nuclear destruction ever present today in international relations.

Thus the principle of non-violence gains a solid theological foundation in the life of the Church — at least officially — for the first time, and must now enter into Christian thought as part and parcel of its doctrine on peace in our day. It must not be understood in a political sense but in conformity with the love of men motivated by the cross of Christ.

SECTION I: THE AVOIDANCE OF WAR

The Council document now proceeds in a logical fashion to outline, in progressive order, the situation now at hand (which is one of revolutionary wars and conflicts) and how to at least attenuate much of its violence and inhumanity. Then on to the question of how to escape total war and, finally, the ideal which is that of a total proscription of all wars as a means of redressing grievances. It is this logical order which the Council will follow in the four paragraphs of this section.

79. a. In spite of the fact that recent wars have wrought physical and moral havoc on our world, war produces its devastation day by day in some part of the world. Indeed, now that every kind of weapon produced by modern science is used in war, the fierce character of warfare threatens to lead the combatants to a savagery far surpassing that of the past. Furthermore, the complexity of the modern world and the intricacy of international relations allow guerrilla warfare to be carried on by new methods of deceit and subversion. In many cases the use of terrorism is regarded as a new way to wage war.

b. Contemplating this melancholy state of humanity, the

Council wishes, above all things else, to recall the permanent binding force of universal natural law and its all-embracing principles. Man's conscience itself gives ever more emphatic voice to these principles. Therefore, actions which deliberately conflict with these same principles, as well as orders commanding such actions are criminal, and blind obedience cannot excuse those who yield to them. The most infamous among these are actions designed for the methodical extermination of an entire people, nation or ethnic minority. Such actions must be vehemently condemned as horrendous crimes. The courage of those who fearlessly and openly resist those who issue such commands merits the highest commendation.

c. On the subject of war, quite a large number of nations have subscribed to international agreements aimed at making military activity and its consequences less inhuman. Their stipulations deal with such matters as the treatment of wounded soldiers and prisoners. Agreements of this sort must be honored. Indeed they should be improved upon so that the frightfulness of war can be better and more workably held in check. All men, especially government officials and experts in these matters, are bound to do everything they can to effect these improvements. Moreover, it seems right that laws make humane provisions for the case of those who for reasons of conscience refuse to bear arms, provided however, that they agree to serve the human community in some other way.

d. Certainly, war has not been rooted out of human affairs. As long as the danger of war remains and there is no competent and sufficiently powerful authority at the international level, governments cannot be denied the right legitimate defense once every means of peaceful settlement has been exhausted. Government authorities and others who share public responsibility have the duty to conduct such grave matters soberly and to protect the welfare of the people entrusted to their care. But it is one thing to undertake military action for the just defense of the people, and something else again to seek the subjugation of other nations. Nor, by the same token, does the mere fact that was has unhappily begun mean that all is fair between the warring parties.

e. Those too who devote themselves to the military service of their country should regard themselves as the agents of security and freedom of peoples. As long as they fulfill this role properly, they are making a genuine contribution to the establishment of peace.

The paragraph starts with a description of the various types of violence which have been introduced in the modern age, the most obvious being that of nuclear weapons which far surpass any firepower the world has ever known. There are missiles presently armed, which alone contain more destructive power than the bombs and bullets of all previous wars *combined*. But aside from this, a new method of warfare known as "guerilla warfare" made popular in our century by the textbooks of a Mao Tse-tung and Ché Guevara, which, by selective terroism and mobility, can defeat an army many times its size. This is, above all, the tactic presently used in the "third world" by both East and West alike, which leaves the peoples of these countries the real victims of both sides of the conflict. This is the situation of fact which the Council describes as a "melancholy state of humanity."

What are the things to be done to promote some sort of humanity and limitation of violence in the modern age? There are, first of all, some tactics which are so immoral (the document mentions genocide of various shades), that nothing can excuse them — no matter what the reasons of state (79b). No "blind obedience" to the nation can excuse individuals from such crimes. Implicit within the text is that soldiers are responsible for their individual actions and when they are commanded to perform such crimes, they are to refuse to obey. The list of such crimes is admittedly very small and of an outstanding nature, but the principle of individual judgment on the actions of a state by civilian and soldier alike comes out clearly in the text. The Nuremberg trials against Nazi war crimes were based squarely on this principle, namely, that individuals are indeed responsible for their actions even in time of war and even when they are commanded to perform various actions in the name of a "higher authority" of the state.

There have also been other limiting conventions and international agreements (treatment of prisoners, the wounded, noncombatants) which must and should be scrupulously followed by all nations. This can serve as an attenuation of the cruelties of modern warfare. (Geneva Convention of 1949, Conventions of the Hague of 1907.) The document appeals here to the basic tenets of "the permanent binding force of universal natural law and its all-embracing principles." It uses the term "natural law" in the sense that Pope John used it in *Pacem in Terris,* namely, an acquired universal consciousness of various actions which are good or bad or, in other words, the general consciousness of mankind in the direction of freedom, justice, and solidarity which are the basic driving principles of the men of our age. We ought not to see here a Thomistic concept of natural law but one that has developed from the 18th century on the fundamental of the freedom and rights of the human person (see the whole analysis of this historic manifestation in *Pacem,* 8-45).

For the first time in an official ecclesiastical document (79c), we have an approbation for those who, for reasons of conscience, are not willing to bear arms. They ought to be excused by civil law rather than be forced to do what is against their conscience. The text makes no distinction as to who such a person may be — Catholic or non-Christian — and with one stroke, the ancient argument about whether a Catholic can be a conscientious objector has been resolved. It was seriously argued in the past that such a thing could not be and that a Catholic as a citizen, lacking full information, was bound to obey (or "trust") the civil authority. The argument was fallacious for the simple reason that all the facts are never in nor do we need them all to make an honest judgment in these matters. The human person is always responsible, because he is a moral person with intelligence and free will. The document does not say that the reasons for conscientious objection must be specifically "religious" but simply appeals to "conscience" which is sufficient —

no matter what the reasons prompting his objection to bearing arms. We must remember that the document is addressed to all men, and conscience is sufficient to cover this contingency for all.

Catholic tradition has not been entirely silent on this aspect, as witness the writings of Francisco de Vitoria in the 16th century who elaborated some very bold theses in this respect. He claimed subjects of a state could not engage in war, if they knew the war was unjust. His witness went unheeded and undeveloped by later theologians; our present document, in a sense, bridges this gap of some four hundred years. Many modern democracies have already made such provisions in their laws (U.S., England, Canada), and it is hoped that all nations will follow suit. In the final analysis, it is the individual person, not the state, who must take himself in hand as morally responsible in such a terrible decision. This does not excuse them from making their contribution to the common good of their country. They must be willing to serve in another capacity such as the Peace Corps, Papal Volunteers, CILA, VISTA, Job Corps, and many other national and international organizations which promote the spiritual and temporal good of the human family. Conscientious objection has thus found its place in theological thought of the Catholic Church, as it has long since been in the theological thought of many Protestant communities.

The Council, however, does see that war, as yet, can be a legitimate method — even today — to protect the rights of any particular country (79d). Governments have the heavy moral obligation to protect the rights of its citizens, even to the extent of having recourse to arms. Those who serve in the army of such a cause (79e) are doing a good work for the protection of freedom. The Council, however, places some very stringent limitations on the conduct of such a war (80). The document indirectly rejects the theory of those who say that nations may no longer have recourse to arms in the legitimate defense of their rights against unjust aggression. This follows the very same thought of Paul VI in his talk to the UN: "As long as man remains that weak, changeable and even wicked being that he often shows himself to be, defensive arms will, unfortunately, be necessary." Complete disarmament and proscription of war becomes, then, a moral ideal which all men of good will must strive for, but which, as yet, has not arrived.

The first great limitation on modern war is the Council's proscription of all types of total war:

80. a. The horror and perversity of war is immensely magnified by the increase in the number of scientific weapons. For acts of war involving these weapons can inflict massive and indiscriminate destruction, thus going far beyond the bounds of legitimate defense. Indeed, if the kind of instruments which can now be found in the armories of the great nations were to be employed to their fullest, an almost total and altogether reciprocal slaughter of each side by the other would follow, not to mention the widespread devastation that would take place in the world and the deadly aftereffects that would be spawned by the use of weapons of this kind.

b. All these considerations compel us to undertake an evaluation of war with an entirely new attitude. The men of our time must realize that they will have to give a somber reckoning of their deeds of war for the course of the future will depend greatly on the decisions they make today.

c. With these truths in mind, this most Holy Synod makes its own the condemnations of total war already pronounced by recent popes, and issues the following declaration:

d. Any act of war aimed indiscriminately at the destruction of entire cities or extensive areas along with their population is a crime against God and man himself. It merits unequivocal and unhesitating condemnation.

e. The unique hazard of modern warfare consists in this: it provides those who possess modern scientific weapons with a kind of occasion for perpetrating just such abominations; moreover, through a certain inexorable chain of events, it can catapult men into the most atrocious decisions. That such may never happen in the future, the bishops of the whole world gathered together, beg all men, especially government officials and military leaders, to give unremitting thought to their tremendous responsibility before God and the entire human race.

What is immediately evident in this paragraph is the manner in which the Council sets the limits to war. It does not mention only nuclear war as being indiscriminate (which it certainly is) but any kind of war — nuclear or conventional — which has as its object the total destruction of a whole village or city or a whole area. We have here reaffirmed the principle of non-combat immunity, since this condemnation would otherwise make no sense whatever. The mere destruction of property could not elicit such a clear condemnation.

In this respect, Pius XII had said the same thing over a decade ago. The Pope — like our present text — was not measuring megatonage, because this was and is beyond his (and also the Council Fathers') competence. Thus from the Pope's message of September 30, 1954:

> Every time the employment of a means entails such extension of harm that it entirely escapes man's control, its use must be rejected as immoral. Here there would no longer be a question of "defense" against injustice and of the necessary "safeguarding" of legitimate possessions, but of the pure and simple annihilation of all human life within the radius of action. This is not permitted on any score.

What were the criteria? Not so much the megatonage, but the indiscriminate massacre of non-combatants. Again the Pope said:

> The atrocities and the illicit use of means of destruction, even against the non-combatants and refugees, against the old, women and children; contempt for human dignity, liberty and life, from which result acts that cry to God for vengeance.
> (December 24, 1939)

It is evident that our present document reserves its moral censure for all types of indiscriminate warfare. The Council has in mind the examples of recent history: Dresden, London, Hiroshima (which Paul VI referred to as "that barbaric atrocity"). Nor is it here a question of "small" wars versus "big" wars (this indeed is relative to the people and place where a war is being fought). Nor is there a distinction made between "clean" bombs and "dirty" bombs, because neither respects the principle of non-combatant immunity. This type of warfare goes beyond all reasonable defense to a simple threat of "city destruction" (these are the words of a secretary of defense) to the total obliteration of the so-called "enemy." This, in military parlance, is referred to as the "overkill" which means that the U.S. and Russia have enough power to destroy each other hundreds of times. Here, we go beyond good and evil to simple absurdity. Such war could never be initiated or conducted in any fashion whatsoever by Christians. Proportion of means to ends, principle of non-combatant immunity and objectives all become one gigantic absurdity which no "reason of state" could ever possibly justify. The Council also notes that — whatever be the final judgment on the concept of deterrence (81) — the simple possession of such weapons is in itself a constant temptation to bring about such a crime. The dangers which come from this sector have been repeated by both religious and secular authorities: proliferation of nuclear weapons to those nations who do not as yet possess them, war by accident or by a malicious third party, and, above all, the dangers which are caused by "escalation" ("a certain inexorable chain of events," says our document). This latter aspect is, perhaps, the greatest of all, as one country may feel it has gone back as far as it can and stands ready to employ any and all means for its defense. We need not search for an example: the war in Viet Nam is a perfect case in point. The document continues:

81. a. Scientific weapons, to be sure, are not amassed solely for use in war. Since the defensive strength of any nation is considered to be dependent upon its capacity for immediate

retaliation, this accumulation of arms, which increases each year, likewise serves, in a way heretofore unknown, as a deterrent to possible enemy attack. Many regard this as the most effective way by which peace of a sort can be maintained between nations at the present time.

b. Whatever be the facts about this method of deterrence, men should be convinced that the arms race in which an already considerable number of countries are engaged is not a safe way to preserve a steady peace, nor is the so-called balance resulting from this race a sure and authentic peace. Rather than being eliminated thereby, the causes of war are in danger of being gradually aggravated. While extravagant sums are being spent for the furnishing of ever new weapons, an adequate remedy cannot be provided for the multiple miseries afflicting the whole modern world. Disagreements between nations are not really and radically healed; on the contrary, they spread the infection to other parts of the earth. New approaches based on reformed attitudes must be taken to remove this trap and to emancipate the world from its crushing anxiety through the restoration of genuine peace.

c. Therefore, we say it again: the arms race is an utterly treacherous trap for humanity, and one which ensnares the poor to an intolerable degree. It is much to be feared that if this race persists, it will eventually spawn all the lethal ruin whose path it is now making ready. Warned by the calamities which the human race has made possible, let us make use of the interlude granted us from above and for which we are thankful, to become more conscious of our own responsibility and to find means for resolving our disputes in a manner more worthy of man. Divine Providence urgently demands of us that we free ourselves from the age-old slavery of war. If we refuse to make this effort, we do not know where we will be led by the evil road we have set upon.

We have now arrived at the most difficult aspect of this chapter: disarmament, about which so much has been said in present times and with such meager results. The Council must face the problem as it exists — not as we would perhaps like it to be: that is, the "balance of terror" particularly between the Soviet Union and the United States really exists and cannot

be wished nor condemned away by the Council. Its main function is not to condemn (as many private groups of Catholics
wanted it to do), for this would accomplish nothing as well as
antagonize the great powers. Its moral voice must be raised
as regards the concrete steps to be taken by both sides to ward
off the impending disaster for mankind. The nations are in
danger of committing the ultimate blasphemy: destruction of
the human race if ever these instruments are unleashed. What
is to be done in the face of this danger?

From one point of view, men see no possibility of defending
their freedom except by having recourse to such instruments
of war; and on the other hand, such instruments can only lead
to total world destruction if they are ever employed.

The reason men accumulate these spiraling arms, says our
document, is the fact that they fear each other for a variety of
reasons — historical, ethical, or ideological. Whatever be the
cause of the fear, it is the fear itself which is the cause, and
armaments the effect. We must eliminate the causes of fear and
mistrust under pain of the illusion that we can banish war by
simply condemning it. The Council will now give a whole series
of arguments in this regard, in order to exercise a certain "moral
persuasion." By gradual and measured steps, one can slowly
arrive at the moral elimination of fear and distrust. How does
our document develop its reasoning?

It, first of all, gives a clear summary of the argument of
those who say that peace can be accomplished only by a "balance
of terror or armaments" (81a). Then it proceeds (81b) to
show the fallaciousness of such a method for accomplishing the
peace ardently hoped for. It passes no moral judgment, one
way or the other, on this argument from deterrence. It simply
recognizes the situation and says we must use the time given
us now to promote by gradual steps the peace we all seek. We
cannot rely on this balance for true peace, and the document
deliberately refers to it as a "trap" twice in the same paragraph.
The reasons for this seem quite clear to the Council. First, the

evident argument, that far from reducing the very causes of war, it simply continues to accentuate and increase mutual tensions and distrust one for another. For any one anti-missile system, the other side must build an anti-anti-missile system for fear of a "first strike"-capability of the enemy. Secondly, the waste of enormous sums of money on arms (e.g., the U.S. has spent over $1,000,000,000,000 on arms since the end of World War II, enough to develop the poor nations twice over), while 2/3 of the population of the entire globe are either actually hungry or insufficiently fed. It is these latter conditions (which our document described earlier) which are among the major causes of disruption and war in the world today. This building of arms, then, is self-defeating, since it absorbs funds which must be spent on those conditions at the source of war itself. Thirdly, this preparation for war actually settles nothing from an ideological point of view, but rather spreads the infection called "the cold war" throughout the globe, thus further enervating the world's difficult condition in our century (81b). The document concludes that this balance which comes from armaments is a fallacious "trap," and can lead only to war itself. We must adopt "new attitudes" which can gradually lead us away from the abyss. We must use the time which God has given us to do this on which the Council will spend the last third of this chapter. We must free ourselves from the "slavery" which has held man captive from the very beginning of his recorded history, and especially, as we saw, at this critical juncture where man must either change this ancient attitude or be in grave danger of total loss of the human family (81c). The object of the Council is truly radical but then humanity has no real choice in the matter. We have here an indirect rebuke to all those who cling to the notion that the safest means of peace in our day is that of reliance on a balance of arms in any form.

We now reach the last stage of the document's view of war and peace in our day, which presents an ideal: the absolute proscription of war in international relations to restore violated rights. We have seen that the document has proceeded in a practico-pastoral way, taking the world as it is; and gradually, by measured steps, it advances toward this ideal. After an examination of the present world, we find it necessary to change its ancient attitudes before we can hope to eliminate war in international relations. The paragraph as cited simply repeats some of the more general means of this slow progression previously exposed from Benedict XV to Paul VI, such as disarmament, a powerful and effective world authority, education as well as a change in public opinion from war to peace in all of the diverse ways that it affects the decisions of political heads of state.

82. a. It is our clear duty, therefore, to strain every muscle in working for the time when all war can be completely outlawed by international consent. This goal undoubtedly requires the establishment of some universal public authority acknowledged as such by all and endowed with the power to safeguard on the behalf of all, security, regard for justice, and respect for rights. But before this hoped-for authority can be set up, the highest existing international centers must devote themselves vigorously to the pursuit of better means for obtaining common security. Since peace must be born of mutual trust between nations and not be imposed on them through fear of the available weapons, everyone must labor to put an end at least to the arms race, and to make a true beginning of disarmament, not unilaterally indeed, but proceeding at an equal pace according to agreement, and backed up by adequate and workable safeguards.

b. In the meantime, efforts which have already been made and are still under way to eliminate the danger of war are not to be underrated. On the contrary, support should be given to the good will of the very many leaders who work hard to do away with war, which they abominate. These men, although burdened by the extremely weighty preoccupations of their high office, are nonetheless moved by the very grave peace-making task to which they are bound, even if they cannot ignore the complexity of matters as they stand. We should fervently ask God to give these men the strength to go forward perseveringly and to follow through courageously on this work of building peace with vigor. It is a work of supreme love for mankind. Today it certainly demands that they extend their thoughts and their spirit beyond the confines for their own nation, that they put aside national selfishness and ambition to dominate other nations, and that they nourish a profound reverence for the whole of humanity, which is already making its way so laboriously toward greater unity.

c. The problems of peace and of disarmament have already been the subject of extensive, strenuous and constant examination. Together with international meetings dealing with these problems such studies should be regarded as the first steps toward solving these serious questions, and should be promoted with even greater urgency by way of yielding concrete results in the future.

d. Nevertheless, men should take heed not to entrust themselves only to the efforts of others, while not caring about their own attitudes. For government officials who must at one and the same time guarantee the good of their own people and promote the universal good are very greatly dependent on public opinion and feeling. It does them no good to work for peace as long as feelings of hostility, contempt and distrust, as well as racial hatred and unbending ideologies, continue to divide men and place them in opposing camps. Consequently there is above all a pressing need for a renewed education of attitudes and for new inspiration in public opinion. Those who are dedicated to the work of education, particularly of the young, or who mold public opinion, should consider it their most weighty task to instruct all in fresh sentiments of peace. Indeed, we all need a change of heart as we regard the entire world and those tasks which we can perform in unison for the betterment of our race.

e. But we should not let false hope deceive us. For unless enmities and hatred are put away and firm, honest agreements concerning world peace are reached in the future, humanity, which already is in the middle of grave crisis, even though it is endowed with remarkable knowledge, will perhaps be brought to that dismal hour in which it will experience no peace other than the dreadful peace of death. But, while we say this, the Church of Christ, present in the midst of the anxiety of this age, does not cease to hope most firmly. She intends to propose to our age over and over again, in season and out of season, this apostolic message: "Behold, now is the acceptable time for a change of heart; behold! now is the day of salvation."

The document first discusses the question of disarmament resuming in a few words what John XXIII had already said in *Pacem in Terris*. The dangers coming from the arms race are too well known to need any commentary. The only thing that might be added here, since the three years which have elapsed since *Pacem*, is the danger of proliferation of nuclear weapons with the added dangers that it poses both for the great powers as well as for the rest of the world. This same appeal was made by Pius XII as far back as 1957, when he said that nuclear weapons ought to be placed under an effective international supervision, and that the United Nations "ought to have the right and power of forestalling all military interventions of one state into another, whatever be the pretext under which it is effected, and also the right and power of assuming, by means of a sufficient police force, the safeguarding of order in the state which is threatened."

The question of effective controls on disarmament has also received some attention, and the same is reiterated by our document. It is true that because of mutual fear and distrust among nations, unilateral disarmament would, in fact, be out of the question. Yet, the Council's words seem to be a bit overly cautious, in the sense that when nations compromise along these lines, at least one nation must — at least to a small degree — take the first step which is an indirect appeal to the other to follow suit and so forth until total and effective disarmament is achieved. In any real disarmament movement, it will never be possible to have a strictly "equal pace" (82a).

The next section (82b) deals with the levels of action on which peace movements are to proceed. There is a hierarchy of important here, starting with the political leaders in each state. It is, above all, on them that peace is dependent — at least for the immediate future, until a viable international political community can be formed. It is perhaps with a bit of good sense that our document starts off with such an emphasis on these political leaders — on their prudence and love of mankind that the very future of the globe will depend. They must view this task as their commitment to the human family as such and not to selfish nationalism and nationalistic parochial interests. This is a difficult task, indeed, since nations today are deeply infected with the cancer of nationalism, where each respective people demands their leaders to seek, first and foremost, their own nationalistic goals. That is why this reminder and encouragement from our document is both realistic and opportune. The Council was thinking along the lines of the now-famous American University speech of John F. Kennedy, when he said in 1963:

> What kind of peace do I mean and what kind of peace do we seek? Not a *Pax America* enforced on the world by American weapons of war. Not the peace of the grave or the security of the slave. I am talking about the genuine peace — the kind of peace that makes life on earth worth living — and the kind that enables men and nations to grow and to hope and to build a better life for their children — not merely peace for Americans but peace for all men and women — not merely peace in our time but peace for all time.
>
> I speak of peace because of the new face of war. Total war makes no sense in an age where great powers can maintain large and relatively invulnerable nuclear forces and refuse to surrender without resort to these forces. It makes no sense in an age when a singular nuclear weapon contains almost ten times the explosive force delivered by all the allied air forces in the Second World War. It makes no sense in an age when the deadly poisons produced by a nuclear exchange would be carried by wind and water and soil and seed to the far corners of the globe and to generations yet unborn.

. . . .

I speak of peace, therefore, as a necessary rational end of rational men. I realize the pursuit of peace is not as dramatic as the pursuit of war — and frequently the words of the pursuer fall on deaf ears. But we have no more urgent task.

Some say that it is useless to speak of peace or world law or world disarmament — and that it will be useless until the leaders of the Soviet Union adopt a more enlightened attitude. I hope so. I believe we can help them do it.

But I also believe we must re-examine our own attitudes — as individuals and as a nation — for our attitude is as essential as theirs. And every graduate, every thoughtful citizen who despairs of war and wishes to bring peace, should begin by looking inward — by examining his own attitude toward the course of the cold war and toward freedom and peace here at home.

Such inspiring words are those of a political leader who seeks a true peace among men as a family and not simply nationalistic goals. These goals of peace are not simply restricted to the "great" powers in the world of our day. It is evident that it is becoming more and more a global problem, as diverse spheres of political influence begin to make their presence felt in the world (e.g., Western Europe, Eastern Europe, Africa, China — which have all been coming into existence over the past 10-15 years). In any case, peace no longer depends solely on the great powers, but on political leaders of other nations as well, and on their prudence and self-control which they exercise at an international level. It is not strange that such an inference is made in our document, since the bishops of the "third world" had a lot to say concerning the text.

Yet there is another important aspect which cannot be neglected but which renders even the best and most magnanimous world leaders helpless. This is the problem of public opinion (82d). The Council wisely views this phase of peace as crucial for the future. No peace, no settlement, no accommodation is possible unless the people of any one nation are prepared for it. If through propaganda, hysteria, or fear, they have come to view a particular nation or group of men in a Manichaean way — that is, as totally depraved and evil — then not only is accommodation not possible but war is inevitable. It is precisely this climate of change in public opinion which the above-quoted speech by John Kennedy hoped to accomplish.

> Let us focus . . . on a practical, more attainable peace — based not on a sudden revolution in human nature but on a gradual evolution in human institutions — on a series of concrete actions and effective agreement which are in the interests of all concerned.

> . . . .

> So let us persevere. Peace need not be impractical — and war need not be inevitable. By defining our goal more clearly — by making it seem more manageable and less remote — we can help all people to see it, to draw hope from it, and to move irresistibly toward it.

It falls, above all, on teachers and educators to prepare the young for changes in such attitudes toward the world around them. The young generation must be trained in an open spirit of tolerance toward those who differ from their own social, cultural, economic, and even political view. They must realize that there is no divinely approved social or political institution on this earth. Everything must be examined to see whether it can serve and promote the human person; for that, in the last analysis, will be the ultimate criterion of their worth. This includes a true inculcation of the basic equality and dignity of the human person, against every form of nationalism or racism. A universal consciousness of the dignity of all men would make it imperative that the young be formed in such a way. Even with those who are our enemies, we must encourage not the stock-piling of bombs so much as a dialogue. This is what Pope John desired, above all, in the promotion of peace among men.

In the now-famous paragraph 159 of *Pacem in Terris,* the Pope developed the attitudes we must have in approaching and encountering each other. The Pope makes a distinction between the good that various movements have accomplished, and the false philosophical notions on which these movements may have been built. In a sense, we have here an attitude regarding change of institution identical to that of John Kennedy whose words we cited earlier. The Church, in her own efforts to avoid war and violence between men, offers herself in the spirit of total service and dedication. It is this cause of dialogue, emphasized by Paul VI in his encyclical *Ecclesiam Suam,* which our document is at such pains to encourage throughout the entire text. For unless fear and hatred can be replaced with mutual respect and trust, then, indeed, we are letting "false hope deceive us" (82e). The Church has no ready-made solutions, no miracle-formulas for curing the ills of violence and war from which the world is presently suffering; but she gives all that she has in the service of men: herself. Her mission is to continuously encourage men to this dialogue, to this conversion of heart which is absolutely necessary for the attainment of peace. She has no guarantee that she will be successful in this matter but only the hope that her administration will be accepted by men of good will.

SECTION II: SETTING UP AN INTERNATIONAL COMMUNITY

We next have a summary listing of the great causes of war and conflict in the modern age (83): injustice, inequality of material distribution, domination of the weak by the strong, not only materially but culturally and politically as well.

83. In order to build up peace the causes of discord among men, especially injustice, which foment wars must above all be rooted out. Not a few of these causes come from excessive economic inequalities and from putting off the steps needed

to remedy them. Other causes of discord, however, have their source in the desire to dominate and in a contempt for persons. And, if we look for deeper causes, we find them in human envy, distrust, pride, and other egotistical passions. Man cannot bear so many ruptures in the harmony of things. Consequently, the world is constantly beset by strife and violence between men, even when no war is being waged. Besides, since these small evils are present in the relations between various nations as well, in order to overcome or forestall them and to keep violence once unleashed within limits, it is absolutely necessary for countries to cooperate to better advantage, to work together more closely and jointly to organize international bodies and to work tirelessly for the creation of organizations which will foster peace.

These causes of conflict are, above all, moral and economic — which *Gaudium et Spes* has developed many times before in its exposition. It avoids a deeper analysis of the sociology of conflict in today's highly urbanized and urbanizing civilization. What is perhaps its most disturbing aspect can be found precisely here. At the root of this malaise in the modern world lies the failure, if not *de jure* at least then *de facto,* of the denial of the dignity and worth of the human person. Pope John XXIII's *Pacem* was built on this principle and made of it the foundation stone of any sane and lasting national and international community. It is evident that the subject of these rights is the person himself, precisely because, writes the Holy Father, he has intelligence and free will, making him capable of and responsible for the realization of his moral destiny. In man's personal being lives the source of his rights, and he is the bearer of these rights. These rights are universal, because they pertain to every person on the face of the earth. Since these rights are not arbitrary, they pertain to what man is and to his fulfillment as a human person. They cannot be granted or denied by the whim of the state. They are inviolable and inalienable, because each person has a destiny which no one else can take or fulfill for him; and if each person must fulfill his destiny, he must have the means, ensured by his fundamental rights, to do so. On this rock foundation, the Pope built his own encyclical on peace; and it is, indeed, a regrettable deficiency in the present text that this path opened by John XXIII was not pursued by Vatican II in its analysis of peace and of the international political authority. Without such a universal and well-founded aspect of the political order at an international level, there is grave danger of nationalism, the very cancer of our age. Not very long ago, entire armies were blessed by the German hierarchy to fight Hitler's immoral wars. Each country drafts God first of all, and the first casualty of the war — any war — is truth. Indeed, now is the time to escape this trap into which so many Christians of the past — all with the best of intentions, serving the famous "Deus Vult" — have fallen; and to rise above this, "to think in a new fashion" (in the words of Paul VI), is to think more and more in terms of the new community of nations and how best to make it into an effective political authority of a universal nature based on the rights and dignity of man. We might as well recognize that the theory of the just war has been dead for a very long time — if ever it was observed by Christians. We must replace it with an international morality corresponding to the needs of our day and age. In this respect, it would be most useful to summon in permanent committee, theologians, sociologists, psychologists, etc., to examine the problem and make recommendations, giving us an in-depth study of the theology of peace.

In the following paragraph, two major types of action for peace are kept for us by our document. The development of international institutions as well as mutual aid between nations themselves — especially between the poor and the rich countries, is advocated. It will suffice to recall the fervent pleas of the popes from Pius XII to Paul VI on the obligation of the rich nations toward the poor countries. This can be effectively brought about today by various international agencies working for this goal:

84. a. In view of the increasingly close ties of mutual dependence today between all the inhabitants and peoples of the
earth, the fitting pursuit and effective realization of the universal common good now require of the community of nations
that it organize itself in a manner suited to its present responsibilities, especially toward the many parts of the world which
are still suffering from unbearable want.

b. To reach this goal, organizations of the international
community, for their part, must make provision for men's
different needs, both in the fields of social life — such as food
supplies, health, education, labor and also in certain special
circumstances which can crop up here and there, e.g., the need
to promote the general improvement of developing countries,
or to alleviate the distressing conditions in which refugees dis-
persed throughout the world find themselves, or also to assist
migrants and their families.

c. International and regional organizations which are
already in existence are certainly well-deserving of the human
race. These are the first efforts at laying the foundations on
an international level for a community of all men to work for
the solution to the serious problems of our times, to encourage
progress everywhere, and to obviate wars of whatever kind. In
all of these activities the Church rejoices in the spirit of true
brotherhood flourishing between Christians and non-Christians
as it strives to make ever more strenuous efforts to relieve widespread misery.

Pope John in *Mater et Magistra* had already mentioned
several such international organizations which were doing great
good in the underdeveloped nations (155-156). Since the whole
of the human family is a true family under the Fatherhood of
God (and this has never been a metaphor used by the Church
and the popes), individual men and nations have a serious moral
obligation to come to the economic aid of those who are less
fortunate or less developed. FAO has helped poor countries to
achieve variety in diet, better balance between agriculture and
trade, longer life span, reduced infant mortality rates, and better
health in general. UN technicians and its various agencies have
helped to improve the quantity and quality of food by showing

farmers new methods such as crop rotation, the use of fertilizer, as well as the use of hybrid seed. All of this and much more has been accomplished by these international agencies, especially by the four to which our document makes indirect reference (FAO, WHO, UNESCO, and ILO). This is important for many reasons, since the Church at her highest level has openly approved and given financial aid to these organizations, in spite of what some Catholic isolationists might think. It is also a fact that the Holy See has an observer at the UN as well. Thus it is in these necessary areas that Catholics and non-Christians can work together "in a true spirit of fraternity" for the good of all men.

Our text explicitly mentions the flight of immigrants as well as refugees. Pope John XXIII in *Pacem* had already recalled (103-108) that many states have not respected the dignity of the human person and encouraged other nations to welcome political refugees and to give them full citizenship in "a sufficient sphere of freedom within which they can lead a life worthy of man" (104). UNESCO has done much to facilitate the placing of such refugees, and our document continues to encourage the same thing as did the Pope.

In any case, our document shows that at least at this level of cooperation on the international level, we have reached a cooperation which will prepare for future political intercooperation. We do have here a beginning — even if very humble — of international integration toward which the world is headed, and seemingly will not be able to reverse. The Council thinks we must support such endeavors in order to strengthen peace among nations. This, indeed, is a part of the process of "socialization" about which the document spoke earlier in its text. We must, however, be sanguine in our hopes. Economic integration does not necessarily bring about political integration (as our paragraph would seem to imply), even if this former phenomenon has a great influence on the latter. The evidence example which comes to mind is that of Western Europe and the European

Common Market. It was based precisely on this thought, namely, that economic integration would be followed, and itself would encourage, political integration. So far it has failed to do so, but it is, as yet, too soon to give a definitive answer to this problem. What can be said is that the two phenomena do influence each other, and that mutual understandings will be built by trade and economic exchange. This is the basic hope regarding the amelioration of relationships between East and West in general and Eastern and Western Europe in particular. There are political problems which must be solved as soon as possible if peace is to be promoted: the problem of Israel in the Middle East; the problem of Rhodesia and South Africa in Africa; of Viet Nam in Southeast Asia; of Kashmir in the dispute between India and Pakistan; between Indonesia and Malaysia in Oceania; even the border disputes between China with her neighbors, India and Russia. These problems need, essentially, a political solution, not a military or an economic one. What can be said is that trade and economic cooperation could help foster feelings of good will and understanding which are a basic prerequisite for any permanent political settlement. It is along these lines that our document is directed.

Paragraph 85 will now deal directly with aid to the underdeveloped nations of the world — a favorite theme of the encyclicals *Pacem* and *Mater* of John XXIII whose teaching is here reiterated:

85. a. The present solidarity of mankind also calls for a revival of greater international cooperation in the economic field. Although nearly all peoples have become autonomous, they are far from escaping all danger of serious internal difficulties.

b. The development of a nation depends on human and financial aids. The citizens of each country must be prepared by education and professional training to discharge the various tasks of economic and social life. But this in turn requires the aid of foreign specialists who, when they give aid, will not act as overlords, but as helpers and fellow-workers. Developing nations will not be able to procure material assistance unless radical changes are made in the established procedures of modern world commerce. Other aid should be provided as well by advanced nations in the form of gifts, loans or financial investments. Such help should be accorded with generosity and without greed on the one side, and received with complete honesty on the other side.

c. If an authentic economic order is to be established on a world-wide basis, an end will have to be put to profiteering, to national ambition, to the appetite for political supremacy, to militaristic calculations, and to machinations for the purpose of spreading and imposing ideologies.

As with this same Pontiff, the reason for aid is once again the "solidarity of mankind" (*Mater*, 155-175). We have already explained this aspect of pontifical teaching (see above, pp. 79-107). In fine, the world's goods and resources have been created for all men, and not for any particular nation; thus the patrimony of the whole human race is the sum total of all the wealth of the individual nations. Within this understanding of the world's goods, the obligation of the economically developed countries to help the underdeveloped nations is a matter of strict justice, and not of simple charity (*Mater*, 157).

Our document also goes into other reasons for the mutual aid between countries. The first and the most important, from a practical point of view, is one that we have already seen: namely, that the disparity between the poor and the rich nations is growing and that this itself is a constant danger to the peace of the world. Poverty itself has never been a revolutionary factor in the world, but the poverty realized as not being inevitable or of fate but rather can be overcome, is, indeed, a revolutionary factor today throughout the globe and particularly in the underdeveloped nations. The only way to overcome this disparity is by a massive drive throughout the globe to eliminate poverty (destitution) as a peril to peace. The marxist would have us believe that this will come about inevitably by class conflict (rich versus proletariat; rich nations versus the poor ones). This is neither necessary nor inevitable, if a sustained effort is made by all. Yet, as with all errors, the marxist thesis does possess an element of truth, in that until the vast chasm between rich and poor can be bridged (in a type of international "middle-classism") then conflict will be inevitable and in an atomic age, no one can safely predict the final outcome.

Secondly, this type of interaid is one in which each individual citizen can immediately and personally engage himself. This can be done in a multiplicity of ways. He can directly make his contribution by engagement in technical services such as in the Peace Corps, Papal Volunteers, World Bank, etc., (see above, p. 311, where our document discusses these international agencies). Or he can contribute, at least indirectly, by money that his nation gives in the form of foreign aid to the underdeveloped nations or to various religious organizations (Bishops' Relief Fund, Jewish Relief Fund, National Council and World Council of Churches, etc.). This is all-important from a psychological point of view, since it lends an important element of personalism in the giving of aid, which can lessen the bane of bureaucracy here.

Thirdly — and this is the theme which permeates almost all of the Council's document — we consider the matter of poverty for all Christians. The Council was conscious of a grave paradox here — where some Christians have so much and others are starving; they found a terrible contradiction which exists among the people of God. They all must be brought to a consciousness of this situation, and if true love and charity are to prevail among these people, then this theme of poverty, of sharing (koinonia) must imbue the Christian consciences of all members of the Church. Without it, the Fathers were convinced — and in this they were merely following the teachings of the gospels — that no true or authentic Christian life could be had by the members of Christ's body here on earth.

Another wise aspect of international aid which is basic and which the Council brings out (85b) is that of balance of trade agreements. It is a well-known fact that it is the poor nations which receive the short end of the deal, because they are at an economic disadvantage. For instance, from the period 1961-1965, all of Latin America exported some 13.5 billion dollars' worth of goods and received only 9.5 billion in return. The reason was the great fluctuation in the basic price of products such as coffee, tin, etc., on which many nations of Latin America depend for their livelihood (monoculture, little development of home industries for processing, etc.). This is a grave problem because it cancels out any other type of foreign aid (e.g., "Alliance for Progress"), and actually makes these nations all the poorer. Price stabilization between the rich and the poor nations is absolutely imperative if these countries are going to progress economically. The basic question is no longer whether there is to be national and international "planning." This is simply a fact. The question today is planning for whom and for what (rich and poor nations). If one country undersells another on the international market, the whole balance of international payments is affected. This situation is becoming more apparent to individual nations in their trade agreements. The "Kennedy Round" of Trade negotiations in 1964, for instance, was a good example of how aid to the economically underdeveloped countries can result in providing additional markets for the goods of the richer nations. In the agreement, a UN-member trade organization was established to help developing nations, thereby narrowing the economic gulf between the "have" and the "have-not" countries. Great Britain suggested a four-point aid program designed to assist the poor nations: an increase in the contribution to the UN technical assistance programs; support for an increase in the UN budget to expand its activities in industrial development; readiness to provide capital assistance to the African development bank; and sympathetic consideration of assistance to other regional development banks. It is exactly along these lines that our document is thinking.

Then the text goes into some practical and useful suggestions on international economic cooperation:

86. The following norms seem useful for such cooperation:

a. Developing nations should take great pains to seek as the object of progress to express and secure the total human fulfillment of their citizens. They should bear in mind that progress arises and grows above all out of the labor and genius of the nations themselves because it has to be based, not only on foreign aid, but especially on the full utilization of their own resources, and on the development of their own culture and traditions. Those who exert the greatest influence on others should be outstanding in this respect.

b. On the other hand, it is a very important duty of the advanced nations to help developing nations in discharging their above-mentioned responsibilities. They should therefore gladly carry out on their own home front those spiritual and material readjustments that are required for the realization of this universal cooperation.

Consequently, in business dealings with weaker and poorer nations, they should be careful to respect their welfare, for these countries need the income they receive on the sale of their homemade products to support themselves.

c. It is the role of the international community to coordinate and promote development, but in such a way that the resources earmarked for this purpose will be allocated as effectively as possible, and with complete equity. It is likewise this community's duty, with due regard for the principle of subsidiarity, so to regulate economic relations throughout the world that these will be carried out in accordance with the norms of justice.

Suitable organizations should be set up to foster and regulate international business affairs, particularly with the underdeveloped countries, and to compensate for losses resulting from an excessive inequality of power among the various nations. This type of organization, in unison with technical, cultural, and financial aid, should provide the help which developing nations need so that they can advantageously pursue their own economic advancement.

d. In many cases there is an urgent need to revamp economic and social structures. But one must guard against proposed technical solutions that are untimely. This is particularly true of those solutions providing man with material conveniences which are nevertheless contrary to man's spiritual nature and advancement. For "not by bread alone does man live, but by every word which proceeds from the mouth of God" (Matt 4:4). Every sector of the family of man carries within itself and in its best traditions some portion of the spiritual treasure entrusted by God to humanity, even though many may not be aware of the source from which it comes.

Such steps are not new; they were already contained to a certain degree in *Mater et Magistra* — but what is emphasized throughout these practical points are two things: one is that these suggestions are geared to having the poorer nations help themselves in their relationship with the richer nations. This is a valuable point, since human dignity and legitimate national pride cannot progress on the good offices or charity of another nation. What the poor nations need, above all, is capital for building basic industries (we must remember that in most of these nations the process of industrialization is rather primitive as yet) and technical training in the modern forms of agriculture, irrigation, seed and crop development, fertilizers, etc. This will ultimately give these nations a capacity for self-development and progress.

Secondly, we must always remember, says our document, that the economic development of a nation exists for man and his dignity and not vice versa. We must not destroy the cultural, moral, or religious heritage of a country by hasty methods of urbanization and industrialization. Man is not just a *homo faber* but also a *homo sapiens,* and, in this respect, modern industrial development must proceed with the greatest care, taking precaution against the destruction of other valuable national values. We must, however, be sanguine here as well. It is a fact that industrialization will necessarily affect and even change various traditional modes of life within a given country. Many of the traditional religious beliefs will either have to accommodate themselves, in evolutionary fashion and incorporate these new phenomena within its theology or they must perish. The Catholic Church went through this agony, and it was not so long ago that she finally managed to "baptize" the whole of modernization (cf. struggles in Church-State relations, religious freedom, evolution and science, birth control, democracy and human rights, etc.). So these religions, (Hinduism, Mohammedanism, Buddhism, etc.), too, will have to undergo an evolutionary metamorphosis.

It must also be remarked that under "c," our document applies the principle of subsidiarity to international relations as well (in traditional social theology this is applied between the singular state and private groups, as is seen in *Mater*, 52-53, 117 and *Pacem*, 26, 66 and 140-141). This is a direct result of universal socialization which has made men and nations of the entire globe more interdependent than ever before. The principle calls for mutual aid between nations when needed, but it also requires that each nation take care and responsibility for its own internal development. It is in this area that the Council condemns that new form of neo-colonialism, namely, economic domination of the poor nations by the rich nations. This would directly violate the principle of international subsidiarity.

The document next deals with one of the most important and crucial problems for the underdeveloped nations: overpopulation.

87. a. International cooperation is needed today especially for those people who, besides facing so many other difficulties, likewise undergo pressures due to a rapid increase in population. There is an urgent need to explore, with the full and intense cooperation of all, and especially of the wealthier nations, ways whereby the human necessities of food and a suitable education can be furnished and shared with the entire human community. But some peoples could greatly improve upon the conditions of their life if they would change over from antiquated methods of farming to the new technical methods, applying them with needed prudence according to their own circumstances. Their life would likewise be improved by the establishment of a better social order and by a fairer system for the distribution of land ownership.

b. Governments undoubtedly have rights and duties, within the limits of their proper competency, regarding the population problem in their respective countries, for instance, with regard to social and family life legislation, or with regard to the migration of country-dwellers to the cities, or with respect to the information concerning the conditions and needs of the country. Since men today are giving thought to this problem and are so greatly disturbed over it, it is desirable in addition that Catholic specialists, especially in the universities, skillfully pursue and develop studies and projects on all these matters.

c. But there are many today who maintain that the increase in world population, or at least the population increase in some countries, must be radically curbed by every means possible and by any kind of intervention on the part of public authority. In view of this contention, the Council urges everyone to guard against solutions, whether publicly or privately supported, or at times even imposed, which are contrary to the moral law. For in keeping with man's inalienable right to marry and generate children, the decision concerning the number of children they will have depends on the correct judgment of the parents and it cannot in any way be left to the judgment of public authority. But since the judgment of the parents presupposes a rightly formed conscience, it is of the utmost importance that the way be open for everyone to develop a correct and genuinely human responsibility which respects the divine law and takes into consideration the circumstances of the place and the time. But sometimes this requires an improvement in educational and social conditions, and, above all, formation in religion or at least a complete moral training. Men should judiciously be informed, furthermore, of scientific advances in exploring methods whereby spouses can be helped in regulating the number of their children and whose safeness has been well proven and whose harmony with the moral order has been ascertained.

It is quite clear that this paragraph stands between the "prophets of doom" for whom the world is already overly populated, and those for whom there is no problem at all — or at least for the foreseeable future. All will admit that absolutely speaking, there is no overpopulation over the globe as a whole. On the other hand, it cannot be denied that in certain countries, there is today a definite overpopulation, at least in a relative way; that is, between the resources at hand (both present and savings for future development of the country) and the present population (both actual and the percentage of yearly increase). To a great degree, as well, this swelling of population in various countries is chiefly due to the reduction of infant mortality by the introduction of modern medical and hygienic techniques. In certain countries, as in Latin America, this increase in population has all but nullified the economic growth made in the past few years. In India, the money necessary to support eight million additions each year has eaten away the surplus capital needed for industrial expansion and, consequently, the economic growth of the whole country. The situation is practically the same in many of the underdeveloped nations (see *Mater*, 187-195). Demographers, however, are in serious disagreement on the number of people the earth could support, if all the resources presently known were fully employed. Their estimates range anywhere from 15 to 100 billion human beings. Yet, as we have mentioned, most demographers do agree that, at present, there is overpopulation only in specific areas. As a solution to this problem, many countries have gone to extremes such as modern Japan. She has undertaken a massive government-support program of abortion, sterilization and birth control. Beyond a doubt, this program has reduced the number of births in Japan from 33.5 per 1,000 in 1948 to 21.5 in 1953 and to a 17.2 in 1957, where it has since stabilized. Abortions there have increased to over a million a year, and the number might well be doubled. The Council here warns against such drastic and immoral means to curtail the population of any one country.

What is to be done? First and foremost, a positive program to increase food-production by methods which are scientific and productive: agricultural and rural reform, fertilizers and modern techniques of farming which can bring to these impoverished areas a measure of immediate relief. This is what Paul VI referred to in his UN speech of 1965 when he rightfully said that the first preoccupation of the family of nations is not to curtail people, but increase the amount of food at humanity's table — a gentle reminder that man's task be positive, above all. The Council makes this positive plea its own (87a).

On the other hand, however, there is the present fact of relative overpopulation on the globe. Nor should the Pope's, nor the Council's emphasis on a positive program be misconstrued to mean an uncontrolled birth rate. The Council's teaching on "responsible parenthood" in Part II, Chapter I should be sufficient refutation of such an interpretation. A limitation of births is a basic necessity in today's industrialized and modern world — of this there is little question among informed thinkers on the situation. But the measures taken should not be those which offend the very dignity of man (87c). Nor is it possible to deny the fact that governments have a legitimate interest in such a basic question which so thoroughly affects the social and economic fabric of the whole country (87b). Methods such as sterilization and abortion are so offensive to the dignity of man, that no excuse can be made to perpetrate such crimes. On the question of birth control, we refer the reader to the Council's teaching on this subject.

Aside from these reservations, the document leaves much latitude for finding a solution to the problem, both by increase of food production by scientific methods as well as a legitimate limitation of population by means which respect the moral law. As a matter of fact, our document encourages governments to study the biological process of reproduction, so as to be of all the more service to those couples wishing to exercise "responsible parenthood" providing them with most modern scientific knowledge in their proper circumstances. The Church here — as elsewhere — has no ready-made solution for this problem and she is permitting experimentation by all who have a legitimate interest in the matter. In this respect, she is neither holding back progress nor giving her approval to every new technique which might come along. Her essential mission on earth is to recall to man the essential human dignity and the sacred character of life. In practical condemnations (she mentions only the most obvious here in the text), she is very prudent, and as in the chapter on marriage and birth control, she has left the door open for further progress and advancement.

The document then goes on to draw the necessary conclusions from what has developed above: mutual cooperation on the part of Christians for the world's poor and destitute.

88. a. Christians should cooperate willingly and wholeheartedly in establishing an international order that includes a genuine respect for all freedoms and amicable brotherhood between all. This is all the more pressing since the great part of the world is still suffering from so much poverty that it is as if Christ himself were crying out in these poor to beg the charity of the disciples. Do not let men, then, be scandalized because some countries with a majority of citizens who are counted as Christians have an abundance of wealth, whereas others are deprived of the necessities of life and are tormented with hunger, disease, and every kind of misery. The spirit of poverty and of charity are the glory and witness of the Church of Christ.

b. Those Christians are to be praised and supported, therefore, who volunteer their services to help other men and nations. Indeed, it is the duty of the whole People of God, following the word and example of the bishops, to alleviate as far as they are able the sufferings of the modern age. They should do this too, as was the ancient custom in the Church, out of the substance of their goods, and not only out of what is superfluous.

c. The procedure of collecting and distributing aid, without being inflexible and completely uniform, should nevertheless be carried on in an orderly fashion in dioceses, nations, and throughout the entire world. Wherever it seems fitting, this activity of Catholics should be carried on in unison with other Christian brothers. For the spirit of charity does not forbid, but on the contrary commands that charitable activity be carried out in a careful and orderly manner. Therefore, it is essential for those who intend to dedicate themselves to the service of the developing nations to be properly trained in appropriate institutes.

Perhaps we have here an example of what could be understood as "grass-roots ecumenism" among Christians. Christian unity will come about ultimately when there is doctrinal unification. But a necessary preparation for such an event must be a psychological unification of all Christians by all Christians through discussion and work together in solving common problems. They will not soon exhaust subject matter in this area, and above all, in their mutual endeavors on the part of helping the world's poor. The recent announcement from Geneva, that the Vatican and the World Council of Churches have agreed to collaborate on famine relief in Asia and Africa, is highly significant, in this regard, and sets the pace for Christians at a lower echelon of cooperation for relief of poverty in the world.

What is very striking in our present paragraph is the fact that we no longer read that Christians must give to the poor out of their superabundance; they must share with them their very essentials. This is a strong statement and shows with what seriousness the Council considers the fact that poverty and alleviation of the world's poor must become an essential of the Christian's vocation in the world. This love of men cannot be just sporadically demonstrated. In a highly technical and organized age such as ours, no aid to the poor will be efficacious, unless it, too, is highly organized to attack the very sources of poverty and destitution. We know infinitely more today about the "culture" of poverty and its causes than ever before in human history. We realize that we must methodically attack the root-causes of this poverty before the poor can benefit from any aid — at least as a long-term endeavor, and not simply "relief."

Many young people in our day are driven by highly motivated sentiments of justice and charity to serve the poor and underdeveloped both at home and abroad. The Council calls this an "evangelical task," since whether they realize it or not, in serving the brethren out of charity, one in reality serves Christ, for Christ can be found in a most particular way in the face of the poor. There are many such organizations — highly trained and technical — which are working in various fields of human development. One may mention such organizations as the Peace Corps, Job Corps, Papal Volunteers, Misereor, CILA. These groups, at least from a Christian point of view, can be regarded as the active presence of Christ among men, as a sign of God's presence among men.

The Church's mission, of course, is essentially the rendering of the very presence of Christ among men. She does so by encouraging her children to take an active role in both religious and secular organizations which aid the poor both at home and abroad (88). We have mentioned some of them above and they are all efforts toward peace in the modern world. She also does this by awakening in the mass of her faithful a consciousness of the world's poor, and encouraging them to make a direct or an indirect contribution to this gigantic problem. We have already seen with what stress the Council has emphasized the poverty of all Christians. Thus the following paragraph:

89. a. Since, in virtue of her mission received from God, the Church preaches the gospel to all men and dispenses the treasures of grace, she contributes to the ensuring of peace everywhere on earth and to the placing of the fraternal exchange between men on solid ground by imparting knowledge of the divine and natural law. Therefore, to encourage and stimulate cooperation among men, the Church must be clearly present in the midst of the community of nations, both through her official channels and through the full and sincere collaboration of all Christians — a collaboration motivated solely by the desire to be of service to all.

b. This will come about more effectively if the faithful themselves, conscious of their responsibility as men and as Christians, will exert their influence in their own milieu to arouse a ready willingness to cooperate with the international community. Special care must be given, in both religious and civic education, to the formation of youth in this regard.

What can the Church do? It was to this question that Paul VI addressed himself in his talk to a group of specialists from Catholic charitable agencies on May 11, 1966. A full-scale alleviation of poverty, he said, would require a transformation of the world's financial and economic system, not to mention "methods capable of multiplying productivity and transforming the mechanism of international commerce" (points which we have seen above). With equal wisdom, however, he observed that changes of this scope and magnitude are well beyond the means of the Church. The horrendous fact of world poverty is that no one institution or one nation can, by itself, do more than scratch the surface. The only hope lies in a genuinely universal movement, drawing on the dedication and resources of many nations and institutions. What contribution can the Church make to all this? It can assist, in the words of the Pope, "to make the stark reality better known, helping to reveal its gigantic dimensions, indicating ways of remedying it and, above all, arousing a lively awareness of the objections deriving from man's universal brotherhood." It is exactly this which the whole Council attempted to do in its emphasis on poverty throughout its documents, as well as in this section (particularly 89) of *The Constitution on the Church in the Modern World*. The Church's function then, is, above all, to serve the world of men, and that is why she must bring these truths to the attention of her children. It is only in serving the poor, the destitute, the aged, the neglected of this world, that we can hope to find the face of Christ.

All this is a far cry from the definition of the Church of the Middle Ages where she was viewed as a "perfect society" being served by the world in imitation of the princes of this world. She is not a self-sufficiency in the world, but a ferment, a light, a guide, working among men in their struggle for human dignity. This theology of the Church's engagement in the world is at the heart of our text. The ghetto-mentality of the Church as an armed fortress fighting off the onslaught of "the enemy" is now a thing of the past. The Church is engaged in human history among men with very human problems. Hers is not a separation from the world (*"fuga mundi"* of the Middle Ages), nor is it an indifference to the agonies and problems of the men of our age. The divine vocation of man cannot be fully accomplished without the development of human dignity in all its forms (*Pacem,* 18-26). It is, indeed, a false dichotomy to separate these two aspects of man in fact, even if we must do so in theory. Grace builds upon nature to the extent that man, as God wills him now, must be promoted in a total sense, body and soul; for God has saved him as a total composite by the resurrection of his only begotten Son. It is in the perfection of man's personal dignity as a son of God, and in the harmonious development of his human inclinations and energies that the Church is interested.

Finally, in this section, we have a moving Christian appeal for the poor as pre-eminently reflecting Christ himself, and thus calling for a concerted and unified effort in this regard on the part of all Christians:

> 90. a. An outstanding form of international activity on the part of Christians is found in the joint efforts which, both as individuals and in groups, they contribute to institutes already established or to be established for the encouragement of cooperation among nations. There are also various Catholic associations on the international level which can contribute in many ways to the building up of a peaceful and fraternal community of nations. These should be strengthened by augmenting in them the number of well-qualified collaborators, by increasing needed resources, and by a suitable coordination of their forces. For today both effective action and the need for dialogue demand joint projects. Moreover, such associations contribute much to the development of a universal outlook — something certainly appropriate for Catholics. They also help to form an awareness of genuine universal solidarity and responsibility.
>
> b. Finally, it is very much to be desired that Catholics, in order to fulfill their role properly in the international com-

munity, should seek to cooperate actively and in a positive
manner both with their separated brothers, who together with
them profess the gospel of charity, and with all men thirsting
for true peace.

    c. The Council, considering the immensity of the hard-
ships which still afflict the greater part of mankind today,
regards it as most opportune that an organism of the universal
Church be set up in order that both the justice and love of
Christ toward the poor might be developed everywhere. The
role of such an organism would be to stimulate the Catholic
community to promote progress in needy regions and international social justice.

The theme of love and engagement for the poor is almost
monotonous in this document. We have already spoken earlier
of the unified action of all Christians in this regard as a concrete
ecumenical gesture of the first order. Cooperation with all
men of good will (90b) is, in fact, included here. But it is
incumbent, especially on Christians, to show this lively sense
of love of the world's poor as a sign of Christ's presence in the
modern world.

    Finally, the Council calls for an organism whose members
and experts would be drawn from the entire Church, in order
to keep before the eyes of the whole Church this fundamental
problem of our day. Many high Church officials from all con-
tinents showed deep interest and strong support for this, and
that is why it was so paramount in our text. Its object would
be a continued study of world poverty and its long-term remedies
to bring this particular concern to the whole of Catholic life
by working in and through and with the existing entities of the
Church — (and not to replace any of them). Above all, the
field of world poverty and world progress is one in which all
Christians can work closely together with a common sense of
commitment and purpose, without becoming entangled in doctrinal and historic differences which would undermine their
sense of fellowship. This vision of Christianity united against
the world of want and poverty and joined to all men of good

will of other religions — or none — is behind our present appeal. It is, indeed, a vision which can have as yet untold effects on world peace. If it can be translated into action, then a decisive step forward will have been taken in the war on poverty. In this way, the moral force of mankind may be mobilized against the greatest scandal of our age. It would indeed help to realize the goal economists tell us is perfectly attainable: elimination of the world's most ancient enemy, grinding poverty, famine and hunger, as a condition of a fuller, more human, more just life for all its inhabitants (90c).

CONCLUSION

The document now reiterates the position already taken, that Christians must cooperate with each other and with all men of good will for the accomplishment of the works of peace in our day — much along the same lines given by John XXIII in *Pacem* (159):

91. a. Drawn from the treasures of Church teaching, the proposals of this Sacred Synod look to the assistance of every man of our time, whether he believe in God, or does not explicitly recognize him. If adopted, they will promote among men a sharper insight into their full destiny, and thereby lead them to fashion the world more to man's surpassing dignity, to search for a brotherhood which is universal and more deeply rooted, and to meet the urgencies of our age with a gallant and unified effort born of love.

b. Undeniably this conciliar program is but a general one in several of its parts; and deliberately so, given the immense variety of situations and forms of human culture in the world. Indeed while it presents teaching accepted in the Church, the program will have to be followed up and amplified since it sometimes deals with matters in a constant state of development. Still, we have relied on the word of God and the spirit of the gospel. Hence we entertain the hope that many of our proposals will prove to be of substantial benefit to everyone, especially after they have been adapted to individual nations and mentalities by the faithful, under the guidance of their pastors.

One important point must be noted in this paragraph. Article 91b does not, in any way, "tone down" what our document has previously exposed. At first reading, it would seem to be doing just that, but this section was added for the simple reason that some bishops feared these practical orientations of Part II would quietly pass as the world changed, and therefore ought to be viewed as properly "doctrinal." This was the special note given in our text by the Council itself with respect to the exposition of the second part of our document:

> By way of explanation: the constitution is called "pastoral" because, while resting on doctrinal principles, it seeks to express the relation of the Church to the world and modern mankind. The result is that, on the one hand, a pastoral slant is present in the first part, and, on the other hand, a doctrinal slant is present in the second part.
> In the first part, the Church develops her teaching on man, on the world which is the enveloping context of man's existence, and on man's relations to his fellow men. In part two, the Church gives closer consideration to various aspects of modern life and human society; special consideration is given to those questions and problems which, in this general area, seem to have a greater urgency in our day. As a result, in part two the subject matter which is viewed in the light of doctrinal principles is made up of diverse elements. Some elements have a permanent value; others, only a transitory one.
> Consequently, the constitution must be interpreted according to the general norms of theological interpretation. Interpreters must bear in mind — especially in part two — the changeable circumstances which the subject matter, by its very nature, involves.

Thus, in no way does this attenuate the authority of the document but it simply draws attention to the fact that these problems of the modern world need constant and vigilant attention, if solutions are to be found for them in an ever-changing and progressing world. Our doctrine must continuously follow such progress, enlightened by the ever-expanding experience of men in the world. It is here that the *"consensus fidelium"* in the development of Christian doctrine finds its efflorescence in space and time of the total life of the Church.

In the following paragraph, the Church goes on to enumerate the "signs of brotherhood" thereby stimulating the dialogue between all men of good will:

92. a. By virtue of her mission to shed on the whole world the radiance of the gospel message, and to unify one Spirit all men of whatever nation, race or culture, the Church stands forth as a sign of that brotherhood which facilitates and invigorates sincere dialogue.

b. Such a mission requires in the first place that we foster within the Church itself mutual esteem, reverence and harmony, through the full recognition of lawful diversity. Thus all those who compose the one People of God, both pastors and the general faithful, can engage in dialogue with ever-increasing effectiveness. For the bonds which united the faithful are mightier than anything dividing them. Hence, let there be unity in essentials; freedom in doubtful matters; and in all things charity.

c. Our hearts embrace also those brothers and communities not yet living with us in full communion; to them we are linked nonetheless by our profession of the Father and the Son and the Holy Spirit, and by the bond of charity. We are not unmindful of the fact that the unity of Christians is today awaited and desired by many, too, who do not believe in Christ; for the further it advances toward truth and love under the powerful impulse of the Holy Spirit, the more this unity will be a harbinger of unity and peace for the world at large. Therefore, by common effort and in ways which are today increasingly appropriate for seeking this splendid goal effectively, let us take pains to pattern ourselves after the gospel more exactly every day, and thus work as brothers in rendering service to the human family. For, in Christ Jesus this family is constituted to the family of the sons of God.

We think cordially too, of all who acknowledge God, and who preserve in their traditions precious elements of religion and humanity. We want frank conversations to compel us all to receive the impulses of the Spirit faithfully and to act on them energetically.

d. For our part, the desire for such dialogue, which can lead to truth through love alone, excludes no one, though an appropriate measure of prudence must undoubtedly be exercised. We include those who cultivate outstanding qualities of the human spirit, but do not yet acknowledge the Source of these qualities. We include those who oppress the Church and harass her in manifold ways. Since God the Father is the origin and purpose of all men, we are all called to be brothers. Therefore, if we have been summoned to the same destiny, human and divine, we can and we should work together without violence and deceit in order to build up the world in genuine peace.

We have already spoken of the dialogue among men (see above, pp. 64-76). Its description follows for the most part that given to us in *Ecclesiam Suam* of Paul VI: dialogue in the Church, dialogue with other Christian communities, dialogue with men of non-Christian religions, dialogue with all men of good will — even with those who oppose the Church for one reason or another, (see par. 40, where the document spoke of the contribution "of other Christian Churches" in the humanization of the world; also pars. 21f and 43c, where many of the points mentioned here were already brought out in our document).

The document concludes in a truly evangelical tone, in that the real Christian is not one who simply sees and judges, but one who acts, as well, in the service of men.

93. a. Mindful of the Lord's saying: "by this will all men know that you are my disciples, if you have love for one another" (John 13:35), Christians cannot yearn for anything more ardently than to serve the men of the modern world ever more generously and effectively. Therefore, by holding faithfully to the gospel and benefiting from its resources, by joining with every man who loves and practices justice, Christians have shouldered a gigantic task to be carried out in this world, a

task concerning which they must give a reckoning to him who will judge man on the last day.

b. Not everyone who cries, "Lord, Lord," will enter into the kingdom of heaven, but those who do the Father's will by taking a strong grip on the work at hand. Now, the Father wills that in all men we recognize Christ our brother and love him effectively, in word and in deed. By thus giving witness to the truth, we will share with others the mystery of the heavenly Father's love. As a consequence, men throughout the world will be aroused to a lively hope — the gift of the Holy Spirit — that finally they will be caught up in peace and utter happiness in that fatherland radiant with the glory of the Lord.

c. Now to him who is able to accomplish all things in a measure far beyond what we ask or conceive, in keeping with the power that is at work in us — to him be glory in the Church and in Christ Jesus, down through all the ages of time without end. Amen (Eph 3:20-21).

It is reminiscent of the teaching of John XXIII in *Mater et Magistra* (234-238). The pastoral concern of both documents is evident throughout. Action is an essential element in the development of a Christian. The Pope there emphasized that the Christian is not only educated *for action but also by action*. Christian education is no longer enough. It must be supplemented by concrete action on the firing line. The Christian is called upon — in fact, is obliged — to become directly engaged in the social, political, and economic activities of the modern world. Our document follows this line of thought rather fully, which, in its turn, is nothing more than the evangelical call to action. We can only love our brother insofar as we place ourselves at his concrete service in all his agonies and needs.

INDICES

TABLE I

TABLE II